Bad ____ ____

By
Suzie Ivy
§
A True-life Adventure

Bad Luck Publishing
Suzieivy@gmail.com
www.badluckdetective.com

Bad Luck Cadet
Bad Luck Series: Book I

Printing History
First Print Edition: May 2012

Dear Reader,

This is the first two books of my adventures as a midlife police officer. Book I - Bad Luck Cadet was written for my blog and I've kept the original flavor and style though edited a word here and there that was missed the first time. Book II – Bad Luck Officer takes you through the first two years of my life in law enforcement.

These books were written because of my lifelong friend Linda Anselmi. She introduced me to the blogging sphere and changed my life. Thank you for years of friendship and support. You are my "Veronica" in the world of writing.

In the world of law enforcement, Tammy IS Veronica. You supported and believed in me when I sometimes didn't believe in myself. My portrayal of you in BLC is of a strong, beautiful and no nonsense woman because you are. You were the first person I told about the crazy notion of becoming a police officer and that's the smartest move I ever made. Thank you!

My blog readers have kept my fingers to the keyboard working on the next two books and penning Stories from Small Town, which can be found on my blog. Bad Luck In Small Town (a true-life murder mystery) will be available fall, 2012 and Bad Luck Detective will be out mid, 2013. Thank you for your comments and encouragement!

Special thanks go to my family. My children are incredible and they allowed me the freedom to be me. You are wonderful parents and I can't wait to see what you will someday do with your middle age dreams. My mother is the reason I dream. Her words to me as a child, "In your lifetime there will be a female president. Why can't it be you?" Keep me believing. My husband is my backbone and best friend. He still thinks I'm crazy but loves me anyway. Thank you all!

To Class 95, the greatest group of cadets to ever walk the halls of any police academy anywhere!

Suzie Ivy

Chapter 1
Accidents Happen

My midlife crisis started with a broken hip that began with a smart horse and a dumb rider. I was forty four years old and forty pounds overweight. My horse was in great shape and enjoyed my pain tremendously. He laughed all the way to his new owners. I cried all the way to the hospital.

I convalesced for two months. During that time, I watched television, read books, surfed the web and ate lots of junk food. My forty pounds soon became fifty and I think depression set in. I never suffered from that condition before so I can't be positive. It may have just been the pain pills.

As soon as I could walk without the walker, I decided I needed to make some changes. But what? What did I want to do with the rest of my life?

An ad on the drugstore bulletin board changed everything:

Small Town looking for a few good men and women!

Must have a crime free background,

Must work well with others,

Must be able to physically undergo the rigors of the police academy,

Must be able to complete what you start.

Must be 21 years old but you're never too old.

Academy begins August 15.

Six months away, never too old! This was for me. I could actually picture myself in a police uniform. I had always looked good in navy.

I stepped back from the police academy ad and my reflection appeared in the glass. Who was this overweight slob looking back at me? I had no excuse. I was forty pounds too heavy before my accident. And I might have under exaggerated the extra ten pounds since the accident.

Things needed to change. I needed to change.

I looked back at the ad. What would my kids say? What would my friends think? My husband would be no help. He would sit in his big easy chair and say, "Yes dear."

I needed Veronica. She's that one friend everyone has, but likes to hate. She's in great shape, she's a vegetarian and she believes volunteer work is good for the soul. Veronica's that kind of friend.

Over the next two months Veronica kicked my butt. She never gave up and felt it was her own personal volunteer goal to see I dropped the weight and got in shape. She agreed not to tell our friends. I agreed to keep her latest nose job to myself. We were both happy but I was in pain. My legs hurt, my arms hurt and my butt hurt.

What I needed was another prescription for pain pills but I knew I would need to pass the urine test and it wouldn't look good to have narcotics in my blood stream even if they were legal. So I suffered through.

As my stomach shrank the small food portions I was consuming became more bearable. My pants became too large and my breasts too small. My husband was the only one who complained. I started to feel like I was in my twenties, well maybe thirties. I had more energy and wanted to exercise all the time. I went to Small Town's police department and picked up an application.

Yes, I lived in the Arizona city of Small Town. It is frequently confused with Nowhere, Arizona. My husband and I moved here ten years ago. He sells widgets to power plants and two of the largest power plants in the country reside here. Norman also had a pilot's license and flew to other large power plants. There was a lot of money to be made in power plant widget sales.

There were two reasons I married Norman. One was because I loved him and the other was for his last name. Ivy just went along with Suzie. My maiden name was actually Suzanna Shultz. Need I say more?

The police application was twenty-two pages long. It required my life history, copies of my birth certificate and high school diploma and it had to be notarized and turned in by the deadline of June 1. Two weeks away. It was time to tell Norman and my kids.

Technically they were not kids any longer. They were young adults just beginning their lives. My oldest, Letty, thought she had finally found the "right man." Roger, the middle child and my only son thought he wanted to be a power plant operator. My youngest,

Cassie, just graduated high school. She would be leaving for college when I left for the police academy.

Norman accepted my announcement like I knew he would. I'm surprised he didn't pat me on the head. I didn't think this was a good time to explain I would be living on campus five hours away and he would be cooking his own dinners.

My kids were a different story. Roger thought I was out of my mind. He actually stormed out of the house. I knew he would be back; he lived with us rent-free. Letty thought I was menopausal, too old and even after losing thirty pounds, too fat. Cassie, bless her heart, sided with me.

"If this is what you want mom, I think it's great." She said.

It actually didn't matter what anyone said. My mind was made up and I'd been working my ass off to reach my goals. I finished the application and turned it in with a week to spare. A few days later, I was called to begin the first round of eliminations.

There were sixteen people in the room not including Sergeant Spears. He told everyone he would begin checking our backgrounds after we passed a written examination. Two people walked out without completing the test. I spent the first hour answering questions and the second hour checking my work. The test wasn't exactly hard but it made you think about and analyze the questions.

I looked around and I realized the applicants were young. All appeared to be in their twenties. Maybe this was not such a good idea. How could I compete? I turned in my test and went home.

A miserable three days later I got a call.

Sergeant Spears wanted to speak with me in person. He scheduled the appointment for 1300 hours. Thank god I was an army brat and knew what he meant. I arrived two minutes early. I didn't want to show my eagerness but I absolutely didn't want to be late. I waited around the corner for thirty minutes before pulling into the parking lot.

I was shown to Sergeant Spears' office. He looked me up and down as I entered. Not in a male female sort of way but in a "she's completely lacking sort of way." He asked me to have a seat.

"What makes you think you can be a police officer?"

"I'm organized, I'm intelligent and I love mystery novels, not the cozies but the real hard core ones."

He rubbed his forehead and then the back of his neck; I didn't think it was a good sign. He shook his head and then looked at me again.

"From what we have found so far you have a clean record. I believe you received a traffic citation five years ago but went to traffic school. As we dig deeper, are we going to find out anything?"

"I'm a Democrat."

There, it was out. I'd been reading up on police officers and they were overwhelmingly Republicans. Not that it would be anything new, I was an out spoken democrat in a town that was prodigiously republican and took its politics seriously.

Sergeant Spears just stared. I stared back without breaking eye contact.

"You scored the highest on the written test. I've been giving that test for three years and yours is the highest score ever."

Boy there must be some dumb kids nowadays.

"If everything checks out you will need to pass a physical, psychological and polygraph tests. You will also be required to meet Cooper Standards for running, pushups and sit-ups. Can you?"

"Yes I can." I said emphatically.

He studied me another minute.

"Okay we'll be calling one way or another by early next week. Be ready."

I held my elation in check as I went out the door. It wasn't hard.

What the heck was a Cooper Test?

Chapter 2
Jumping Hurdles

The week dragged by as I waited for the next stage in my police academy entrance tests. My husband could do nothing right. My kids were driving me nuts, my son most of all. He actually told me I was an embarrassment to our family. My palm itched, but I knew if I slapped him he would call the police just to ruin my near perfect background record.

I looked up Cooper Standards on the Internet. It is divided by sex - male and female, factors in age, then gives levels for superior, excellent, good, fair, poor and very poor standards. If I used the good category for my age and sex, I needed to be able to perform one 17.7 inch vertical jump, 28 sit ups and 15 pushups in one minute; run 300 meters in 72 seconds, and 1.5 miles in 13 minutes and 58 seconds.

Were they out of their cotton picking minds?

I was averaging a 14-minute mile and thought that was good. The sit-ups and pushups wouldn't be a problem. But I had no clue as to my abilities on the 300 meters or the vertical jump.

Well, now was the time to find out. I decided to head over to the high school's track and start timing myself. Maybe I could push everything up a notch or two in the time I had. I called Veronica for moral support. It took me five minutes to get there. She was already waiting.

It was probably my hardest workout. I was beginning to think I might not have it in me. Veronica was a drill sergeant and wouldn't let up.

The entire week continued this way.

In the end, I managed to shave a whole minute off my mile. But I was sure that extra half-mile was going to kill me.

My phone rang at precisely 0800 hours on Monday morning. I was asked to meet at the track at 0800 the following day. I decided to give my body a rest and take it easy. I jumped on the scale and was down another five pounds. I had fifteen more to go.

The following day was overcast, cold and gloomy. I again arrived early but this time got out of my car and went to do my stretches. Veronica had taught me the value of stretching my old tired body. She just looked so much better doing them than I did.

Everyone began arriving. There were only five of us, three men and two women. The other female was a spunky little thing. She didn't say much to me, mostly just flirted with the guys. I'll call one Mr. Muscle, and the other two, Curly and Mo. Miss Pony Tail rounded out our crew. Sergeant Spears told us we would be doing the pushups and sit-ups first.

The other four recruits (see I was learning the terminology) chose each other as partners. I was left with Sgt. Spears. I actually finished in the excellent category according to Cooper. Next was the vertical jump. I managed 18 inches and raised Sgt. Spear's eyebrows. It was the only test I beat Miss Pony Tail on. Next, we had the 300-meter run. I finished in 70 seconds, two seconds to spare. We then had the mile and a half run. I gave it everything I had. It didn't matter that I finished last I just wanted to finish under my time.

Mr. Muscle stopped running about halfway through and walked a lap. He still beat me. Curly also walked part of the way and finished before I did. I missed my time by 35 seconds. It put me in the fair category. I didn't know if it was enough, but I knew I had given it everything I had.

Sgt. Spears said he would call us all the next day. I went home and ate a bowl of ice cream. I then ate another bowlful, but added chocolate syrup on top. I hid my crime by washing and drying the bowl and spoon. I didn't try to disguise the empty ice cream carton. Everyone would assume it was my son's handy work.

Torn between dread and anticipation, I tossed and turned for most of the night.

Before my husband left in the morning, he told me not to feel bad that I hadn't accomplished my goal. He said I needed to pick something a little more attainable the next time. I'm sure somehow he thought that would make me feel better.

The call came early and I was asked to come into the station at 0900.

I was the only recruit there. Sgt. Spears did not look happy. He asked me to sit. I sat.

"Look, I don't think you have what it takes. I don't think you'll survive a week at the academy," he said. "You don't seem tough enough and this is a tough business. I think you showed guts though by going this far. I had two young strong men stop running yesterday and take it easy when they could have done better. I don't think you could have done better but you never stopped. Those two men are out of the program. That leaves three of you. I'm going to include you in the poly and psych tests. I also want you to have the physical exam. I'll give you a chance. You showed 'heart,' and sometimes as police professionals, that's all we have."

That was it. I thanked him and told him I was available for the tests.

I called Veronica as soon as I got to my car. I invited her to meet me for a thank you lunch and then gave her the news. I was not 'in' yet, but I was a step closer. Veronica began crying and told me that she was so proud.

And in that moment, I was happy Veronica's mother hadn't drowned her at birth for being so perfect. She was just what I needed.

Chapter 3
I Think I'm Crazy and a Liar

I was scheduled for my psychological examination in Phoenix on Thursday morning and the polygraph test on Friday. It's a bit of a drive so I decided to stay Wednesday night in the city. I loved visiting the city and the biggest reason was Starbucks coffee. Venti hot mocha, non-fat, with whip, it's the only thing I order.

My Starbucks and I arrived early for the exam. I finished my caffeine chocolate combination and hid the evidence. I didn't know what the psychological exam entailed but I didn't want them to know I needed caffeine to feel human every morning.

I was shown to a small room with four tables and two chairs at each table. I took a seat. Miss Ponytail and Mo came in a few minutes later. Miss Ponytail took a seat with a good looking military type guy and Mo was forced to sit by me. He at least said hi. Miss Ponytail and I were the only females.

A woman came in and told us we would start with basic timed tests. We were each given a bubble page and then our exam. We were told not to begin or look at the test until told and then the ten minutes began.

This was easy.

Question 1: 1,3,5 – what number comes next?

And on it went. The questions were basic sequencing problems. They weren't all as easy as number one, but I actually enjoyed doing them. Before the ten minutes were over I had finished but Mo was having problems. He turned to me and whispered, "What happens if we don't finish? Will they make us leave?" His voice held absolute panic.

I told him to take his time and finish what he could. I was beginning to understand what the tests were about. When you're forty you've taken so many tests in your life it doesn't throw you to be under pressure or not know an answer. You just go to the next question. Being young, you return to those dreaded achievement tests in high school. Just how smart are you?

For once it was nice to be older. I might not be in the best physical shape compared to others in the room but I had it made when it came to these questions. Five more timed tests were given. I didn't answer every question but overall I knew I had done well. Poor Mo was dripping sweat and feeling the pressure. Miss Ponytail was flirting with her table partner and didn't appear any worse for wear.

After the sequencing and math tests we started the hard part. I've always felt I had a strong head on my shoulders and was pretty self-assured. At the end of four hours I was feeling quite disturbed. We were given three main tests, each with 200 questions. The questions on all three were only slightly different. I could see if you lied in any of the first test questions you would be in trouble. I don't know if my answers were correct but I answered honestly.

I was asked over ten times if I loved my mother or if my mother is deceased, did I love my mother. I answered yes every time. Next, do I love my father and if my father is deceased, did I love my father. Every time I answered no.

Now I was starting to sweat. Was I a horrible person because I didn't love my father? My father was a no good jerk. He left my mom and his three children when we were young. He needed some space and wanted a different life. He died when I was in my twenties. I never really knew him. I didn't hate him any longer but I don't remember ever loving him. I was such a terrible person! I knew they wouldn't want me as an officer. What a stupid test.

We were called one by one into the room with the psychologist. No one ever came back into the testing room after being called. I was last. This was an omen; I knew it. When I was finally called I went into another small but quaint room with a couch and chairs. I sat on the couch and the Doctor sat in a chair. He went through my evaluation and asked me questions. He never questioned the dislike of my father he just asked about general life questions. I left feeling crazy.

I slept poorly but had to be up early for the polygraph. After hitting Starbucks, I checked in and was given a questionnaire. It covered everything from juvenile shoplifting to drug use. I don't remember ever shoplifting. My mom would have killed me but I remember my best friend stealing a purse and the guilt I felt because I was with her.

Drug use was another no brainer because I didn't know what most of the drugs were. Marijuana, cocaine, yes, but mescaline, crank, and methamphetamine, I had no idea. I guess it didn't matter because the bottom line was I hadn't ever used any. I figured I was just boring.

I finished and was shown into the testing room. Rob Thomas introduced himself as my polygrapher. He began by hooking me up to electrodes. My chest, finger and arms were wired and he explained I was sitting on butt plates so they could measure how my butt clinched. I was mortified. My butt cheeks were getting firmer but they still had wobble. I knew they would give a false impression. This was not going to be good.

Rob asked what police department I was testing for and what academy I was going to. I told him Small Town and PAFRA (Police Academy For Rural America). He told me he was also attending PAFRA in September. I explained I would be starting in August. Rob was not aware there was a class starting in August and I knew he felt I had told my first lie. I think the ad said August. I had looked up PAFRA online but it didn't give very much information.

The test began. I was asked the same questions from the questionnaire I was given earlier. Rob stared at his computer screen while the test continued. I answered every question honestly and began relaxing. It was finally over. I was waiting for Rob to re-question me because on the testing information it stated any questionable answers would be re-asked. It never happened. I told Rob I would see him at the academy. His answer, "We'll see."

What if every question showed I was lying?

I drove home feeling sad. I knew it was my jello cheeks. Whoever thought they'd measure butt clenching on a polygraph test?

I was exhausted when I arrived. My husband was out of town until Sunday, my son was spending the weekend camping and my daughter went to bed early. I made a Tom Collins and listened to music until I was tired and then tried to sleep. I wondered when I'd receive the news good or bad.

Chapter 4
Good News, I Think

It happened on Tuesday morning. The call came in and essentially I was IN. I would begin the police academy on August 13. I was told there was a lot to do and they wanted to see me later that same afternoon.

I arrived at the police department and sat down next to Miss Ponytail. I found out her name was Stacy and she was from Montana. She told me she had always wanted to be a police officer and had seen the ad online. Mo was nowhere in sight and I was pretty sure it was not good news for him.

Sgt. Spears asked us both to step into his office. We were given an academy letter laying out the specifics of what to expect and what would be needed. We were told we would be issued a check for our uniform allowance and from that we would be expected to purchase what we needed. He told us to get our identification cards as soon as we left his office, a secretary would issue them. He also said we would begin being paid on the following Monday and would be expected to be at the police department at 0800 Monday through Friday until we left for PAFRA.

Sgt. Spears explained Small Town Police Department (STPD) was in need of female officers and we would be the first if we succeeded at the academy. I had lived here for over ten years and never realized there were no female officers. I believe Sgt. Spears was setting his star on Stacy and did not think I would make it. He seemed to be speaking to her and I was only a side bar.

Stacy and I made plans to head to Phoenix for a uniform store the following morning. We needed to do a turnaround trip so it would make for a long day. Stacy seemed more likeable as I got to know her. She was 26-years-old and had a 7-year-old daughter. Her daughter was living with her ex-husband while Stacy attended the academy. She told me she was very nervous and heard the academy was difficult.

I had put a lot of pressure on myself about getting to the academy but thought very little about actually being there. I would probably begin getting nervous a few days before we left but for now I was just relieved. Stacy said she had always dreamed of being a police officer and this was the beginning of her dream.

That evening I had to break the news to my husband. I made his favorite dinner. Cassie my youngest daughter and my son Roger were home for dinner as well.

"I have news." This was said in a determined voice lacking any excitement.

Everyone looked my way and dinner came to a standstill.

"I'm leaving for the police academy on August 12th. It begins on August 13th. I'll be gone for 18 weeks and you will all be fending for yourselves."

Cassie jumped up and gave me a hug.

"I knew you could do it mom."

Roger just stared. He then got up from the table and left the room.

My husband asked, "Is this what you really want?"

I looked at him and said, "Yes."

"Well congratulations I'm sure you will do great. What's this about 18 weeks?"

I explained I would be living in a dorm and weekends off were up to the academy staff. I told him I would come home anytime I could.

Norman and I met my freshman year in college. He was in his third year studying to be an engineer. We fell in love, one thing led to another and then we had one of those talked about moments when the condom actually broke. Nine months later Letty was born. Norman married me as soon as we discovered there were consequences to our actions and went with me to tell my family. I dropped out of college and discovered I loved being a mom. Norman finished college and began his career. Those first years were lean but Norman felt if I wanted to stay home and raise Letty, he would do everything he could to make it work.

I loved being a mom up until Cassie started high school. These past four years were difficult. I knew I either needed to finish college or decide what I wanted to do now that I was all grown up. The midlife crisis did not really set in until this past year. Middle age and Cassie's final year of high school seemed to do the trick.

Roger came back out and said he had been reading online about what was expected at the police academy. He said I would need to jump a six-foot wall. I could tell he was feeling rather smug about it.

"So I'll jump a six foot wall." I replied. "Is there anything else you're worried about?"

"Mom, you're being ridiculous. You can't possible think you'll make it through the police academy?"

"That's enough," interjected Norman. "What your mother does or doesn't do will be up to her. She's worked hard and she deserves a chance. I will not hear one more negative word out of your mouth."

Roger left the room again.

Have I mentioned how much I love my husband? He's just a great guy. I would miss him and realized we had never been apart for more than a week during our marriage.

After Cassie left the room, I asked him if he wanted to go to bed early. We cleaned up the dinner table together, left dishes in the sink and went to bed. Hours later, I was trying to fall doze off but all I could think about was a six foot wall.

Was Roger lying?

Chapter 5
Being Late Will Get You Fired

Over the next three weeks, Stacy and I felt like we were getting our first experience at what being a police officer was like. We were issued wallet police badges, by a secretary, to take to the academy and we were also issued our batons, handcuffs and firearms.

Guns, this was one thing I hadn't thought about. I had never shot a gun before. It looked huge. It was a .40 caliber Glock 35. I was told it had an extra-long barrel and was great for target shooting. P-R-O-B-L-E-M! It barely fit my hand.

Sgt. Spears took us to the range for shooting instruction. I screamed, with the gun practically jumping out of my hands on my first shot. Sgt. Spears looked like he wanted to scream too. He was patient but I pushed him to his limit. He told me if I made it far enough, the academy would straighten out my problems. Of course, Stacy did an excellent job.

The night before I left for the academy, Norman gave me a party. He invited Veronica and a few of my close friends. They baked a cake for me and wished me well. My daughters were both in attendance but Roger made his excuses and stayed away. I didn't let him ruin my great evening. Everyone wanted to know if I was nervous. By then I was past nervous and had gone straight to petrified.

Stacy and I left Small Town first thing in the morning. We stayed in a hotel in Phoenix that night and were expected to be at the academy at 1300 hours the following afternoon. Our hair had to be up and off our collar; we wore white dress shirts with black ties, black pants and black shoes. We had to carry our duty belts minus the guns and gear. We left our suitcases in our police issued unmarked vehicle and went inside. There were about thirty people standing around dressed like us. I only saw two other women.

Everything was going well until a military drill sergeant arrived. He was short, squat and had a loud voice.

"What are you doing?" He bellowed, "Get in formation NOW, NOW, NOW!"

He had several "helpers" with him. They were yelling as well. We began lining up and were told to count off. The first five people got it right but number six missed his turn.

"What the hell is your problem? Did you learn to count in kindergarten? Start over and this time, get it right."

We made it to twenty-two.

Stacy blew it. Her eyes were huge and I thought she would cry. After more yelling we started over. This time we made it. There were thirty-five of us. Next, we were marched outside. The weather was expected to be 115 degrees that day. It felt like 120. Our stiff white shirts and ties were drenched with sweat within five minutes. About half of the cadets didn't bring their duty belts with them, and the rest of us were made to stand at attention, in the hot sun, while they were given five minutes to run out to their cars.

We were placed in two lines, by numbers. We were marched around the campus. PAFRA was located on a college campus. Students would not be arriving for another week. We would have the place to ourselves for now. We ran "double time" in the heat while the library, gym and cafeteria were pointed out. We ended about ten minutes later at the far west end of campus. Our classroom was stadium style. There were six rows and I was the third person in the fifth row. Stacy was next to me and a male cadet was first in our row. We would become squad five. There were seven total in our squad.

We were told we had one minute to get a drink of water and were sent to the fountain by squads. No one did more than wet his or her lips.

I was just getting my heart rate under control when the back door at the top corner of the room flew open. A metal garbage can was kicked down the classroom stairs and our class Sergeant stormed in. I thought the other guy was the sergeant but soon discovered my error. The new sergeant made the other look like a pansy.

"On your feet, I'm Sergeant Dickens and you will stand when I enter a room. You will address me as sir." He had our attention. "Don't eyeball me; you will look through me and not at me. Do you understand?"

"Yes Sir," It came out weak. I wondered what the hell he meant, through me, not at me? I guessed I would be learning.

"What did you say? Is everybody here capable of saying yes sir? Or maybe you don't understand. Do you understand?"

"YES SIR," We were louder this time.

"If you have military experience I want you front and center immediately." About ten guys started for the front of the room. "I didn't tell you to walk. For the love of God, get down here now." Their pace picked up.

Squad leaders were appointed and all sent back to their desks. Some seat shuffling went on as the squad leaders took the far right seats in each row. We were in luck; our guy already had the correct seat. Next, we were told to come forward when our names were called and we were given a nameplate on yellow cardstock paper along with two large white paper filled binders.

Before my name was called, a young man dressed like us, looked into the room. One of the Sergeant's helpers noticed him. "Who are you?" She asked.

"Mike Todd." He answered.

"And what are you doing here Mike Todd?"

"I'm supposed to be in this class."

"What time were you to be here?" She asked.

"1300 hours."

"What time is it?"

Mike looked at his watch and said, "1342 hours."

"And you think you can come in late? Does this look like kindergarten? Sergeant Dickens, this fine young man is late."

Sergeant Dickens walked over to Mike and got in his face. "Are you eyeballing me Mr. Todd?"

"No sir."

"You were eyeballing me and now you're a liar as well as late. You have no business being here; get out. Go back and tell your department you were late. See how they like it. Now get the hell out of my room."

Mike left. We never saw him again.

I learned two very important rules; don't be late and double time means run like hell.

I also realized I had been thrown into the Hollywood set for the remake of Full Metal Jacket. I just wondered who would end up being our Pvt. Pyle and hoped it wasn't me.

Chapter 6
You Will Be Sent Home

After we received our academy study binders, Sgt. Dickens reviewed the class rules. We would be spending eight hours a day in the classroom. Everything we learned throughout the week would be covered in a test on Monday mornings. We were expected to get a seventy percent or higher. If not, we would be given one retake. If we did not pass the retake with a seventy percent we would be sent home immediately.

We were also expected to pass the POPAT (Police Officers Physical Aptitude Test):

A 99-yard obstacle course

Body Drag – Lift and drag a 165 lb. lifelike dummy 32 feet

500-Yard Run

Chain Link Fence – Run 5 yards; go over fence and run an additional 25 yards

Solid Fence Climb – Run 5 yards; go over solid fence and run an additional 25 yards

The nightmare six-foot fence that Roger taunted me with was now on the table.

Each event was timed and scored with higher points given for shorter times. The minimum passing score was 384. Men and women were scored equally. Age did not matter. If we scored a 383 we were going home. I think I liked the Cooper Test better.

Oh, and yeah, we had to pass the Cooper Test as well.

More rules. There would be no fraternizing with the college men or women on campus or among the cadets. If caught we would be sent home. We would tell the truth at all times, if we were caught in any lie we would be sent home. We would attend every class. If we missed more than three classes, we would be sent home. There were so many "you will be sent home rules" it's hard to remember them all.

We would keep our dorm rooms spotless and have a dorm inspection weekly. All homework would be turned in on time. Our notebooks would be inspected weekly. We would be given daily uniform inspections. We were to be outside on the classroom deck at 0745 each morning; inspection ready.

Monday, Wednesday, and Fridays we would meet in the gym at 0530 hours for Physical Training (PT). On Tuesday and Thursdays we would meet at the same time for Defensive Tactics (DT). These classes would last an hour and a half, giving us 45-minutes to eat breakfast, change into our uniform of the day and arrive for inspection on the deck. Infractions would be severally punished.

Punishment hill runs (whatever that was) would take place after class at 1700 hours daily. We were not to leave campus unless we had permission. There was an absolute ban on cell phones during the day.

After this set of rules and instructions were yelled out, we were marched to the gym. It was time to learn a few military formations and some of the terminology. Sgt. Dickens continued to yell and we eventually got it. It was hot in the gym. One hundred and fifty degrees was what it felt like. I'm pretty sure we were dying.

Eventually the first cadet dropped. He passed out in a dead faint. I could see the look of satisfaction on Sgt. Dickens' face. An ambulance was called and we got a break. There were two water fountains and we took turns getting water and wetting our heads and necks. No one spoke; we were all being watched closely. The "lucky" cadet was taken to the hospital about 15-minutes later.

We were told it was time for our first inspection. We lined up by squad. This would be our formation throughout the academy. The orders were being yelled out; about face, parade rest, attention, forward march, etc. The Sergeant and his helpers yelled at once. My head was spinning. We were told not to lock our knees or we would be visiting the emergency room. I tried locking my knees but it didn't work, I just couldn't pass out.

The two Sergeants and their helpers (a.k.a. our squad advisers) began going person to person and finding something wrong. My hair was barely staying up and I could feel it touching the back of my neck.

I could sense someone close behind me and then the back of my hair was tugged, hard.

A female voice, "Sgt. Dickens, it appears we have a bird's nest in squad five." It was yelled into my ear.

I couldn't help it, I giggled. A woman pulled my hair and compared it to a bird's nest. What could possibly be funnier?

Sgt. Dickens was in my face before I could choke back my laughter.

"Cadet, are you laughing? Do you find this funny? Give me twenty push-ups now. As a matter of fact, I want the entire class to give me twenty pushups. Quarter right turn, assume pushup position. Begin."

What the hell was a quarter right turn? Thankfully, I was getting good at mimicking the cadets around me. I can't believe the police ad at the drugstore had not stated, "Military training a must."

We were so tired. Someone stopped doing push-ups at the count of fourteen and we had to start again. The inspection continued and so did the punishments. When finished we had done over one hundred pushups. I couldn't feel my arms and they wouldn't stop quivering.

After inspection, we were shown the location of our dorms at the eastern end of the campus. We didn't get a change to stop and admire our dingy living quarters; we were immediately marched to the cafeteria. Not a word was spoken. We huddled together miserably at whatever empty seat we came to. The Sergeants and advisors sat at their own table. It was 1800 hours. We had only been at it for five hours. This sucked.

I tried to eat. I could barely lift my fork to my mouth. I ate very little. After about twenty-minutes, we resumed our formation outside. We ran like hell -- I mean double-timed it, back to the dorms. I was thankful I hadn't eaten much. We were finally released for the day, and told to be at the gym at 0530 hours.

Getting our room assignments, unpacking, and arranging the shower schedules were done next. There were only four female cadets. Our dorm was tiny with two sets of bunk beds. We decided to rotate every two weeks so we would each have a turn on the top bunk. There was only one small bathroom for the four of us.

After getting situated, Stacy left the room with her cell phone in hand. She came back an hour later and said she was going back to Montana. She wasn't crying or acting anything but determined. She left. I never heard from her again.

Have I mentioned how much this sucks?

Chapter 7
Are We In Hell?

Day two at the police academy began at 0430 hours. A squad leader had knocked on our door the previous evening to inform us we would need to meet before physical training the next morning and work on straightening up our marching and formations. And there were some, like myself, that needed to learn basic commands.

We were in front of the dorms at 0445. It was already warm. As we lined up, the space beside me was noticeably empty. Another cadet asked where my partner was. I explained what happened the evening before. Everyone moved down one spot.

Stacy was one of two cadets to drop out the first day. The other was a male cadet from squad three. It was at this point that I swore to myself I would complete the academy. I had never given up on anything and I wouldn't begin now. I was not a quitter.

We marched and learned: about face, quarter turn, marching while turning a corner, and standing at attention with our toes pointing out so the Sergeant could stand between our feet and inspect us up close and personal.

It was now time to march to physical training. As much as I would come to dread our early morning workouts, the marching was great. We marched and sang to cadence. One of the cadets, fresh out of the military, knew every cadence imaginable. They were funny, entertaining and inspiring. Our voices rang across the campus.

Sgt. Dickens was waiting when we arrived. The yelling began and we were introduced to our PT instructor Sgt. Listberg. He turned out to be a great guy but we weren't aware of this on the first day. After warm ups we went on our first run. Sgt. Listberg told us it would be the last mile we ever ran at the academy.

He was correct. Wednesday we ran two miles.

It soon became apparent I was a slow runner and I was put in front to keep the pace. Another female, Cadet Higgins, was put in front beside me as well. She ended up dropping back due to her asthma and barely finished the mile run. I finished but could tell my pace did not offer a challenge to the other cadets. I had work to do.

We were taken into the weight room next and put through Sgt. Listberg's idea of a power workout. There were thirty-one torture stations set up. Every sixty seconds he blew his whistle and we moved to another station. Arms, legs, wrists, butts and thighs were all given a workout. The only good thing was Sgt. Listberg also turned on some great 70's rock and roll music. Through the pain I remember George Thorogood's Bad to the Bone and Joe Walsh's Life's Been Good, blaring through the speakers.

After the workout, we were taken to the gym bleachers and made to jump with both feet together to the top, then we ran back down and began jumping our way back up again. This went on until the end of class. Do you have any idea how your teeth clack when you land on both feet? My head was killing me. We double-timed it back to our dorms, changed into our shirts and ties, and then headed to breakfast.

Eating was again a difficult task due to my shaking arms and hands. God forbid we spilled anything on our ironed white shirts, it would mean changing before inspection. Somehow I managed to get some food in my mouth.

We three female cadets sat together and a few male cadets joined us. Our "cliques" were already forming.

Cadet Chavez sat next to me. He was obviously as stressed as I was. I found out he was an emergency medical technician sent to the academy in order to be part of a SWAT team. He was twenty-seven years old, fifty pounds overweight and worried about what he'd gotten himself into. He was told the academy would be a piece of cake, but he was having doubts.

I had doubts too. We made a pact to complete the academy and help each other out. We weren't such an unlikely friendship, we were both in over our heads and both needed to lose weight. It felt great to have a friend and he was also in squad five along with me. We would suffer together.

Our first inspection was horrible.

Sgt. Dickens as well as all six squad advisers were in attendance to find something wrong. And they found plenty. Our ties were the improper length. Our shoes were not shined to a high gloss. We had lint on our black pants. Several of the guys did not have a close enough shave, due to shaving the night before to save time this morning.

In all we were given eighty pushups and six hill runs. The pushups were done on the spot and the hill runs would be executed after class. I also found out why we practiced a duck stance early that morning. Sgt. Dickens placed one foot between my boots, put his face an inch from mine and began the inspection from the top of my head down to my toes. I know my last OBGYN appointment was not this thorough.

It was a relief to enter our classroom and begin learning.

The first two hours every Monday would be with Lieutenant Griffin for report writing. He talked and told stories more than he taught us report writing but we enjoyed him tremendously.

Our binders were explained to us. A schedule was located in the front of the first binder and encompassed the entire eighteen weeks of the academy. All our lesson plans were outlined, which explained the four-inch thickness of the binders. We were told we would get a break every hour but most importantly we were not to fall asleep in class. We could stand up in the back of the room but there would be hell to pay if one of us was caught sleeping.

Our first lesson from our binders was on the history of policing. Robert Peel created the first organized police unit in England called "Bobbies" in 1829. He was our founding father and his ideas lived on in modern policing.

After a lunch break, it was back to the classroom. Sgt. Dickens stuck his head in and did some yelling on a regular basis but learning was the focus. We had different instructors for different lecture modules. My brain wanted to explode by the end of that first day in class. I actually wish it had, because waiting for us were our six hill runs we'd earned that morning during inspection.

The hill consisted of a quarter mile of switchbacks up a steep, rocky dirt path to a water tower. It looked like a nightmare. And it was. Add in the 109 degrees outside and it was hell. I decided I needed to straighten up my ways. I didn't want to go to hell if it is anything like these hill runs.

We had water bottles at the bottom and took drinks between runs. I was the second to last person to the top on the first run. We were all going at our own pace. One of my roommates slipped and fell. She twisted her knee and sat out the last few trips to the top.

We were all focused on the hill and didn't notice when Sgt. Dickens showed up. I was taking my last trip upward.

"What the hell are you doing?" He yelled at the cadets waiting at the bottom for the stragglers to finish.

"Are you individuals or a team?" He demanded, "I want your punishment done as a unit. Start over and get it right this time."

Higgins, Chavez and I turned around and went back for our classmates. We formed two lines and ran six more hill runs together. We were then released for the day. I was too tired to eat and went back to my room. I ironed my shirt for the following day, tried to shine my shoes but fell asleep.

I slept until 0430 hours the next day, woke up, and did it all again. We were given 110 pushups at morning inspection and ten hill runs. I could barely move my arms during class and taking notes was excruciating. I thought Friday would never come. I was gigged (gig is like a demerit) for my boots every day. Our class could do nothing right.

My thinking began to change that week. I had always respected police officers but my admiration for them was growing as well.

We were constantly under stress. It was explained as being similar to what it would be like as an officer on a patrol shift. Being a police officer was stressful as well as deadly and if we couldn't handle it we needed to leave. It was not shameful to decide this was not right for you. It was smart, or so they told us.

I struggled with my decision to become a police officer on a whim. Did I have what it would take? Could I handle the stress?

Friday finally came and we were released at 1600 hours. I was too tired to make the drive home. I called my husband and begged his forgiveness. I spent the weekend working on my shoes, typing my notes and organizing my binders.

Sunday evening at 2000 hours we had a study group in our classroom. All but two cadets showed up. The two missing didn't show up for physical training on Monday morning as well. They had decided being a police officer was not right for them. My roommate with the hurt knee was one of the two not returning. I was down to one bunkmate. The bathroom schedule became much easier.

Cadet Donna Higgins, Rocco Chavez and I were becoming a team. We were the slowest, most un-police like cadets at the academy and we bonded. We weren't treated badly by the other cadets, but we knew they didn't think we would make it.

Our first classroom test was the next day. If we didn't pass, the decision to stay would be taken out of our hands.

Chapter 8
The Worst Possible Enemy

The day of our first classroom test had arrived. After more
torture at morning physical training, then breakfast, then inspection
where we earned eight hill runs, we sat down for our test. Bubble
sheets again. It was multiple choices, but for every question there
were at least two possible answers.

We were able to leave the room when we finished. I was third
out the door and felt I had done well. Cadet Clark, our classroom
leader, who we had elected the previous week, was the first to finish.
There was a machine for grading in the secretary's office outside the
classroom. When approximately ten bubble sheets were turned in,
they were gathered and run through the machine.

My test was handed back and I only missed three out of eighty-
six. We all managed to pass but there were quite a few scores in the
seventies. We were told this was the easiest test we would be given
and we needed to study harder. It felt good to be out of the bottom of
the pack for a change.

Next, each squad was given a package of stencils and one black
cloth marker. We were told we needed to stencil our last names on
the back of our white physical training t-shirts. The top of the letters
had to be two inches down from the collar.

It was a disaster. The male cadets made mistakes left and right
and t-shirts were thrown in the garbage. When it was my turn to
stencil I had no problems. It was easy. I wasn't a housewife and
homemaker for nothing. Word got out. It was decided I would
stencil while cadets shined my boots. What a great trade off.

The next morning, for the first time, Sgt. Dickens said, "Nice
boots cadet."

We could carry a backpack for our binders and classroom
supplies. I carried everything but the kitchen sink in mine.
Ibuprofen, Kleenex, band aides, sun block and chemical icepacks
were only a few of the items. As word got out on this, Cadets began

raiding my supplies regularly and I earned the name Momma Ivy. I think we nicknamed everyone. It was our way of making our group a family. We became proud of those names.

Tuesday and Thursday mornings were defensive tactics. Sgt. Tillman was our instructor. He was in his late forties, in fantastic shape, and basically kicked the shit out of us. We were hit, knocked down and handcuffed until our wrists were raw. I had bruises everywhere. Ice packs became my new best friend. My roommate and I bought a small refrigerator for our room and I was able to keep the packs frozen. It was cheaper than the chemical packs, though I still carried those for emergencies.

During the first and second weeks of defensive tactics we learned how to fall. We were tested on falling forward from a standing position, turning our heads to the side (so we didn't break our nose), and landing just on our palms and toes. It's hard not to use your knees to break your fall, and some of the cadets had difficulty but eventually we all succeeded.

We also started learning pain compliance techniques; wristlocks and joint control. The painful part for us was practicing on each other.

Proper search techniques were taught as well. I learned men like to hide things in their "junk." This means I had to search their "packages" thoroughly. The male cadets had a harder time searching the women than we did the men. We all had to get over our mental rebellion and learn to grope and be groped. The TSA had nothing on us.

My arms were twisted and I was thrown to the ground too many times to count. I would limp to my room after training, take some Ibuprofen, apply ice packs while changing my clothes and then head to breakfast.

Rocco and I began skipping dinner, eating a power bar and working out. We were barely keeping up in physical training and our POPAT practice was beginning the following week. By the end of my second week I had lost ten pounds and Rocco twenty-three.

My roommate Donna and I were becoming good friends as well. She had been in the army for four years and worked at a grocery store before coming to the police academy. She was thirty-two years old and wanted a better life for her son. She was single and her mother was keeping her son while she attended the academy. She told me she didn't really like the military but dreamed of being a police officer. She was getting her asthma under control and had moved to the middle of the pack when running.

Once a week, we did not run together but did a personal best run. I was proud of Donna's advancement, but this put me dead last. Rocco finished about a quarter mile in front of me and everyone else was able to cool down while waiting for me to cross the finish line. I was then given two minutes to rest before hitting the weight room. Physical training was my worst nightmare.

I was also struggling with pushups. Sgt. Dickless, I mean Dickens, had pointed me out as a weak link for his class. He seemed to spend more time on my morning inspection than on other cadets. He loved giving us all pushups for my infractions. I didn't get his exclusive attention but it was apparent he had it out for me.

The entire class referred to Sgt. Dickens as Sgt. Dickless -- when we were out of his hearing. And it became second nature to call him by this nickname. I was also incorporating the "F" word in my vocabulary. It seemed to be how every cadet talked and it was becoming just another word. I never swore a lot before the academy but the only way to describe a hill run was to call it a "fucking" hill run. No other word did it justice.

Sgt. Dickless decided I was doing improper pushups and not going down far enough. He told the class he was adding five hill runs every day until I could do them correctly. The class was pissed and I was getting angry glances.

Class leader Clark said he would help me out that evening. He showed me a proper pushup and I could barely complete ten. If Sgt. Dickless was going to be watching me the entire class was in trouble. I added pushups to my nightly workout routine.

That week we did five extra fucking hill runs every day with Sgt. Dickless screaming at the bottom about whose fault it was. Mine, because I was a forty-five year-old woman who couldn't do a proper fucking push-up.

By Friday, I was beyond spent. We did our hill runs at the end of the day, including the extra five for my improper push-ups. Cadets began heading to the dorms to collect their things for the weekend. I was walking next to Rocco.

"Sgt. Dickless," I said with feeling, "is a fucked-up piece of shit."

I was grabbed by the arm and spun around. Sgt. Dickens stood there, veins popping.

"I will see you immediately in my office!"

Rocco gave me a look of complete terror. I gave him a small push in the direction of the dorms and immediately turned myself in the direction of Sgt. Dickens' office and began marching. This was like being in grade school all over. I was forty-five years old and being sent to the office. I swore I would not cry.

Sgt. Dickens was staring at his computer and waited about five minutes before speaking to me. I knew this drill. I'd used it on my own children.

His voice was low when he finally spoke, "Why are you here Cadet Ivy?"

Before I could answer he went on.

"You can't run, you're overweight, too old and you are not cut out to be a police officer. Is this a joke to you?" he demanded, "Will your social club give you a certificate if you complete two weeks of the academy? How about making it easy on everyone by going home today and not coming back on Monday? Let me add this, if you come back on Monday I will make your life a living hell."

I believed him. My stomach was a quivering mass of jelly, but I looked him straight in the eye.

"I became a police officer because I can do the job. I apologize for my lack of respect today but I will be back on Monday."

He shook his head and told me I would have ten personal hill runs on Monday. He then dismissed me. I didn't cry, at least not until I was in my car and heading home.

I had now made the worst enemy possible.

Chapter 9
I Will Never Call Dickface Dickless Again

My weekend consisted of lazing around and doing as little as possible. It didn't matter that the house was a mess. Keeping the ice packs in place under the ace bandages on my arms and legs was my first priority.

I finally felt better by Saturday night. My husband took me out to dinner and, with the help of couple of margaritas, I regaled him with an edited version of events. I didn't tell him what awaited me on Monday. I made the entire academy experience sound like a lark. He was glad I was doing so well.

I left at two in the afternoon on Sunday and made it back to campus for study group. My class adviser had the short straw that week and he was in the classroom ready to prepare us for the test. His name was Corporal Tsisonnee, pronounced Tis-on-knee. He was quiet and had not interacted much with the class. I needed advice, and decided to speak with him after we finished.

He told me he had been informed of my transgression the previous Friday. He asked what I was going to do about it. I told him I needed to change Sgt. Dickens' mind, and somehow redeem myself. Corporal Tsisonnee told me it would be hard, and it would take a lot of heart.

There was that phrase again. Sgt. Spears from STPD had used it as well. Corporal Tsisonnee said he believed in me, and I could succeed if I truly wanted to. I left feeling better.

The following morning no one was looking at me. Word had spread and I was not a person you wanted to be seen with. Rocco and Donna were my only allies. I think everyone else was surprised I'd returned.

For physical training we headed out to the POPAT training field. We were taken through the obstacle course, and I got to drag the dummy for the first time. It wasn't easy.

Next, we headed to the fences. The chain link was not a problem because you could get a toehold in the fencing. The six-foot wall was a nightmare. There were five of us that couldn't make it over. Rocco was one. Donna, though, made it over on her first try. Rocco and I decided we would head back out that evening and work on the wall some more.

Morning inspection was a nightmare. My shoes were perfect but not according to Sgt. Dickens. He stepped on my toe, and then complained I had dust on my boot. He also complained about my hair wisps touching my collar. It didn't stop there. He gave the entire class twenty pushups for each infraction I had. He watched me like a hawk, and I managed to pull through the punishments.

During our first week, we were given school identification cards. We attached them to our shirt pockets. We were told if we lost an ID card it would be like losing our police badge and the punishments would be endless. A cadet reported his missing badge to our class leader, and Cadet Clark reported it to the sergeant. Sgt. Dickens told us to be at the running track for lunch.

Before the lunch punishment, we had to take our weekly test. I only missed five of eighty-five questions and had the fourth highest score in the class. It was a relief, but I was more worried about what was ahead because of the missing ID card. We double timed it to the track and saw Sgt. Dickens waiting for us.

There was a flock of large black birds on the football field, and Sgt. Dickens told us one of the birds had our ID card. We all started chasing the birds. Sgt. Dickens then shouted we needed to be begging the birds to give us back the card.

We started begging loudly saying, "Here birdy, birdy, give us back our ID card please."

We ran across the field and through campus following those damned birds. The college kids got a real kick out of us yelling at the birds. This went on throughout the entire lunch hour.

Sgt. Dickens then told us the birds had left the ID on the hill at the water tower and we could look after class. Starving and dehydrated we headed back to the classroom.

We ran the hill that day until we couldn't see straight. I think the only reason we were allowed to stop was that several cadets looked as if they would pass out.

When everyone left, I stayed behind to do my ten punishment hills. Cadet Clark told me he had to stay and monitor me and he waited at the bottom of the hill. A young Cadet by the name of Philip Rodriguez (P-Rod) stayed behind as well. He told me he didn't want me to do the hills alone, so he ran by my side.

As we ran, he told me about himself. I was incapable of speech at this point. Every breath was a struggle. Cadet Rodriguez was twenty years old, and would be turning twenty-one in a few weeks. He'd worked at a county jail, and had waited until he was old enough to attend the police academy.

He said he admired me for coming when I was so old. I didn't take offense. I was feeling particularly ancient and just happy to have someone with me. He chatted the entire time and didn't seem to mind that I didn't have the breath to spare for any encouraging remarks. Fortunately, I didn't have any food in my system to throw up or I would have. I did spit up some foul tasting liquid that I assume was bile.

Cadet Rodriguez told me he was struggling with the weekly classroom tests, and asked if I would tutor him. He said he would shine my shoes nightly if I was willing to help. So we made a deal.

That night, after the run, I went to Rodriguez' room with my notes and boots in hand. His roommates were busy shining their boots and said they wanted to participate as well.

My boots were passed around. As the weeks went by we fit about eight cadets nightly in that small room and I also had a study group at my breakfast table on Monday mornings before our tests.

The next day I began the Pushup Club. During every break I worked on my pushups. We added one pushup daily to the total we did at each break. I kept track of our totals for the entire day, week and month.

Including our morning punishment for inspection the Pushup Club did 843 pushups our first week. It started with just Rocco and me but we soon had about ten cadets joining us. I don't think they needed to do the pushups but the Sergeant and advisors were noticing our efforts. Anything that made us look good was on the agenda, because we were told repeatedly we were pieces of shit and not fit to wear a badge.

We were finally given permission to put on our duty belts. We were also issued "blue guns" and told to practice our draw. Blue guns are hard rubber imitation firearms, matching our department issue gun. Thank god I had gone out shooting before the academy and knew what kind of gun I had. It was nice to wear our belts and not carry them everywhere.

By the end of the week my fellow cadets were treating me normally, but Sgt. Dickens was not happy. On Friday I was given an additional ten hill runs for dropping a piece of paper on the floor in the hallway. We only had five hills to run as a group that Friday, and the entire class ran my ten with me. As I ran, there was a litany going through my head.

"I will never call Dickface Dickless again. I will never call Dickface Dickless again. I will never..."

And on it went. I knew this recitation would probably come out at the worst time and I was doing myself more harm than good. But saying those words got me up those fucking hills when I didn't think I could make it.

Sgt. Dickens was right. He had made my life hell. But I had survived.

And I only had fifteen more weeks to go.

Chapter 10
I Have An Egg Head

After my week in hell, courtesy of Sgt. Dickens, I finally broke down and told my husband everything going on at the academy. He was sympathetic and gave me a fantastic full-body massage that night. When I told him of my plan for returning to the Policy Academy on Sunday, he helped implement it and encouraged me through my tears.

Sgt. Dickens could point out anything he wanted at Monday morning inspection, but he would never again be given the chance to complain about my hair touching my collar. I loved my hair, and so did my husband, but I was determined to finish what I started. I took my inspiration from Demi Moore and G.I. Jane and decided that if sacrificing my hair would help; it was a small price to pay. My resolve only grew stronger with every snip.

I arrived at the study session Sunday night with a shaved head.

I just wish I was one of those women that looked good bald. My head looked like an egg with a nose.

Monday morning at physical training, I made it over the six-foot wall for the first time. I was so excited I forgot to run the twenty-five yards to complete the event. It didn't matter, the entire class was cheering and Sgt. Listberg gave me a huge hug. Everyone said it was because I was ten pounds lighter without my hair.

Sgt. Dickens never batted an eye at my shaved head. He only found a piece of hair (not mine) on my back pocket and gave us ten pushups. I knew I wasn't out of the woods, but it was nice just to have some of the pressure off. Unfortunately, my roommate became the next target.

If we wanted to communicate with our advisors we had to write a memo. We were given light blue paper, told to print in all capital letters and not to scratch out or erase anything. The blue paper showed the erasure lines. Misspelled words were another no-no. When we finished with our memo, it was given to our squad leader and he in turn gave it to our class leader. Both would review and correct each memo, giving back any they found had problems.

Donna decided she was tired of Sgt. Dickens and squad advisors coming into the classroom and monitoring us when we needed to be concentrating on schoolwork. If an infraction was seen during class we were pulled outside on the next break and given pushups. We all held our breath when one of our superiors came into the room. Donna was right; it made it hard to concentrate.

Donna wrote this in a memo to the academy staff. It was first given to her squad leader and next to our class leader, it was then turned in. The next morning was the reprisal.

During morning inspection Donna was asked to step front and center. She was then asked if she wrote the memo. It had her name on it but I guess Sgt. Dickens was making a point. Her squad leader was called up next, and asked if he read the memo, and if he agreed with Donna's analysis. He stated he did and yes he agreed. Cadet Clark, the class leader was called next. He also stated he agreed.

Sgt. Dickens asked if anyone disagreed with Cadet Chavez. Not one person stepped forward.

"The entire group of you," said Sgt. Dickens, "is nothing but a class of fucking babies. I'm embarrassed to be your Sergeant. I'm embarrassed you think you can be police officers. Not fair?" his voice screamed, "Not fair? I'll show you 'not fair!' You will all turn in a ten page memo by tomorrow morning on what is not fair in life. You will proceed with one hundred pushups this morning and twenty hill runs after class to give you a start on your memos. One of us will now be in the classroom at all times and you will learn what 'fair' is all about. Cadet Higgins you may lead the class in pushups."

And so it began. If we stopped or got out of sync, Sgt. Dickens was in our face. We all struggled through. During class we weren't just pulled out during break we were pulled out during classroom time and told to do more pushups.

The Pushup Club did not exist that day.

After our classroom torture was finished, we headed to the hill for our twenty hill runs. Once those were accomplished, we headed back to our dorms to begin writing our memos. I didn't go to bed until 0230. Donna cried for hours. She felt horrible about the entire class being punished for her memo. I tried to explain to her that Sgt. Dickens was psyching her out and she had to pull through.

We turned in our memos before breakfast to our squad leaders. Some were returned, and cadets spent breakfast rewriting the page that had mistakes. It helped that we all remembered our old grade school trick of writing in large print. The memos were eventually turned into the Sergeant, but our classroom time continued to be hell that week. I lost count of the number of pushups we did.

Wednesday, according to our calendar, was expandable baton training and we were told to bring them to morning physical training. There was no inspection and we spent the day learning the ins and outs of controlling someone with a baton.

My biggest fear was having my baton taken away and getting beaten with it. But we learned techniques for keeping the bad guy from accomplishing this. I also learned why we did so many pushups. I could barely hold the baton by the end of the day and I'm sure I couldn't have just three weeks before. Having completed baton training, we were given permission to carry our batons on our duty belts.

Donna was talking about not returning after the weekend. I made her promise she would come back, but I had my doubts. Sgt. Dickens was singling her out during inspection and she could do nothing right. The psychological abuse was terrible but for some reason I think my age played a huge factor in it not affecting me as much as the younger cadets.

It was the physical requirements that were overtaking me. My body was breaking down. My back was killing me, my joints were unbearably painful and my muscles cramped continually. My age had caught up with me.

Friday finally came and we left for the weekend.

I called Donna several times and she said she would return. I wouldn't believe it until I actually saw her Sunday night at the study session.

Chapter 11
The Red Shirts Bring Pain

I managed a quick trip to my chiropractor's office over the weekend for a readjustment and a water additive to help replenish lost body fluids. But I was on pins and needles to see if Donna would return.

I was able to have lunch with some friends including Veronica on Saturday. She was invested in my hell and completely understood why my head was shaved. My other friends were another matter. I don't think they knew what to make of me. I was a more self-assured Suzie with a toned and muscled body to go with the new me. Veronica gave me a big hug when our lunch was over and told me how proud she was.

Donna arrived for Sunday night study session. I was extremely relieved to lay eyes on her. She told me she was okay when we walked back to our dorm room together.

I felt overwhelming relief to keep my roommate and friend. Donna and Rocco were my rocks and I realized I was theirs as well. Stronger more "cop like" cadets had fallen, but we were still standing.

The start to week five was ominously easy. Sgt. Dickens failed to show for Monday morning inspection, so there were no pushups for improper hair, shoes, clothes, etc. Everyone passed the Monday morning class test. We even managed to skate through the day without a single punishment hill run.

Tuesday morning we were presented with our guidon. This is a flag representing our academy and class. Sgt. Dickens made quite a production and we all took pride in the presentation. The flag was yellow with PAFRA and class number 95 in large black letters. A cadet was chosen to be our flag bearer and it was quite an honor. He would carry it at all times including physical training and defensive tactics. Our flag was to be the symbol of our pride. Nothing was to happen to it or we would be punished like no punishment we had yet seen. We were told we needed a class slogan by the end of the week.

Our academy polo shirts and workout clothing had arrived and were passed out. We were told to wear the workout clothes and academy shirts on the following Monday morning. Class ninety-six would be starting on Sunday. They would move into available dorms and be using the classroom beside ours. We were told to stay away from them. We had our new polos and the new cadets would be in white shirts and ties. For a change it was nice to be us.

The day wasn't over. It was time for OC gas (o-chlorobenzylidene malononitrile) training better known as tear gas. The "red shirts", looking like SWAT commandos, came in directly after lunch. There were three of them. Their muscles were bulging beneath their red t-shirts and they acted like they had the best job in the world. They were deceptively cheerful. We learned to identify "red shirts" with pain, beginning that day.

The training session started out as a lot of fun. The "red shirts" blew things up and taught us about making bombs. We were able to play with plastic explosive. One of the cadets made a penis and it became a contest to see who could make the best one (academy humor at its finest). We were also shown videos of crowd control and actual mob scenes with police intervention.

We were then marched outside and taken about a mile out into the desert. We were issued side-handle batons and learned "hands on" crowd control. We split into two groups with one side being the "out of control" crowd, and the other being the officers. It was a great learning experience, and the psychology behind crowd control is fascinating. We took turns pissing off the other side and then a turn as officers getting the troublemakers under control.

The fun part was over. We were run in a slow jog for a mile to open our pores (this was to make the gas burn more on our bodies). We were then lined up in our squads, but instead of being spread out, we were told to stand shoulder to shoulder. It had been explained the cans of tear gas would reach over 1400 degrees in temperature and we were not to touch them. We were also told we had to keep formation until a whistle was blown or we would start over.

The cans were tossed around us. We tried holding our breath but it was impossible. Water was pouring from our eyes, nose and mouth and breathing was unbearable. I felt someone at my feet and I grabbed his shoulders and held on for dear life. We were not going to break our formation and start over. It's hard to explain the panic that sets in when you can't breathe. There was fire in my chest. I didn't think even getting out of the tear gas would enable me to breathe again. The burning in my eyes was so bad I couldn't keep them open. I could hear my fellow cadets coughing and choking. I seriously thought we would all die before that whistle was finally blown.

The shrill noise sounded and we all ran away from the gas. Besides coughing and choking we were also throwing up. Everyone had tears, snot and saliva running down their faces. I'm still amazed at the amount of mucus we expelled. It was not a pretty site, but we had succeeded. And that is all that mattered.

Our skin was still on fire, but after about ten minutes our breathing returned to normal. We were marched back to the classroom.

Sgt. Dickens came in.

"I am so fucking proud of you! This is what I've been waiting for. You are a team. You are Class 95. You are my Class and you should be proud of yourselves."

And we were. It was a great moment. We were all smiling and laughing and ready to take on the world. It didn't matter that our lungs were scorched, our skin was still burning, and our eyes and noses hadn't stopped running. On that day our Sergeant could have led us anywhere, and told us to do anything, and we would have followed.

This was how soldiers were made. I was forty-five years old but entirely susceptible to the phenomenon. We all wanted to go out and fight evil and we felt we had earned the right. After everyone showered, we gathered outside and talked and laughed until late in the evening. We didn't want the day to end.

Throughout the rest of the week we spent every available minute trying to come up with a suitable class slogan. Our first slogan was rejected by the Sergeant Dickens as being inadequate. We worked late into the night on Thursday worried that our hard work would be rejected again and our positive week would be ruined.

Friday morning, when called to attention for morning inspection, we belted out.

"Class ninety five is the best by far.

We smoke all the rest like a cheap cigar. Ugh."

Sgt. Dickens liked it and gave his approval. The new class 95 slogan was officially added to our drills. We had succeeded

I didn't drive back to Small Town that weekend. My husband was away on a business trip and it was easier to stay on campus and relax.

I took a trip to the drugstore on Saturday to get some cream for my head. It itched like crazy. I was getting used to what I looked like in the mirror but if I had scratched like this when I'd had hair everyone would have thought I had lice. I bought a couple of scarves as well and experimented with no luck. I couldn't scratch with the scarf on and even with the lotion my fingernails needed access to my scalp.

I ate dinner in the cafeteria Sunday evening with a few fellow cadets. We watched as Class 96 marched in with the same looks on their faces that we'd had on ours that first day.

It sucked to be them.

Chapter 12
Small Acts of Defiance

Week six began with us sporting our new polo shirts and the sounds of Class 96 being yelled at by their Sergeant. It was nice to breathe without a tie around our necks and Sgt. Dickens lowered his voice and tried to pretend we were human. Inspection went smoothly. We were only given twenty pushups and not a single hill run. Our Sergeant wanted us to appear superior and leave 'the hill' for Class 96. It wouldn't last, but that week we suffered very few punishments.

We took our weekly academic test Monday morning. Nine cadets did not pass. After the retake test the following day, all passed but two. Cadet Rodriguez barely scraped through. Out of the original thirty-five cadets, we were now down to twenty-nine.

I was lucky, the academic training came easy for me. The physical and defensive tactics training did not. I had never been last at anything in my life. During my childhood, I was athletic and competitive. At the academy, though much stronger than when I started, I felt like a loser.

Wednesday morning we were marched to our dorm rooms before class for a surprise room inspection. We were made to stand outside our room, with the door open. We could not enter the room before inspection began.

This was not our first room inspection, and Donna and I were finally at a point where we felt confident in having our dorm ready for inspection each morning. We had learned through prior error that all shirts in our closet had to be facing in the same direction (buttons east), all shoes pointing outward and beds made to pass a military quarter bounce.

For every room gig (mistake), our entire class was lined up in formation and made to do ten pushups. We'd had as many as fourteen gigs in one inspection. If you do the math it means one hundred and forty pushups. We learned very fast to fix the problems.

Donna and I were lucky at this point because our room contained just the two of us. It made it easier to keep things organized, or so we thought.

When we arrived at the dorms, I opened our door and realized the radio was blaring. I looked at Donna, who had panic written all over her face. She said quietly that she had left the radio on. We had a dilemma.

The rules of dorm inspection were simple; open your door, do not enter the room and stand at ease outside the door. Either our Sergeant or an Advisor would arrive and begin the inspection. The first Cadet seeing one of them come around the corner would yell, "Staff on deck," and we would immediately come to attention.

As we stood outside the room listening to the music, our panic increased steadily. I thought Donna was going to pass out.

I looked around and couldn't see our Sergeant or any class advisors. I ran inside the room and shut the radio off. As I turned around to head back out, I heard those fateful words, "Staff on deck." There was nothing I could do but step out of the room and face the music, literally.

Sgt. Dickens was staring at our room and watched me come out and get into position. I think I might have been the only cadet in his history of him being Class Sergeant that defied him. His face was red and he looked like he was ready to explode.

I was already in trouble and suffering a moment of rebellion. I stared him straight in the eye. Yes I remembered, "Stare through me not at me." I'd had enough. Hill runs, pushups, papers to write, even after an easy week, it just never ended. I went into the "fight or flight," mode. My decision was made and it was time to fight.

I stood my ground looking into Sergeant Dickens' eyes. I did not have long to wait for the explosion to happen.

"Cadet Ivy, what the hell are you doing? Do you know the rules, are you stupid?"

Now how do you answer that question? Was I stupid? I didn't think so; I thought I was helping a friend. I understood the rules but had made the choice to break them. Did this mean I wasn't good officer material? Again I didn't think so.

My response was simple and answered his questions, "I entered our room to turn off the radio, yes I know the rules, and no I'm not stupid." Humble I was not.

Sgt. Dickens' face reddened even further.

"Cadet Ivy you will leave the dorms and go wait outside my office immediately." He said in a soft voice.

This was even scarier than if he had yelled. I turned and left the area heading to his office.

He kept me waiting for an hour. It was hard not knowing what was happening back at the dorms. The longer I waited the more stupid I realized I was. It must be an age thing. Middle age was not meant to be a subservient time in your life. It is a take charge and be a leader time. Sgt. Dickens was approximately thirty-two. He didn't understand. Or maybe I didn't.

I also had another problem with my age. I needed to pee frequently. It had been over two hours and like an idiot I hadn't made a detour on the way to his office. I was regretting it with every minute that went by. I knew if I went to the restroom now, he would return as soon as I was out of sight.

I waited. When he arrived, it was hard to come to attention. Before he was there I could at least jump around a little bit.

Sgt. Dickens never even invited me into his domain. I was chastised in the hallway. The following one-sided conversation took place. I did manage a, "Yes sir," here and there.

"Cadet Ivy, you've surpassed none of my expectations (that was eloquent). You can't follow orders, you can't keep up physically with the rest of the class and you have authority issues. I will have a ten page memo on, "Why it's important to follow orders," on my desk tomorrow morning and you will run ten hills after class today. Now go back to the classroom and stay out of my face."

That was it. Ten hill runs and a ten-page paper. I detoured to the restroom and then entered the classroom. A few cadets gave me smiles. I'm sure they wondered why I was still in the academy.

It was a long day and an even longer night. Donna ran the hills with me and we made up a cadence along the way.

"Sergeant Dickens is a pill. Made me go and run the hill. At the top I slipped and fell. May Sergeant Dickens go to hell."

Not so original but it passed the time. Class 96 was running their hills while Donna and I were doing ours. They laughed the entire time and we were rather pleased with ourselves.

My rebellion continued as I sat down to write my paper. I remembered the hell Donna went through so I made mine subtler.

I started my paper with, "Following rules is important. When I had my first child the doctor told me not to push. I didn't listen. This was a bad time not to be following rules. I split wide open and the baby popped out. Another time to follow rules is when you are reading the directions on a cake box. My cakes kept falling in the middle and it took three disasters to understand that there are directions for high altitude on the side of the box. I had to learn that an asterisk under the directions was a rule to follow."

And on it went. I actually had fun and Donna laughed while shining my boots. She thought I was crazy but we both enjoyed our small acts of defiance. I told her I would take the retaliation if it came.

My last thought as sleep overtook me was one of satisfaction.

Chapter 13
Gun Fights and Car Chases

We had been told several weeks before that our defensive tactics gunfight was coming. This seemed to be a highlight for the instructors. We didn't know what to expect and I was already exhausted. Thursday morning turned out to be the day.

We were each paired up with someone of similar body size. This left Donna and I as a pair. She was in better shape and I felt it an unfair match. At the same time, the odds that I would ever have a fight on the street, for my gun, with someone my size was extremely slim.

We had been shown police video of officers in fights with angry speeders, drunks and assorted bad guys over their guns. It is a deadly serious scenario. You have thirty pounds of equipment including vest, gun, Taser, pepper spray, and baton. Each one of these is potentially deadly in the wrong hands. And each one weighs against you in the fight.

Our training exercise began with the cadets forming a circle around two fighters to keep them on the mat. If the fighters got too close to the mat's edge they were none-too-gently pushed back on. The only rule was "There are no rules." We were given no mouth or head protection, since we would have none on the street. The fights were brutal and the blood on the mat had to be cleaned off between each match.

One "blue gun" is placed at the center of the mat. Both fighters lay down prone, facing each other. First one fighter takes a grip on the gun with one hand and then the second fighter does the same. Then the first fighter places their other hand on the gun followed by the second fighter. Once all four hands are on the gun, a whistle blows and the fight begins.

When it was our turn, Donna and I did as instructed. The guys had been waiting for this and catcalls and friendly cheering ensued. I had been watching the other fighters closely. It seemed a lucky elbow in the nose ended the fight sooner. A head butt did too, but was devastating to the recipient.

As soon as the whistle blew I pulled my face out of the way. Donna and I were wrestling on the floor with everything we had. I was determined to get my feet underneath me. I had figured out if I had the leverage, to pull away while she was on the ground, I could win.

We continued wrestling and our legs and elbows were doing each other damage. The adrenaline was keeping us from feeling the majority of the pain. Donna got in a good hit to my chest with her knee and it knocked the wind out of me. I had suffered the feeling several times in my life and knew not to panic. The air would be back before I passed out. The strike enabled her to get her legs beneath her and pull up using the mat to stabilize her legs and establish a backwards momentum to possibly win.

This was it, do or die. I swung my body around on the mat and planted my legs on either side of her chest. Before she could kick me in the groin I shoved with everything I had while holding on to the gun for dear life. My chest expanded at the same time. Donna was shoved to the outer rim of the mat with no gun in her hands.

I had won. I rolled over on my side trying to get more air in and trying to get my arms and legs underneath me. It would have been easier if I released the gun, but I had won it and I wasn't letting go.

Our fight lasted four minutes. It was the longest four minutes of my life. The guys were cheering like crazy. What is it about a girl fight that gets them going?

When everyone's match was finished, we were divided into two groups; the winners in one and the losers in the other. The winning group was congratulating each other and I was getting a lot of back slaps. I don't think any of them thought I could beat Donna.

We didn't expect what happened next.

The losers were given a punishment. They had to write a letter to their families telling them why they died that day. The letter had to be turned in the following morning to our squad leaders.

Up until this point we had been taught we never die. When we put our uniforms on to head out for duty, our number one goal was to return to our families. Staring at the other group and thinking about what those letters would be like was devastating. You could see defeat on their faces.

We silently left the gym.

Later that afternoon, we noticed some unusual activity in the hallway, outside our classroom door. The leader from squad six and our class leader, Cadet Clark, were called to Sgt. Dickens' office. About twenty minutes later Cadet Clark came back into the room and collected the squad leader's personal items. We never saw the squad leader again and a new one was chosen for squad six.

The rumor would later circulate that the unfortunate cadet was caught lying on his police application, and when his background was closely examined, the lie came out. He would never again be eligible to apply as a police officer in the state of Arizona. We were now down to twenty-eight cadets.

That evening, Donna typed her letter. This was psychological torture for her and I watched her cry the entire time. She wasn't angry at me. Donna had a six-year-old son at home, and addressed the letter to him. She cried for hours and I had a hard time getting her out of her funk. The letters were never sent to family members, but it was a hard lesson whether you won or lost.

Friday was uneventful. There was no retaliation for my smart-ass paper on following orders. But I didn't feel as satisfied with my wit any longer. Reality was crashing down.

I headed home to spend time with my husband. He was lonely without me and I managed to pull myself out of a pain-induced stupor and take a day trip with him on Saturday. I cleaned my house on Sunday morning and then headed back to the academy at noon for some much needed study time.

It was now the beginning of week seven and our first in a two-week driving course. Our classroom time was cut in half and we headed to the speed track.

Before the training I thought I was a good driver, but I learned an entirely new way to approach driving situations at the academy. I never considered the difficulties of police driving -- that is, having to turn the stirring wheel with one hand, while holding a microphone in the other and trying to speak into it, without getting everything twisted up. Like everything else at the academy, the training was very intensive but it was fun as well.

The phrase "stopping on a dime" had to have been invented by cops. We learned to stop, swerve, and make "J" turns, while being shot at with paintball guns. Our windows had to be down so we could actually be hit if we didn't do what we were shown. It was fun, exciting and for some cadets painful.

Driving instruction made the two weeks speed by (pun intended), but it didn't stop our anxiety over the approaching ninth week. We were facing our three-hundred question midterm test and our first practical tests, where we would have to act out pretend scenarios with play actors. This was all "do or die" testing. If we didn't pass the midterm we would be sent home. If we didn't pass the practical tests we would be sent home.

Oh yeah, we also had our first official POPAT agility test. We would be given two times to pass POPAT, the first was week nine, and then a final time one week before graduation.

I stayed at the academy that weekend practicing POPAT, studying, and applying ice packs. My stress levels were at their breaking point.

Chapter 14
Testing Hell Week Begins

Monday morning brought our midterms. It would take half the day. We all attended the previous evening's study session and I had a review at my breakfast table that morning. For the first time two other tables were pushed closer and about half our class participated.

It was a long and grueling test, but everyone passed. Cadet Rodriguez actually did very well and was twenty-second in the class. I was ninth and not very happy. Our academic rankings were posted on the wall and I wanted more than anything to be in the top five. I guess I should have been satisfied that at least academically I wasn't in last place, but I was not happy.

Tuesday was POPAT and our schedules showed no morning inspection. We were to be at the training field at 0800. We double timed it over at 0745.

The Police Officers Physical Agility Test starts with running a ninety-nine yard obstacle course. You next scale a six-foot chain link fences followed by a six foot solid fence, then drag a 165 pound "body' 32 feet and when you're good and tired you get to run 500 yards. Our POPAT testing lasted until lunch. I didn't know if I'd made it or not. The results would be available that evening.

The rest of the day was spent on defensive tactics to help prepare us for the practical tests beginning the next day.

Twenty-two feet is considered the safety zone for a suspect with a knife. Even when you know he's going to be coming at you it's almost impossible to pull your gun and fire at the twenty-foot range. We were made to stand with our arms at our sides, with an attacker twenty feet away holding a large rubber knife. As soon as the attacker starts running towards us, we were to draw our guns and fire (this is done by making the bang-bang sound). We were all stabbed. Twenty-two feet is not easy either but at that distance we all managed to shoot. There is no room for error.

I said "stabbed" not "killed" for a reason. For the past eight weeks it was drilled into our psyche we would never die. No matter what happened we were to continue fighting. This mind set is what will save your life. People have died from non-life- threatening gunshot wounds simply because they knew they'd been shot. The only exception to this rule had been our fight for our guns and the "I died today" letters that were written to family.

That evening we gathered in front of our dorms when we heard the results for POPAT were in. Cadet Clark made the announcement that all but one of us had passed. My heart sank.

"Cadet Chavez, can I speak with you in my room? All the rest of you did a good job, and scores will be posted tomorrow in our classroom."

I'd passed. I couldn't believe it. This was the one thing I'd been most worried about. If I was injured and could not complete the final POPAT this score would stand and I would graduate. I passed on my first try.

I waited for Rocco. We cried together. He missed the magic score by twenty-four points. He told me he needed to lose more weight and he was determined to pass. He wouldn't be given the chance until a week before graduation. If he didn't pass in week seventeen he would go home. It was heartbreaking. I told him we would work at POPAT every night and I was not graduating without him. We'd made that deal the first week at the academy.

Non-academy personnel began arriving that evening for the practical tests beginning the following morning. Some would be staying in empty dorm rooms. They were all police officers volunteering their time to help us train. I hoped if I made it through the academy, I would be given the opportunity to come back and help other cadets.

The officers were nice and relaxed. It was strange after weeks of being treated like we were less than human. One officer told me I didn't need to call him sir. That was impossible. I now even said, "Thank you sir or mam," to Starbuck employees during my weekend splurge.

Wednesday morning it began. We were divided into different groups and placed in separate "station" waiting areas. For my first test, I was given a police radio and dispatched to an unidentified man standing on our parade deck. I was told a neighbor called him in because she could see him out her front window and he was making her nervous.

I approached. The man had a large boom box in his hand. I identified myself and asked what he was doing in the area. The man simply stared at me. I asked him for some identification. He laid the boom box down and placed his hand in his pocket. I could see a bulge in the pocket and I asked him to keep his hands where I could see them.

He finally spoke, "Then how you spect me to give you identification?" (He even had the lingo)

I asked if I could pat him down for my safety and explained I just needed to feel the outside of his pockets for a weapon. He complied and I asked him to turn around, keep his hands where I could see them and spread his legs apart. I stepped forward and performed the pat down. My hands were shaking.

He had a large wallet in his front pocket and I asked if his identification was inside. He told me it was. I stepped back and asked him to retrieve his wallet. He gave me his identification and I told him a neighbor called because he was making her nervous.

He then told me he lived down the block and a friend was picking him up here, on the street corner. The scenario was ended. The two judges came forward and told me I did a good job. I was told I should have noticed the bulge in the pocket earlier but I passed and they liked the way I spoke to my suspect.

This scenario was meant as a non-violent confrontation, but it would have turned aggressive if my demeanor warranted it.

Between scenarios we were sent to our station waiting areas. Our dorm meeting room was one of the waiting areas. There was a television, couches and small kitchenette with a microwave and toaster oven. We cadets didn't normally use this area because the college kids used it as a hangout. We were not allowed to talk about any scenarios we'd finished. So we watched a movie we were too nervous to pay attention to while we waited for our names to be called.

There were two scenarios taking place at this station. I was only able to complete the first before lunch. It was a man with a baseball bat threatening to kill his ex-wife, while he was pounding on her apartment door (an empty dorm room).

I drew my gun upon seeing the bat, and had to talk my suspect down from there. I made an arrest and placed him in handcuffs.

After the completion of the scenario I was asked why I drew my weapon. I explained my suspect had a bat and it was a deadly instrument. I was asked if I would have fired if he came towards me with the bat. I said yes and was given a pass on my second scenario.

It was time for lunch. I was excited but several cadets were upset and said they failed their morning practical tests. I couldn't ask which ones they'd taken, but it made me more nervous about what might be ahead for me. I thought both my scenarios had been rather easy.

After lunch, there was another domestic violence scenario at the dorm rooms. I passed it with flying colors. I'd finished the day and did not need to perform any remedial training. It had been a good day for me but too many cadets had failed scenarios.

I knew I probably would not be as lucky on the second day.

Chapter 15
You're Not Dead Until I Say You're Dead

I wish I could say the next two days of Practical tests went as smoothly as the first, but they didn't. I struggled with two of the scenarios, and completely failed one of them. In the one I failed, I was driving a patrol car and came upon a vehicle pulled to the side of the road with its hood up and a man standing with his head buried in the engine. I pulled over behind the vehicle, activated my emergency lights, and called dispatch with my location.

I approached the man, asking if I could help. He straightened up and began shooting at me with a cap gun. The gun looked and sounded real which scared the hell out of me. I stumbled back a few feet trying to remove my gun from my holster as the man continued walking towards me and firing. I probably took six bullets directly to the chest, before my gun was in my hand. I stood my ground, firing two shots, but the guy just stayed where he was firing back at me. I turned to the instructor and said the fatal words, "I'm dead."

All hell broke loose. Sgt. Dickens was standing to the side of my vehicle, and he blew a gasket.

"You are not dead, you never stop fighting. You're a fucking loser Cadet Ivy, and I should kick your ass out of the academy right now."

I stood frozen. I wanted to bury my head in the dirt and cry. Sgt. Dickens told me to get the fuck out of his sight and I left. What a disaster.

I felt I was lucky to even be given a second chance but I was. During the remedial scenario things were changed up. I walked into a "store", answering a dispatched call for a disorderly female customer. I could see the clerk and problem maker ahead of me but I was stopped by a man coming from behind, placing his arm around my throat, and putting a gun to my head. The disorderly female pulled a gun and shot the clerk. I did as I was trained and grabbed the barrel of the gun at my head, pushing it away from my head, turning in my captor's arms, shoving him away with everything I had, and then running for cover while pulling my gun.

The significant difference that allowed me to pass the second scenario was running for cover while removing my gun. The first time, I had stood frozen, while going for my gun and never sought to get away or find cover, to continue the fight. In real life I probably had little chance of surviving either scenario but the instructors wanted to see our thought process during the events. Standing my ground and shooting was not what they were looking for.

It wasn't until I found out that three quarters of the class failed that first specific practical, that I felt somewhat better. I'm surprised Sgt. Dickens had a voice left; apparently he yelled at all of us and threatened to kick everyone out.

My other mistake of the day was missing a small gun while searching a suspect. The gun was on a chain around her neck, in her cleavage. I managed to grab the gun as she was pulling it out to shoot me, but I was pissed at myself. I had performed a bad search on a female suspect of all things. After that incident, my searches were extremely thorough and I found two additional guns during the following scenarios. One was literally underneath a suspect's penis. I located it, removed it, and found some satisfaction in shaking everyone's hand before I was able to wash the ball sweat off.

My last scenario on Friday was with simulated weapons (SIMs). A small group of us were waiting outside the driver's track building and we were able to pick partners. Rocco was in the group so we partnered up. When our turn came we geared up with head, chest and groin protection. I could barely breathe in my facemask. We were also handed SIMs guns with rubber bullets. These guns fire and launch a rubber bullet and leave a colored chalk mark on what they shoot. We were warned it would be painful if we took a hit.

When it was our turn, we walked to the front of the building, and were told to enter the abandoned building to search for a trespassing vagrant. Rocco and I began the search. The building was dark and we used our flashlights. We had our guns drawn, looking and listening, although all I could hear was my loud, too fast breathing. We searched room by room. There was a small closet and Rocco opened the door as I peered inside. My gun came up and I began shouting commands. There was a man standing inside, next to a water heater. He had his weaponless hands, visibly crossed, in front of him. He put his hands up and complied as we talked him out of the closet. The scenario was over and so were the practical tests.

Rocco and I went back to the classroom and it took about an hour for everyone else to finish up. We were all telling each other which tests we had passed and failed. Everyone made mistakes. We were all upset over the popgun incident and no one felt as if they'd aced it. Donna had not returned and I didn't find out how she did until we were released, she came into the classroom and sat down right before our scolding started.

Sgt. Dickens came into the room after we were all assembled. He was pissed off and stated there were forty-three guns missed in searches. He asked everyone that missed a gun to stand up. Everyone stood. Some cadets missed more than one. We were given forty-three hill runs to be completed the following Monday.

Sgt. Dickens also told us two cadets shot an unarmed man and these two cadets needed to consider if police work was right for them. He told us in real life the two "officers" would not only lose their police certifications but would be prosecuted for homicide.

The judges next reviewed specific scenarios and we were praised on how we handled ourselves throughout the two days. We were told to be proud of the job we had done. This was hard due to the angry look on Sgt. Dickens' face.

Donna and another cadet were called to the Sergeant's office when we were given permission to leave for the weekend. I waited for Donna before taking off. She was crying when she entered the room.

She told me she shot the unarmed man in the closet with her SIMs gun. Sgt. Dickens told both cadets they needed to think long and hard over the weekend about being police officers. I consoled her and said Sgt. Dickens was an ass. We both packed our laundry and took off for our homes.

Donna called me that weekend and told me she was not returning. She was sorry to leave me alone, but she could not take it anymore. The thought of being prosecuted for homicide was more than she could handle and her mind was set.

My son also announced he had taken a job in Phoenix and would be moving out in two weeks. He barely spoke to me and refused to ask about the academy. I loved him dearly but his attitude hurt. I didn't know if he would ever see me as my own person and not just his mother. My daughters were both proud of me. Letty, my oldest had announced her wedding date a few weeks earlier. She already had an apartment of her own. Cassie, the youngest, was doing well in her first semester of college. She had left for Tucson when I left for the academy.

With Roger moving out, my house would finally have just my husband and me under the roof. In some ways this was a blessing but it was sad as well. My husband would be alone during my last nine weeks at the academy. I worried about him. He said he would survive but was counting the days until my graduation.

Driving back to the academy that Sunday was hard, and I had a heavy heart. My friend would not be there, waiting for me. I cried for her and myself. I realized becoming a police officer was about inner strength. I made the drive slowly not wanting to face my empty dorm room. I still had Rocco and I was determined he would pass POPAT. I was not graduating without him, and I planned to graduate.

Chapter 16
No Jerking Off On My Range

Returning to my dorm room on Sunday evening was depressing. All signs of Donna were gone. I went in search of moral support. Rocco hadn't arrived yet. Cadet Rodriguez, known as P-Rod was looking a lot worse for wear. Philip Rodriguez is the cadet who ran my ten punishment hill runs with me and it was hard to be down when around him. He's one of those "Life is wonderful people." I think I was one of those people before the academy, but the stress was wearing me down. It never seemed to bother P-Rod and I felt lucky to run into him.

He said he got extremely drunk on Saturday night in celebration of his twenty-first birthday and lost his virginity. He was a good-looking, hardworking guy. He told me he thought he was in love with the lucky girl. I was impressed he'd held out until he was twenty-one.

I told Rodriguez about Donna not returning. He told me he had seen my determination that first week at the academy and never doubted I would make it. He said he never saw the same resolve in Donna. And when she wrote the famous memo about our Sergeant bothering us during classroom time, he was surprised she hadn't quit then. He said she didn't have the nerve to handle the job.

Hangover or not, this young man was wise beyond his years. I would miss Donna terribly, but I was learning daily this job was not for everyone. The other cadet (besides Donna) who shot his SIMs gun at an unarmed man returned to the academy. His department would be informed of his faulty judgment call but they would allow him to remain. We had now survived half our training and were down to twenty-six cadets.

Monday we were given our department issue duty weapons minus bullets. These had been kept in the classroom vault. We double-checked everyone's guns, including instructors, to make sure none were loaded. For me, even this small step with guns was huge.

I had never owned a gun in my life. Going out with Sergeant Spears, before coming to the academy, was the full extent of my firearm handling experience.

We spent the day in the classroom learning about our weapons and "dry firing," which is aiming at a target and pulling the trigger with no bullets in the gun. Different videos were played on the front classroom screen to simulate shooting scenarios. We would shoot our guns at the front screen when appropriate. At the end of the day we were taught to dismantle and clean our weapons. They were then returned to the vault.

We were divided into two groups. Group one would head to the range the next day while group two would stay and have class lecture. I was in the second group. We would alternate activities and days so that each group went to the range twice a week. Range days would start after physical training or defensive tactics and go until evening.

It seemed odd on Tuesday with half the class missing, but it was also very stress free. I was saving my panic for the following day at the range.

Wednesday morning we headed to the range and were issued our weapons and ammunition. Our guns and two extra magazines were loaded. Range rules were drilled into us. If we deviated from a single rule we would be asked to leave permanently. The old, "You will be sent home" mantra was back in force.

There were four range instructors for thirteen of us. The instructor assigned to me was becoming frustrated. And so was I but couldn't help it. I was not a very good shot. And I was worried that shooting would be the death of my academy experience and my police career.

Lieutenant Hurd was head instructor in charge of firearms training. He stayed mostly on the opposite end of the range. At the end of the day Lt. Hurd pulled me aside and asked how I did.

"With all due respect sir," I said, "I sucked."

"You don't suck and believe me I would rather have a new shooter than someone that is unwilling to learn the proper way of handling a gun. I can mold you into someone that is confident and smart with their firearm."

I was having difficulty with his assurance.

"Honestly I think my biggest problem is being afraid of guns. I don't like them."

Lieutenant Hurd laughed and said, "We have a lot in common. I still have a very healthy respect for guns and I'm not a gun fanatic like many officers. I wasn't raised with guns. In the long run you and I have less chance of having an accidental discharge of our weapons. We always respect them. A little fear is a good thing. Always keep in mind that guns are made to kill. They really have no other use."

"But if I suck so badly and can't hit the target, I don't know what good it will do being armed out on the street. I may be able to hit a vehicle or the broad side of a barn door but that's about it."

He laughed again and told me he would help my group come Friday. He said he would fix my problems and not to worry about it. I felt better but continued having concerns. My fear didn't seem to affect Lt. Hurd at all. I would try keeping his lack of worry in the back of my mind and think positive thoughts. Yeah right.

On Friday we began with a practice shoot and then were told we would start learning our qualify drills. The instructor from Tuesday stayed clear of me. He was a stereotypical healthy, in excellent shape, clean cut, bigoted cop, the stereotype that had clearly defined ideals of cop material. And I didn't fit it. My very presence seemed to annoy him and his "type" endlessly.

Lt. Hurd finally came over as promised. He stood beside me and said I needed to relax as I was shooting. He told me I was jerking off. Was he kidding? Before I could decide to be offended, he explained I was anticipating my shots and jerking my gun. He smiled and said he did not allow jerking off on his range. I smiled and relaxed a bit.

He asked for my pistol and then asked me to turn around. I did as instructed. After a moment he handed my gun back and told me to face my target again. He instructed me to fire one bullet. I fired. My shot went wide. He told me to fire again. I did. This time the only thing that happened was my hand and gun jerked up but no bullet exited the barrel. I was jerking my hand in anticipation of the gun firing. This was my problem. He had put blanks in my gun to show me. I fired again but didn't jerk. I hit the target and then hit the target again. The next shot was a blank. My gun did not jerk.

Now that I knew what I was doing wrong and why, I began to improve. Whenever I would forget his lesson and my hand jerked, I would hear him shout, "Ivy, you're jerking off on my range again." It would put me back on target and keep me smiling.

Rocco (nickname, The Rock) was a good shooter and we both began enjoying our time on the range. Again, I learned why we did so many pushups. We shot over six hundred rounds every time we went to the shooting field.

The weeks flew by and we were finally at week four, time for our firearm qualifiers. I was improving and consecutively shooting in the 240's. We needed a 210 to pass with a 250 being a perfect score. Several of the cadets shot 250's on a regular basis. I passed qualification day with no problems and was feeling proud of myself. Friday night we would return to the range for our qualification.

On the day between our qualifiers, we had a lesson in traffic control. It began with a twenty-minute classroom lecture about hand signals. We were then bussed to a major intersection in the city. The traffic lights were turned off along with the crosswalk signals. One by one we were thrown into the street with a traffic vest and a whistle.

Talk about on the job training. The saving grace was that there were signs posted, "Police Training in Progress."

Each Cadet directed traffic for ten minutes. It took the first five minutes to learn the ropes while traffic backed up. The next five minutes were actually fun. I think a little control created a small monster in most of us. It was comical. Some drivers just tried to ignore us while others shouted obscenities or laughed out their windows.

I waved cars forward and stopped them at my leisure. A pedestrian dared to cross before I gave him permission. I told him to get his ass back to the curb and I made him stand for an extra minute before giving him the go ahead. He complied, which was a smart move on his part. If not, I may have taken out my rubber gun and said, "Bang-bang."

We had a few near misses but overall it was a great experience. I always appreciate those comical officers on television that make directing traffic an art form. I was not one of them. But I did get the job done.

After lunch on Friday we headed back to the range. There were different scenarios set up and while we waited for the sun to go down we did a lot of tactical shooting, which is running across the range and shooting at different targets.

During one test, pylons were set up every six feet. Six small metal targets were spaced twenty feet in front of us, six feet apart between pylons. We could not stop moving between the first two pylons until we hit the first target. We would then move to the next two pylons. Back and forth we ran in a six-foot space until that fateful "ping." For safety's sake we went through the course one at a time. By the time we were at the last three targets it was easier and our speed picked up. The test was timed and the scores would be added to our overall range rankings.

As hard as I felt some of the shooting tests were, by the time the sun went down, I was ready to shoot at a non-moving target. I passed with a good score and was not last. For me, this was something to celebrate.

My confidence was increasing and the end to my academy days was in sight. Only five more weeks and I was holding on to my determination for all it was worth.

Chapter 17
The Police Perspective

The academy was changing me, mentally, as well as physically.
Physically, I didn't just have arm bicep muscles. I had muscles in my forearms, thighs and butt. No jello cheeks for that polygraph seat now.

Mentally, I was now seeing things from the "police perspective."

This was pointed out to me by an old friend I saw during a weekend stay in the city. We went to Starbucks for breakfast. She asked what I would do if someone walked in and robbed the cashier. I told her I would be an excellent witness and observe everything he or she was wearing, along with noticing facial and body features. My friend asked what I would do if I was actually an officer, off duty with my gun. I told her I would do exactly the same thing and I wouldn't take out my gun unless the suspect started shooting.

My friend was floored. She didn't understand. I was going to be a cop and she expected me to act like the cops on television. I explained my reasoning. I had to look at the amount of people in jeopardy if I opened fire, the people sitting behind me if the suspect opened fire. The suspect getting away with some cash was very small compared to an innocent person being killed.

I don't think my friend "got it." I just looked at things differently now. A motto drilled into us daily at the academy was to go home to our families every night. Be smart and be safe. Police Officers are not like firemen. When we're off duty we don't advertise that we are officers. It's dangerous.

During those last academy weeks we watched a movie that talked about keeping your family safe and teaching your children to not say anything about you being a police officer. The film shows a boy and his father at a hotel getting off the elevator and seeing two men fighting. The father tries to get his young son back into the elevator when the son says, "Do something dad, you're a cop." Both men turn; one pulls out a gun and starts shooting at the boy and his father. End of video.

I think this was something none of us ever thought of. Our children should be proud to have an officer for a mom or dad. In real life, "cop" families don't advertise who they are. When they are with fellow officers and their families it's a different story but when not on duty and out in public, it's important to remain anonymous.

I see firefighter t-shirts everywhere. I seldom if ever see a police t-shirt unless it's the rock-n-roll band "Police."

On the east wall of our academy classroom Sgt. Dickens posted the "Officer Down" memorial page of every officer, in the United States that was killed in the line of duty, while we were at the academy. Without a word, he would walk into the classroom during our instruction time with the "page" in hand. Silence would descend. With measured dignity, he would post the page and then walk out.

Another officer dead. Another family left to grieve. Fellow police officers across the country left to mourn.

The longer we were at the academy the more pages appeared on that wall. During our breaks we would read the latest officer's page and mourn in our own way. Two officers died in Arizona during our eighteen weeks. The sadness was overwhelming but until it happened to one of our own, I don't think we understood the sense of loss that we would forever feel.

Four months after we graduated the academy, I got the call at six in the morning. It was from one of the guys I sat with in the classroom.

Through tears he said, "This is Mike, P-Rod is dead."

My mind didn't seem to want to process the words.

Deputy Philip Rodriguez (P-Rod as he was known at the academy) was only twenty-one years old and just beginning life, engaged to the incredible young woman he gave his virginity to. He always had a goofy smile plastered on his face. He got a great amount of teasing from his fellow cadets, but he took it all in stride and we loved him. He was the baby of the class and he had so many hopes and dreams for his future as a police officer.

P-Rod was also the incredible young man who ran beside me through all ten punishment hill runs when I was at my lowest point. And he was the one who bolstered my determination when Donna quit the academy.

While crying, Mike told me P-Rod was heading to a code-3 (lights and sirens) call, when he lost control of his vehicle and was ejected. He died at the scene.

I stayed on the phone with Mike as we both cried and tried to find some sense in P-Rod's death. There was none to find, but we needed each other.

I went into work that day to request time off for the funeral. I was asked if I needed to see a counselor and told one could be made available before or after the funeral. I was shocked it was even offered but I would grow to understand what it meant to be part of a police department and wear a badge.

Deputy Philip Rodriguez' funeral was held in his high school auditorium to accommodate the large amount of mourners. The stands were filled with his high school classmates and friends. On the floor of the gymnasium were hundreds of chairs filled with police officers and deputies from Arizona and surrounding states.

We, his classmates at the academy, all sat together. The academy classmates working at his department were his pall bearers. When the service was over we walked up together to say our last goodbyes. We were in groups of three and fours and all holding hands.

When I turned to walk away I saw Sgt. Dickens at my side. He was crying. I let go of the hands holding mine and tightly hugged Sgt. Dickens. The day before graduation he had made us all promise to always wear our seatbelts while on duty. We all swore. P-Rod broke his promise and you could see the hurt over this young officer's life in Sgt. Dickens' eyes.

We walked out to our vehicles to line up for the procession. Mike rode with me.

P-Rod was buried at the top of a hill in a cemetery overlooking the valley. I was about twentieth in line and as we came to a stop, at the top of the rise, Mike told me to turn and look down the hill. As far as you could see, there were hundreds of police vehicles with red and blue lights flashing.

At the cemetery, all officers lined up to give Philip our last solute. All the drills we had not performed since being out of the academy were used as we were called to attention. Every Officer knew the drill no matter how many years they had been on the streets. We saluted Philip and his family.

We were then told to turn on our portable radios. The dispatcher on duty, during the time of Philip's death, announced his final call. His "End of Watch" was recognized and his watch was turned over to us. We would take his duty and live up to his dream of what it was to be a police officer.

Philip Rodriquez' memorial page is at http://www.odmp.org/officer/18852-deputy-sheriff-philip-anthony-rodriguez. Philip's time as a detention officer before going to the academy is included with his time of service. He held the detention officer job until he was old enough to begin his dream of being an Officer. His time of service as a Deputy was four months.

Yes, I was changing. Even before Philip's death I was a different person than I had been when beginning the academy. I watched everything around me with a new eye. I had a different perception of the world. I was tougher and more secure in who I was. During those last weeks at the academy the world shifted and I began knowing I had what it takes. This was no longer a whim. This was the beginning of my life as an officer.

Chapter 18
The Most Popular Cadet

Graduation day was only five weeks away. I wish I could say
the academy was easier at this point, but it was only getting harder.
Sgt. Dickens never thought I would make it this far and now,
concerned that I just might make it all the way through to the end, he
was out to get me.

Police Chief Varnett and Sergeant Spears from Small Town PD
attended an academy luncheon. The luncheon was an opportunity for
individual police departments to speak with class Sergeant Dickens
about their cadets. We cadets were not allowed anywhere near the
event. Later that evening, Sgt. Spears called and asked me to meet
him outside my dorm. We then went for a long walk.

He began by congratulating me for making it as far as I had. He
told me he was proud of my determination. He then dropped the
bomb. He and my Chief had been told by Sgt. Dickens that I was not
officer material. I was, according to Dickens, physically and
mentally unfit to wear a badge. I was devastated.

Sgt. Spears told me Sgt. Dickens wanted me removed from the
academy immediately. I held my breath as he continued to talk.

"Suzie, I didn't have to send you to the academy. I questioned
my decision repeatedly but I saw something in you. I see it now. I've
discussed it with the Chief and he is deferring to my judgment.
You're staying. Be aware your class Sergeant has it in for you and he
is not happy with our decision."

I hugged Sgt. Spears. I could tell he was uncomfortable with my
emotion, but he patted me on the back and returned the hug.

"I won't let you down." I promised.

We continued to walk, and he asked me questions about my
experience. He told me a little about his journey through the same
academy. He talked about sneaking out at night and drinking alcohol
at the top of the water tower. Alcohol was banned on the college

campus and he would have been kicked out of the academy if he'd been caught.

By the time I returned to my dorm, I felt I had a new friend In Sgt. Spears. I knew I was not Sgt. Dickens' favorite cadet but I felt he had let up on me slightly. I had always thought of myself as a likable person but I realized Sgt. Dickens did not just dislike me; he wanted me gone. This was a hard realization but at the same time it just added that extra spark to my determination. I had come too far to even consider quitting and I wanted to be a police officer like nothing I had ever before desired in my life.

During morning physical training, we were now running six miles. Once a week we ran our "personal best." This is when we would run on our own, not as a group and our times were recorded. My "personal best" time had gotten much better but I continued to finish well behind the rest of the class.

One morning, as I was running alone through our desert trail, I noticed a vehicle parked in the distance. I could see a man looking through binoculars and watching me run. It was Sgt. Dickens. I continued running and actually pushed myself harder. He would not catch me slacking.

I spoke to my squad advisor about the incident and he confided that Sgt. Dickens suspected I was walking, when no one else was around, during my personal best runs. It was not true and I was pissed off he would think so. It was just another sign of his dislike.

At the beginning of week fifteen, we were told to wear our department uniforms. It was exciting to actually put on my police uniform. None of us looked the same as we did when we started at the academy. We looked like real police officers and deputies, if you could look past the rubber guns in our belts. The "baby" class, class 96, was now allowed to wear their academy polo shirts and it was great to see them out of white shirts and ties.

The first day of week fifteen, Sgt. Dickens came to early morning physical training and was waiting for cadets to finish our personal best runs. The entire class had finished but me and I was nowhere to be seen.

I was running along minding my own business, when suddenly the rest of the class appeared. I saw them coming and wondered if we were being made to run the course again. But they all turned around when they reached me and started kept pace by my side.

Rocco said, "Don't ask!"

It was impossible for me to run and talk anyway so I continued over the finish line. I later learned that Sgt. Dickens had asked everyone where I was. When informed that I was still running, he started yelling.

"You call yourselves a team? Have I taught you nothing? You left a fellow cadet on her own. What if she's injured, been bit by a rattlesnake? You don't know where she is or what she's doing."

Later at morning's inspection, Sgt. Dickens told us to march back to our rooms and put on the white shirts and ties we wore when we first came to the academy. We did as told and returned to the inspection deck. We were then told we were not a team and we would walk everywhere through campus holding hands until we were a team. It was never explained what our infraction was and we didn't ask. We had learned early on that a reason didn't matter. It always seemed to depend on the Sergeant's mood.

On lunch break, we made our first walk to the cafeteria holding hands, all twenty-six of us. It was embarrassing but comical as well. I was the most popular person in the class. Every guy wanted to hold my hand. I switched places over the next two days during every formation march. The college students got a big kick out of us. We were kind of like the ROTC and it was fun to ridicule us.

I was finally getting a true sense of how incredible my classmates were. It was fun to be fought over during our marches but I was also feeling they wanted me to make it to graduation. I'm not sure when the entire class transformation began but they let me know they were behind me. I might not have been the ideal cadet but I had become one of them and we took care of each other.

As the week progressed I began getting a bad head and chest cold. I was having trouble breathing during any physical activities we were assigned. I wasn't the only cadet suffering but it was slowing me down physically, which I didn't need.

Sgt. Dickens again showed up at morning physical training and took over our instruction. He told us we were to run around the track and every cadet was to finish within two minutes, or we would start again until we all accomplished the desired time.

I couldn't do it. I tried. Every cadet would finish and then run back to where I was and cheer me on. My lungs were about to explode, I couldn't catch my breath and I thought I would die if I did not get air. We ran three laps, with me being the only one not able to make it, within the two-minute time limit.

On the fourth lap something amazing happened. Two cadets ran beside me, lifted me under my arms and began carrying me. They ran about twenty yards and two more cadets took over, and on it went until I was around the track.

I don't know if we made it in under the allotted time, but Sgt. Dickens told us to change back into our uniforms before inspection and he walked away. His lesson was cemented in our minds.

We were a team. And, while I hated being the "weak one," I was a part of that team and now my academy class had proved it.

Chapter 19
Pepper Spray Me; I Shoot You

I made it through another seven days. It was now the week of
Thanksgiving. We would have a four-day break from the academy.
But before that break came, Wednesday, pepper spray day. A day I
had been dreading like no other. I had hated our CS (tear gas)
training and everyone who had previously encountered pepper spray
said the pepper spray, also known as OC spray, was much worse.

Almost daily, we were performing scenarios enacted by our
squad advisors and overseen by Sgt. Dickens. I was becoming
known as a shooter. In one scenario, I was told a fellow officer had
entered a home and was not answering his radio. I knocked on the
door and heard yelling from inside. I drew my gun and pushed open
the door. The officer (a life like dummy) was lying on the floor and a
man was standing over him and hitting the officer in the head with a
bat. I shot and killed the suspect. The scenario was immediately
ended and Sgt. Dickens began yelling "articulate your reasons,"
wanting to know why I shot.

I calmly said, "He had a bat. I did not know if the downed
officer was dead but he was obviously unconscious. I shot the
suspect because I was the only chance the officer had to survive. The
suspect had already taken down one officer, and was armed and
dangerous."

Although said grudgingly, Sgt. Dickens replied, "Good job."

We were always yelled at when we had to defend our decisions.
It was part of thinking under stressful conditions. The words
"articulate your reasons" were used throughout my academy
experience. I learned to articulate very well.

For some reason, I was always justified in my "Kills." I would
explain my reasoning and pass each time. Other cadets would not
shoot so fast. Some would even fail the scenario because of this.

During one of these scenarios, our defensive tactics instructor
punched a fellow cadet in the eye and then when he didn't lift his

hands to defend his face he was punched in the other eye. I don't mean soft taps here. The cadet had two black eyes for days after the incident. I was not punched because I shot the bad guy (our defensive tactics instructor) and then defended my decision correctly.

These incidents only seemed to piss my Sergeant off more. I wasn't sure why but my fellow cadets laughed because I passed all the scenarios by shooting.

Rocco and I continued to work on POPAT together. I had no doubt he would pass the next testing and his confidence was at its highest point. He'd lost over fifty pounds and was kicking my butt in all the physical activities we did.

During these last weeks at the academy things began to get lighter when it came to inspection and penalties for unknown infractions. I no longer had that feeling of dread in my stomach when Sgt. Dickens walked up to our parade deck for morning inspection. We would manage to get through the morning with only twenty to thirty pushups.

I continued to miss Donna and I thought of her often. Rocco and P-Rod became my support. I feel they gave more to me than I could ever return. The three of us were acing our Monday morning tests and Rocco and P-Rod excelling physically at everything put before us. I too, was doing better, though my body continued to fight me, and the four day break coming up would again be one of icepacks and Ibuprofen.

Pepper spray Wednesday rolled around. We were marched out to an area beside the track by the "red shirts." We had learned during our earlier academy experience with CS gas that these men (officers) in red shirts signified pain. Yes, it was necessary but they seemed to get great enjoyment from what they would be bringing our way.

Pepper spray could not be put off and many cadets had their remedies with them. Small portable battery operated fans, bottles of baby shampoo, and so on. They'd been told by previous pepper spray survivors that these items would help with the burning.

We were made to stand and recite our full name and police department name and address. During this recitation we were sprayed directly in the eyes with pepper spray. We were then attacked and hit with a square pad held by an instructor. We had to successfully fight the attacker off and then the instructor would back off and grab a weapon. It could be a knife, gun or baton. We would then need to radio our location to dispatch, tell them we were under attack, and identify the object in the instructor's hand, while he threatened us. Depending on his weapon we would take the appropriate action.

Within ten to fifteen seconds after being sprayed our eyes were swollen shut, and burning like nothing we'd ever felt. We had to use one hand to pull our eyelids apart just to see, and yell the commands into our radios, all the while yelling at our attacker to obey our commands.

My turn came and I was sprayed and then attacked with the pad. I used my radio correctly and then I lucked out and my attacker had a gun, which I identified. I shot him. My turn was over. I had passed, though the pain was not over. I was led by fellow cadets blindly to a water hose and helped to point it into my eyes to thoroughly flush them out. I was then left alone, so the cadets could rescue the next victim. My hands and fingers were burning where I'd touched my eyelids. The effects would last for hours.

We were told to be careful when taking a shower that evening and to wash our heads and faces with our bodies standing away from the stream. This kept the pepper spray from running down our bodies and burning everything it came in contact with. Advisers described which body parts would be the most painful if the pepper spray connected. I couldn't even imagine the spray in that particular area. We were also told to be careful washing our clothing because the pepper spray would reactivate in the wash. I think the worst part was the fact my skin burned for hours. Nothing helped the burning but time. I tried the baby shampoo and even a fan. Time was the cure.

All this torture was lifesaving preparation. If a suspect managed to get our pepper spray away from us or had his or her own to spray, we needed to know how it would affect us. It was also possible when using pepper spray on a suspect, to have the wind blow it back on us. I now knew the pepper spray was practically incapacitating. If I had to shoot a suspect due to any of these previous scenarios, I could articulate my reasoning due to my experience. This would be the most painful single experience I would have at the academy. I never wanted to be pepper sprayed again.

Thanksgiving break at last. The police department in Small Town, Arizona was having its annual Thanksgiving banquet on Saturday and my husband and I were invited. I was nervous. It would be my first time meeting most of my department, and I worried about what they would think of me.

With a potluck dish in hand, my husband and I arrived and were introduced around to everyone. There was no way to remember all the Officers' names much less their spouses' names. The Chief and Sergeant's wives were great. They were excited to finally be getting a female at the department. The officers stayed back. Besides saying a brief hello, during introductions, they kept to themselves. I was not deterred. I had won over my fellow cadets at the academy and I had no doubt I could get along with the officers I would be working with. The situation would also improve once I was actually wearing a badge.

There would be plenty of challenges coming my way in a department that had never before employed a female cop. But I was looking forward to them. Now all I had to do was finish my last three weeks at the academy.

Chapter 20
Electric Erection

The end of our time at the academy was in sight. We could all see it and we were feeling it too. Everything was being thrown at us at once. We were preparing for the AZ-POST (Arizona Police Officer Standards and Training Board) exam. This would be our final. We had to pass in order to be certified as police officers in the state of Arizona. It covered all the material we'd learned since entering the academy. We were hitting the books hard.

We were also preparing for our "stop and approach" practical tests. These are an even more grueling set of scenarios than the ones we had in our ninth week. Then, on the Friday morning of stop and approach week, we would be given our last PO-PAT (physical) test. Our nerves were shot and we were all tense.

Even with everything being put on our shoulders, the environment at our dorms in the evening was relaxed. We spent time sitting around in a large group talking about our academy experience and singing songs. A couple of the cadets brought guitars and we listened and joined in whenever we knew the words.

The cadet who sat on my left in our classroom finally opened up and told me he did not think I had a chance in hell of making it through the academy on that first day. He had just gotten out of the military when he was hired by his agency and was in top shape.

He sat next to me all those weeks and was always pleasant but he didn't really warm up to me until those evenings we sat around talking, laughing and singing. He was a great guy and had a great career in front of him as a law enforcement officer.

I also spoke quite a bit with Class Leader Clark. I had so much admiration for him. He was the smartest guy I had ever met. Before coming to the academy he was preparing to take his L-SAT (Law School Admission Test). He made a last minute change and decided to go into law enforcement. He had a wife and four children waiting at home for him. The fate of our class rested on his shoulders. I don't think any other cadet could have handled it as well as him. He had backed me since day one and I would never forget his encouragement.

My body continued to give me problems and during one of my chiropractor visits, I was set up with a TENS machine to help relieve my back pain. The TENS unit gives off electronic pulses and interrupts the pain signals going to the brain. One evening I brought it out to our nightly group session and we started playing with it. When turned up high it gave quite a jolt.

We would hold hands and see how many cadets the current would affect when we made a circle. One of our goofier cadets started connecting the prongs to different body parts. He would then have me turn the settings on high and see how long he could take it. He placed a probe on either side of his foot and ended up falling backwards over the bench he was sitting on when I turned up the unit. We couldn't control our laughter and it became a contest to see who could follow in his footsteps and repeat what he did.

These were young guys, mind you, most in their twenties, and it didn't take long before the probes were going under clothing on unmentionable body parts. We were laughing so hard we were crying. We called it the electric erection. We were like a bunch of kids, good friends and family. For that short amount of time, I felt like a kid again and not old enough to be these mens' mother.

On another one of these evenings, my friend Veronica drove down to check out the academy. She brought along Betty, another one of my good friends. They were able to eat dinner in the cafeteria with me and I showed them around campus. After dinner they asked if I could go out to a bar. I told them I would have needed to get written permission several days in advance. We walked around the campus for a while and I finally said, to hell with it. If Sgt. Spears from my future department could sneak up to the tower and get drunk, I could sneak off campus.

We made a break for it and ended up at the bar inside Chili's Restaurant. Betty was our designated driver so Veronica and I tied one on. I'm not sure how many pitchers of margaritas we had but I could barely walk by the time we left.

I stumbled into my dorm room at 0100 hours. I was up at 0445 hours, or at least that's when the alarm went off. I struggled to get out of bed and somehow managed to get myself to physical training. My head was spinning uncontrollably. I showered fast, brushed my teeth and shoved gum into my mouth (also against the rules). My stomach was turning and I was thinking a night of disobeying orders was not the best of ideas.

After warming up, I ran to the bathroom and puked my guts up which helped. I then went back out and struggled through a six-mile run and weight training. Thank god no one smelled alcohol on my breath. I know it was a lot to risk, but I needed to cross the line. I had done everything asked of me, and this act of rebellion felt great, although my stomach and head didn't. I will always love Veronica for bringing out my wild side and helping me break the rules. I had earned this small break in routine.

I waited all day for Sgt. Dickens to mention I was seen leaving campus but it never happened. The week ended and there were only two weeks to go. The following week would be the hardest we had yet to face. Sitting in my classroom on Friday, I looked around at all these hopeful young men. I couldn't imagine one of them failing at this late date. I was thinking the same of myself.

We had all come so far and everything we had learned was coming together. This had been the longest sixteen weeks of my life. Two more to go and I did not plan on letting anything stop me.

Chapter 21
Failure Is Not An Option

After what seemed like a short weekend, Monday came around. It was the day of our last weekly test. I had studied hard and did well. We all passed. The rest of the day was spent in the classroom reviewing for the final exam, which would take place the following Monday.

Tuesday was our Defensive Tactics final. We had to know the names of all the major pressure points and major nerves on the body. We had to demonstrate proper take down procedure as well as handcuffing techniques. We all passed this test, as well.

Stop and approach scenarios would begin on Wednesday. As they did last time, all the volunteers arrived the evening before. We had been hearing horror stories of what we would undergo in these final practical tests. We were told the staff and volunteers had taken it easy on us during the first set of scenarios. Stop and approach was do or die and would take every bit of knowledge we possessed to pass.

Sgt. Dickens told the class he already knew two cadets would not be passing because they didn't have what it took to be officers. I knew I was one of those cadets. I just didn't know who the other person was. I felt he had made up a second person because he could not just point me out.

Wednesday finally came and the tests began. My first test involved a man caught shoplifting at a convenience store. He was in a "red man" suit, which caused my heart to speed up even more. A red man suit is a padded, head to toe covering, used in demonstration exercises. The suit is always red. It has a face guard as well as foot guards. It can take a lot of punishment but the person wearing it can give it back as well.

The suspect was sitting in a chair and holding a medium sized box. The instructor pretended to be the store manager and said the gentleman was caught walking out of the store with the contraband. I walked over and asked the man if I could see his identification. He started yelling and threw the box at me. I pulled out my baton and told him to turn around and place his hands behind his back, he was under arrest. He complied and I handcuffed him. The scenario was ended.

These type scenarios were used to be sure we did not use excessive force when it was not necessary. The suspect was in the red man suit to increase our anticipation of violence. I passed and moved on to my next test.

I was sent to the campus gym. We had to wait outside and again we were able to partner up. A young cadet went in with me. It was pitch black inside and we turned on our flashlights. Mats had been used to section off areas and we faced blind spots at every turn. We then heard a scream.

We kept our cool and continued slowly towards the screams. Our first suspect came at us on the last turn. My partner took him down as I watched our backs and kept an eye on a female crouched against a wall screaming. After the first guy was secure, I walked towards the female telling her who I was. A second man came around the corner and was on me before I could blink. I hit him in the head with my blue gun, which was in my hand (it had to have hurt). I then placed him in handcuffs. The scenario was ended. Again, I passed.

After my lunch break, I went to my third test of the day. It was a vehicle speeding away after the occupants inside the vehicle had robbed a bank. I performed a "high risk vehicle stop." This is a training we spend days perfecting. It's done the same throughout the country and saves officer's lives.

The driver of the vehicle jumped out and began running up a hillside beside where his vehicle was stopped. He was firing a SIMs weapon at me as he ran. I returned fire but kept an eye on the others remaining in the vehicle. I radioed back to dispatch and told them one of the occupants had taken off running to the north and he was armed with a gun. I then sat in the "V" of my car door's front seat. I watched the vehicle occupants as well as the hills where my other suspect had run. The scenario ended. I was told I did a great job.

My adrenalin was sky high. It's true: police officers are adrenalin junkies. I didn't understand until I went to the academy. It was like no other feeling on earth. I was flying.

Next I headed to the dorms and underwent domestic violence scenarios. I spoke with fellow cadets while we waited. Not everyone was doing as well as me.

The Class 96 Sergeant was talking to some fellow instructors as I walked up. I didn't know her well and I was surprised when she asked me to walk a short ways away from everyone and talk to her. I replied, "Yes mam," and followed her.

"Cadet Ivy do you understand what is happening today?"

"I hope so." I replied.

"Do you understand you are not meant to pass the stop and approach tests?"

"Yes ma'am."

"I want you to fight and when you don't think you can fight anymore I want you to pull out everything you have and continue fighting. Do you understand?"

My eyes had tears when I replied, "Yes ma'am I do."

She walked away. To this day I will always remember her support. Her words inspired me and gave me strength. What an incredible Sergeant. She was promoted about a year later to Lieutenant.

I didn't do as well on the domestic violence scenarios, as I had on the first set weeks before, but I passed. Day one of stop and approach was finished.

Thursday was more of the same. The scenarios continued throughout the day. The only one of note before "the disaster" was the SIMs building search. This time I was going in alone and was geared up in protection equipment. I was handed my SIMs gun and I entered the building. I went into the first room on the right. As I was exiting a man came towards me pointing a gun at his own head. He was screaming and I yelled several times for him to stop. He continued to advance and I shot him three times in the chest. The scenario ended. I was asked why I shot and I explained the man continued to approach, disobeyed my instructions to stop, and he could have turned the gun on me at any moment. I was then asked what the man was yelling and I told the instructor I had no idea.

We had been taught about tunnel vision and loss of hearing when our adrenalin was high. I had just experience the hearing loss first hand. I was told to stand to the side of the first door as the next cadet entered for his test. I watched and listened. The man holding the gun and pointing it at his own head was approaching the cadet saying, "I hate fucking cops and I will kill every one of you." Wow! What a thing to miss and what a wakeup call. I passed the scenario but was upset over what I had not heard. The instructor told me ever cadet fails to hear those words and it was normal but also a learning lesson.

The day continued and I had one scenario left. It was another red man test. Cadet Clark came up to me after he finished and said for me not to worry, I would pass it with flying colors.

When I started the scenario, I was told there were some unidentified noises coming from inside a building. I entered. There was a "red man" hitting a woman with a large club while she was trying to fight him off. I attacked. I don't know why I didn't shoot him but I didn't. I flung him to the ground and tried to gain control of his arms. I was unsuccessful and he got up and came at me with the club. I took him to the ground again and continued fighting. He continued to get up. We continued on as I gave everything I had to get him under control. I was fighting for my life and I refused to give up.

I don't know how long this went on but the instructor finally yelled, "Fucking shoot him! What's wrong with you?"

I pulled out my gun and shot.

The scenario ended and I had failed. The instructor was screaming at me. Sgt. Dickens was in the room watching. I was holding back tears trying not to cry. The instructor continued to yell at me until he kicked me out of the room.

Cadet Clark was waiting outside. He couldn't believe I'd failed. I will never forget his words.

"We all knew you would pass this one. You always shoot."

I was devastated. Could failing one scenario keep me from graduating? I didn't know but I knew if it was possible Sgt. Dickens would make sure it happened.

Sgt. Dickens yelled at us for an hour. According to him the entire class should be sent home. I could see the pitying looks from the volunteers. Several walked out refusing to listen to our scolding. They did not understand that we were used to this treatment by our Sergeant. Before it was over Sgt. Dickens announced there were five cadets he would be speaking to the following day and only one was for doing a good job. I knew I would be on the first list.

We missed a total of twenty-four guns and were told we had to run twenty four hill runs the following morning before POPAT. I looked over at Rocco and knew he was the other cadet chosen to fail.

What our Sergeant did not know; failure was not an option for either of us!

Chapter 22
I Would Not Cry

The following morning we lined up at the bottom of the hill to complete our twenty-four hill runs. Before we began, class leader Cadet Clark made a speech. I could not have said it better myself.

"We've all been through hell together. We've wanted to make our Sergeant proud. We've wanted his approval. Well, it's kind of like the alcoholic father who never thought we measured up. He would never give us praise because the failure was in him and not in his children. We are those children and the only praise we will ever get is what we give ourselves. You have all done an incredible job and I am proud of you. We have all earned the right to have our badges pinned on our chests. I would be proud to serve with each and every one of you. Now let's do these hill runs and then kick some ass on POPAT!"

We cheered loudly with hoots and hollers. It was an incredibly inspiring speech. We ran the hills and then marched to cadence on our way to the POPAT field. We were all required to participate, though Cadet Chavez was the only one that would be going home, if he didn't score at least 384 points. Each and every one of us was determined to see Cadet Rocco Chavez pass.

First up was the obstacle course. Several of us stood ready at the last turn and ran alongside Rocco, pushing him to run faster. It worked he ended up lowering his time. The fences were also not a problem. He had worked so incredibly hard and it was paying off. Those twenty-four hill runs hadn't slowed him down. Rocco had his goal in sight and nothing would stop him.

We kept track of Rocco's score as we went along so we all knew the outcome before the official posting. Rocco didn't just pass, he killed it. He came through with a great score. I was so proud of him. We headed to lunch and had a mini celebration.

After lunch we went back to the classroom. Sgt. Dickens called five names. Mine was on the list. The five of us exited the classroom and then waited outside his office as each cadet was called in. I was the last to enter his office.

It didn't matter what he was going to say, I told myself I would not cry. I knew I could make it as an officer. If he was throwing me out, I would come back to the academy and do it all again. I was willing to go through this hell again if that's what it took to become certified. I had prepared all my speeches. I was ready for Sgt. Dickens.

I entered the office and sat in the only chair available when he gave the command to sit. Sgt. Dickens then asked if I knew why I was there. I told him no.

I looked him straight in the eye and waited to have my world shattered. I would not cry. I would not cry!

Sgt. Dickens' face was stern.

"Cadet Ivy, "He said, "Rarely am I surprised by a cadet. I've followed you and your intent to become an officer closely. I've been very hard on you. Quite frankly I did not see the mindset required to become a cop. This job takes absolute conviction that you will never give up and you will fight with everything you have. I hadn't seen that in you and I didn't feel you had what it takes. I was wrong. You failed the scenario yesterday but one thing came through. You physically fought with everything you had. You continued fighting and you refused to give up. You should have gone for your gun and ended the scenario but I needed to see that even without a gun you could and would protect yourself. You showed me you could. I'm damned proud of you and I think you will make a great officer."

I sat there for a moment in shock and then I did what I swore I wouldn't do. I broke down and cried. And once I started, I couldn't seem to stop. Sgt. Dickens handed me his Kleenex box and, looking very uncomfortable, waited for me to regain control before dismissing me from his office. I gave Sgt. Dickens a huge hug and then headed back to my classroom.

I wonder to this day if I am the only cadet who loves this alcoholic father. Sgt. Dickens changed my life. He put me through hell but it was what I needed. He understood what I would face on the streets. He understood this job is not for everyone. I entered the academy on a lark. I didn't have a clue what I was getting myself into. I didn't have the mental toughness or physical toughness to be a cop. But I had changed and I'd become police officer material.

Maybe no other cadet needed Sgt. Dickens to be an asshole, but I did. During my career, the lessons I learned from him have saved my life again and again. I will never forget those lessons or the man that bludgeoned them into me. The mental toughness he gave me would get me through rough times and in particularly a highly publicized case I worked that required everything I learned from Sgt. Dickens to keep me going.

When I entered the classroom everyone looked at me. They could tell I'd been crying. But I didn't dare speak and tell them the good news. I knew I would start crying all over again. It wasn't until after class that I was able to share my fate.

The majority of us stayed at the academy that weekend and studied. I was not really worried about passing the final but I wanted to help the cadets needing extra attention. We hit the books hard.

Monday morning the final began. The "Arizona Peace Officer Standards and Training" testers showed up and we could feel the importance of what we were about to undertake. It lasted more than five hours and was given in three segments. We would not get our results until that evening. We all walked over to our classroom when we were told the results were in.

Cadet Clark gave us the news. Three people did not pass. The three names were given out. Two had failed one unit and one person had failed two. Cadet Rodriguez had passed with the rest of us. We were relieved but upset about the three. They would be given another chance the next day. They only had to pass the unit(s) they failed.

On retakes the next day, two passed but a third Cadet did not. Unlike the previous tests, the final could be taken three times. But if you failed the third attempt, you did not pass the academy. The department representing the Cadet, that still needed to pass, decided to not have him graduate with our class, but instead, send him to a tutor. We all felt bad for our classmate but it was hard not to contain our excitement over our personal accomplishments.

Our class party was Wednesday night and we all headed to Chili's. We basically took over the bar and drank ourselves under the table. Like good police officers, we made sure we had non-drinking cadets that could get us back to the dorms.

Hung over, but still riding high on our collective success we spent the day getting our individual and class photos taken. Then we practiced for our graduation.

We reserved the dorm lobby television and watched movies that night. First up, Super Troopers. I was turned on to this movie at the academy and it was probably the tenth time we'd watched it. Even now several years into my career in law enforcement, this movie is quoted again and again. If you want a good dose of cop humor, it's a must see. We drew names for the next movie. To the groans of all the cadets, my movie won. It was The Princess Bride. The guys had a good time making sarcastic remarks in the beginning, but by the middle they were laughing and cheering. I knew they would love it.

I barely slept that night. It was almost over. I couldn't even imagine what it would be like to be home again. I missed my husband and I was looking forward to the empty nest I'd once dreaded. The following week, I'd begin working as a police officer. Thirty-five Cadets started down this long road. Only twenty-five cadets would be graduating.

All I had left was the ceremony the following day and then my true dream would begin.

Chapter 23
Endings and Beginnings

Waking on that last morning at the police academy was great, even without sleep. We attended a breakfast put on by the 100 Club. It is an awesome organization (www.100club.org) that comes to the aid of families of Fire and Law Enforcement when a loved one is killed in the line of duty.

After breakfast, we went back to our rooms to begin the process of dressing in our "Class A" uniforms. These are the uniforms set aside for special occasions. Our boots were shined to a high gloss and our uniforms were cleaned and pressed.

Final inspection took place on the school campus by the college flagpole and was carried out by all Police Chiefs and Sheriffs in attendance. It was long and grueling but exciting just the same. Our guidon was retired and we shouted our class motto for the last time.

My family and friends were in attendance, all except for my son. He had called the night before to explain he couldn't get the day off from his new job.

"I know I haven't supported you mom and I'm sorry." He said, "I didn't agree with your decision to attend the academy but I am proud of you."

I was impressed. He was in his early twenties, and to be fair he was a spoiled kid. I had made him that way. I think as a parent you want to give your children everything you didn't get as a child. For me it was tangible objects. My family did not have much money growing up and I tried to make up for it with my children. My son had tried to bridge the gap created by his age and my midlife crisis. I was proud of him.

Class 95 marched to the auditorium to begin our graduation ceremony with heads high. It was wonderful to show off the drilling techniques that we had practiced so diligently.

Speeches were made and cadets were given awards for shooting, academics, and outstanding performance. I didn't receive any, but was so incredibly proud of the cadets that did.

Before our swearing in, we left the stage and went to the front seats in the auditorium to watch our class video. It was funny at times, and sad at times, but most of all it was inspiring. When a clip of me going over the wall was shown, my youngest daughter called out, "That's my mom." We all laughed.

After the video, Class 95 again took the stage and we were officially sworn in as Peace Officers for the State of Arizona. Next was the badge presentation. Every Police Chief and Sheriff took the stage to hand our graduation certificates to us. Spouses, mothers and fathers actually pinned on our badges. My husband represented the one and only male spouse to do the honors and pin on my badge.

We left the auditorium and tearfully said our goodbyes to one another. Class leader Clark told me he would never forget my incredible journey through the academy. I felt the same way about him. We all promised to stay in touch but I knew as our careers began it would slowly fade away, although Deputy Clark is one of the guys I've managed to stay in touch with.

My husband and daughters helped me carry out the accumulation of items and luggage I'd amassed during my eighteen weeks at the academy. The small, bare, quarters of my dorm room offended my daughters' standards of living. They should have seen what it was like when there had been four of us crammed in.

We had reserved hotel rooms for my family to stay at during my last evening in the city. My son came to dinner with us and I had a great time. In the morning we would head back to Small Town and on Monday morning I would begin my first shift as a police officer at 0800 hours.

I was nervous and excited at the same time. I would be in training for the next few months as an officer, but I was up to the challenge and ready to take my next step. This would also be an entirely new way of life for my family and me. And I hoped they were ready for the challenge, too.

My journey as an officer was about to begin. But becoming an officer was only the first leg of the road I had mapped out for myself. I would soon realize law enforcement was in my blood. I would make new friends and become part of a larger family. One month shy of my two-year anniversary as an officer, I would become the first female detective in Small Town's history. Although my career path hasn't been without a few bumps, I love my job and will forever remember that ad on the drug store bulletin as being my fate.

During that first year as an officer, my knack for sex crimes would become apparent. I would attend training sessions around the country perfecting my ability to help the victims of this violent crime. In every annual review, I am chastised for getting too involved in my cases and taking them too personally. The day I change is the day I will turn in my badge.

One day after being promoted to detective, Small Town was faced with a double homicide. It would be my first case as a detective. Nine months later, with the support of my Sergeant, we would solve the murder of a teenager and discover the killer had struck twice before, in another town. We would solve those murders as well.

Along the way a fellow officer tagged me as the Bad Luck Detective. I've enjoyed a good bit of teasing over his comment, so I couldn't pass up using it to write about my adventures in law enforcement.

Statistically one-third of officers graduating from the academy will not be in law enforcement five years later. Unfortunately Class 95 is following those statistics.

Three officers failed to pass their field training programs directly after graduation. For two of them it ended their career in law enforcement. Class leader Clark left law enforcement and is now working in corporate America. He keeps his finger in the pie and volunteers as a reserve officer. Rocco has remained a firefighter and even with pressure from friends like me, he feels firefighters have it better. Cadet Rodriguez died in an accident, while on duty, four months after receiving his badge.

The poor economy is hitting small, rural law enforcement departments especially hard. With current local budget cuts, the officers in my department have not received a pay raise in three years and I fear more good officers will look to other careers and turn in their badges. There are plenty of more lucrative and less dangerous jobs available to raise a family, but I have never regretted my decision.

Sgt. Dickens continues to train new cadets at the academy. I often want to visit and hear his voice beating obedience into his class, but my job has kept me busy. I will get there someday and I will doubly appreciate being on the outside looking in.

Thank you for sharing in my academy adventures.

During those eighteen-weeks at the police academy, I sent a weekly email to my friends and family telling of my daily tortures. This online journal offered the remembrances I needed to write this story. I ended each of those emails with, "Cadet Ivy signing off." I proudly leave you with the signature from my last email:

Officer Ivy signing off

Bad Luck Officer
By
Suzie Ivy
§
A True-life Adventure

Bad Luck Publishing
Suzieivy@gmail.com
www.badluckdetective.com

Bad Luck Officer
Bad Luck Series: Book II

Printing History
First Print Edition: May 2012

This is a true story but ALL character names have been changed to protect victims. In some cases, gender and age are altered.

Chapter 1

He was sitting in the middle of a quiet road on the edge of town. There were no cars backed up due to his presence. No pedestrians loitering to see what was going on.

Just Sgt. Spears, myself, and a Mr. Dwaine Piskett, 92 years of age, who sat squarely in the center of the paved roadway with a big-ass rock in his lap.

"I don't want to speak to you." Mr. Piskett said to Sgt. Spears, "You is a ugly man an' God done handed out the looks the day you was digging through the garbage."

I stayed in the background at a ready position. During our ride to the scene Sgt. Spears explained my role, "This first week, you are to stand back, observe, and let me do all the talking. Above anything else, don't get yourself killed or, God forbid, get me killed. Keep your eyes and ears open and think officer safety. Got that?"

Now, with the morning temperature hovering around 25 degrees and a bright winter sun shining, I was trying to appear professional on my first official call for duty as an officer. Inside, I was thinking-- *I must be out of my mind!*

I'd had this thought repeatedly since early morning when I'd uniformed-up for the first time. While I dressed in matching black sports bra and panties, a black long-sleeved undershirt, dark blue freshly ironed uniform pants, uniform shirt, and my black basket-weave duty belt, I thought it. While I checked for the nth time that my duty belt was fully equipped, with baton, one set of silver handcuffs, pepper spray, flashlight, gun, and two extra magazines of ammunition, I thought it. While I put on my outer bulletproof vest with a bright shiny new badge displaying my police officer status to the world, I thought it. *I must be out of my mind!*

And while I had thought I was equipped for anything, I definitely was not ready for this old man and his rock.

As ordered, I let Sgt. Spears do the talking.

"Mr. Piskett, you need to get up and move out of the road,"

"This is my road." said Mr. Piskett. "It's been my road for a hundred years and I can sit in it if I want to." His head bounced and a small patch of maybe five, white, inch-long hairs swayed back and forth. I kept one eye on my first suspect while glancing nervously up and down the road to assure myself no cars were approaching.

Sgt. Spears kept his cool. "We've been through this before, Mr. Piskett. You can't sit in the middle of the road. Put aside the rock and let's get you moved."

"This here rock is a gift from God. It's my rock and you can't have   it."
Between checking the roadway, I was checking Mr. Piskett from head to toe for possible weapons, not disregarding the threat the rock itself posed. His sturdy leather work boots were well used and scruffy. They matched the condition of his clothing.

"Okay Mr. Piskett," said Sgt. Spears, playing along. "But I need to move you out of the road. You can carry the rock if you want."

"Are you blind? You're nothing but a stupid ugly piece of kennel poop. I can't lift this rock."

Sgt. Spears' voice tightened slightly, "Then how did you get it over here?"

"I rolled the damn thing, but at soon as I got here, God told me I couldn't roll it no more."

Sgt. Spears looked at me with a slight question in his gaze and then turned back to the man cradling the rock.

"Well Mr. Piskett, this pretty lady here was sent by God to move your rock. I've been sent by the Small Town Police Department to move you."

Mr. Piskett looked at me and asked me if I was sent by God. I tried to look godly, but who was I kidding.

"God wants me to help you with the rock," I said to Mr. Piskett, "and get you out of the road."

He got up, allowing the rock to roll from his lap and said, "I'll help you lift it. God said not to roll it, so it needs to be carried, and since God wanted it moved it shouldn't weigh too much."

I stood shoulder to shoulder with the musty smelling Mr. Piskett. He attempted to help me lift the roughened stone but the majority of the weight landed in my arms. I pulled the stone to my body and rested it against my previously pristine uniform and duty belt. Mr. Pisket was wrong about God lightening the load and I was thankful for every pushup I had to do at the academy. I carried that big-ass rock over to the side of the road and dropped it. I slapped my hands together, dislodging rock dust and larger bits that had bitten into the skin of my palms. I tried to use my somewhat clean hands to dust off the front of my uniform and belt and remove the rock particles caught in the crevices of my gear.

Sgt. Spears' voice snapped me out of my grooming. "Angel Ivy, I need you to get a citation out of the car." It was said with humor although he maintained a straight face.

I followed instructions and Sgt. Spears helped me fill in the appropriate information. I then walked over to Mr. Piskett. He was now sitting on the side of the road, out of traffic. His plaid jacket and blue jeans were covered in the same dust I'd divested myself of.

My voice cracked slightly as I gave the recitation I'd learned at the academy, "Mr. Piskett, without admitting guilt, I need you to sign this citation and agree to appear in court on the date I've written."

He scrawled his name and then looked up. I could see two missing bottom teethe in his smile of assurance, "God bless you, Angel Ivy."

He glanced back down at the court date then tipped his head my way. His wrinkled chin moved as he spoke, "I'll see you in January if God is willing."

If I hadn't been paying close attention, I would have missed the lowering of his left eyelid. The old coot actually winked at me. His hazels eyes then looked away as I walked off with Sgt. Spears.

As I returned to my seat in the patrol car, I was quiet, trying to understand exactly what had just happened.

Sgt. Spears laughed. "You did a great job. There's no explanation for Mr. Piskett. He'll stay out of our hair, until after the court date, because he's friends with the judge, and Judge Forsyth will not forgive two citations so close together. We'll get a small break from him and then God will give him a new task and I'll let my new angel sweet-talk him into another citation.

The tension in my shoulders started to loosen and I began to smile. I'd survived my first official call, my welcome to the Small Town Police Department was complete.

Chapter 2

After our little adventure with Mr. Piskett and his rock, the rest of the morning was uneventful.

The sun continued to shine and the temperature warmed slightly as Sgt. Spears cruised through town. I was now seeing Small Town as an officer and everything looked different. It wasn't quite sinister but I was waiting for crime to jump out and bite me. I imagined the decrepit trailers, dispersed throughout town, were filled with drug runners and piles of illegal contraband. It surprised me when a small elderly woman stepped out her door onto a rickety front porch of one of my imagined drug trailers and waved at our police car. I waved back and decided to rein in my imagination.

We ate an early quiet lunch at Paychecks restaurant. Sgt. Spears took a seat in the back corner facing the door. "I have your back." He said with no further explanation and then went on "I like to get in before the noon crowd. Most of the city employees eat here and the place becomes a zoo." Sgt. Spears didn't say much after that, he just ate.

We finally returned to the department and parked on the side of the building under a "police only" sign. I followed Sgt. Spears into the squad room and he pointed out my desk. It was bare except for a computer keyboard and mouse. I wasn't given time to admire my new   space. "Come with me, you'll spend enough time here later."

I followed but couldn't help glancing over my shoulder with longing. I passed other desks decorated with pictures, calendars and knickknacks. I wanted my desk equally adorned. We arrived at Sgt. Spears' office and I was told we would serve a search warrant in the afternoon. Until then, he gave me the task of familiarizing myself with Arizona Revised Statutes (A.R.S.). This is the book of law for the State of Arizona. It covers both criminal code and civil traffic code, weighs about five pounds and has white tissue thin pages laid out like a Bible. I was to study it, not only because I needed to know the information, but, as Sgt. Spears explained, "It will keep you out of my hair while I get caught up on paperwork."

As told, I sat at a small table outside the Sergeant's office. Since I was more familiar with criminal code, I concentrated on civil traffic code -- seat belt requirements, license restrictions and right-of-way. It was like being a cadet again at the academy, but without all the shouting, pushups or lonely dorm room. I would now have a home with the sympathetic ear of my husband at the end of the day.

The afternoon dragged on. My eyes were blurring over from all the regurgitated information when my fellow officers began arriving for the search warrant.

I could not yet put names to faces. I met most of these men at the department's annual Thanksgiving potluck, which my husband and I attended, while I was still at the academy. My fellow officers were considerably younger than my forty-five years.

The stern group didn't acknowledge my presence as they walked by on their way to the squad room. Their silence made me miss my fellow cadets and I wondered how they were fitting in. I shook off my feelings of loneliness and admired their gear. It was way cooler than mine. They were in full tactical regalia -- tactical pants and shirts (lots of pockets), drop down leg holsters, kneepads, radio mics, ear buds and military boots that meant business. I could even smell the scent of gun oil trailing behind them.

They looked and smelled like deadly serious professionals. I, on the other hand, was wearing, thanks to Mr. Piskett, my wrinkled dress uniform, dust incrusted duty belt and scuffed boots. No tactical uniforms for me. It was Small Town Police Department policy that during the first year, a rookie was required to dress in Class A (long sleeved formal uniform) or Class B (short sleeve formal uniform). I would look as out of my element as I was.

I entered the squad room and moved to the back. I could feel the testosterone weighing down the room, with my small bit of estrogen being eaten up. The officers had pulled their desk chairs around a large table. Sgt. Spears walked in and glanced around as he took his place standing at the head of the table. His eyes finally rested on me.

"Officer Ivy, I need to check your weapon." He said.

Six heads, with military cropped hair, turned my way and looked. I could feel the blush on my face but I was well trained and followed the order without comment. I took my gun out of the holster, pointing it downward. I removed the magazine, removed the round from the chamber and locked the slide back. I walked to the front of the room and handed my weapon over.

"When did you last clean this?" Sgt. Spears asked. He was looking at my gun with a frown of disappointment on his face.

"I cleaned it yesterday Sir." I had spent three hours the previous night shining my boots, ironing my uniform and giving my gun a thorough cleaning. It was the gun issued to me while I attended the academy and would remain mine.

He called another officer over and ordered him to clean my gun correctly and check the magazines.

I could feel the heat in my face and I knew my blush was now a deep red. I heard snickers from the men.

My weapon and magazines were taken away. I stood there awkwardly, as they spoke among themselves, wondering if I learned anything helpful at the academy. I had worked diligently to make sure my weapon and magazines were perfect.

They were finally returned and I placed them tentatively back on my belt. My face continued to burn. I could barely look at anyone. Were my fellow cadets going through similar humiliations on their first day of duty? The only thing I knew the academy had taught me at this point was not to cry.

Just a few short months ago I would have been in tears. The new Suzie Ivy did not cry. She sucked it up, moved forward, and learned from her mistakes.

"Everyone, attention front and center." This from Sgt. Spears. All small talk ceased and I went back to my spot, standing alone.

Using a whiteboard on the wall behind him, Sgt. Spears laid out our strategy for the home invasion. He gave assignments to everyone. The bedrooms, bathrooms and back door were to be covered by the entry team. I, as the rookie, was to enter first and cover the front room. I was also to guard the backs of the officers as they fanned out into the other rooms of the house. Sgt. Spears would enter directly behind me as the keeper of the battering ram in case it was needed.

The strategy meeting came to an end and we filed out the back door of the squad room. I rode with Sgt. Spears as we converged on the crumbling rundown home. My adrenaline was pumping and my sweaty hands were shaking as the entry team gathered at the front door. I was in the lead as ordered. My gun was drawn with my trigger finger riding the barrel as I had been trained. I was terrified but ready for action.

Total and complete tunnel vision obscured my mind. I was focused on that front door and what might lie behind it. The rest of the team was behind me breathing almost in unison. I kept my eyes pinpointed at the flaking gray paint on the door.

Sgt. Spears reached his hand around me and slowly turned the door handle. It was unlocked and the battering ram was not needed.

He gave the order softly, "On the count of three -- one, two" We entered with yells of "Police, we have a warrant."

I hardly noticed the bare concrete floors of the empty room, my eyes were straight ahead. Immediately, two men came out from the hallway and opened fire. The sound of bullets was deafening. I felt my gun going off in my hands. I don't remember my finger sliding over the trigger or pulling it. Pop, pop, pop, the noise was all I could hear.

I have no idea how many rounds I fired. I wasn't even thinking of impending death. The two men fell. I wasn't sure if I shot them or if someone else had. My heart was pounding so hard I felt it was going to explode. I was worried about the possibility of other bad guys being inside the home so I held my stance while I tried to figure out what my next move should be.

I sensed my entry team moving out from behind me. I thought they were heading to other parts of the house to secure it. I didn't even take a moment to look down and see if I had been shot. I knew if I had, the pain would begin momentarily and right now, I needed to cover my guys as they converged on the other rooms.

A weighty hand descended on my shoulder. My entire body jumped. Then I heard laughter.

I turned my head slightly, with my gun in my hand still ready to fire, and found myself semi-surrounded by laughing faces. The team hadn't proceeded to the back of the house. They were all looking at me.

What the fuck!?

I was still running on adrenaline and fear. Reality was slow to sink in.

When it did, I didn't want to cry, I wanted to scream. My heart was beating hard and my brain barely functioning. My gun was still out in front of me and a hand gently pushed it down to my side. I felt another pat on my back and I slowly noticed the smoky familiar smell of sulfur.

"Welcome to Small Town PD Ivy, you did great." said Sergeant Spears.

By now everyone was laughing, cheering and clapping, including the two "dead guys" who had gotten to their feet. What a bunch of dickheads.

They were all talking at once. My ears continued to ring from the pop sounds that exploded during the "shoot out". I was finally computing things in my head and guessed the pops were the product of cap guns, which generated the sulfurous odor. These guys were out of their f-ing minds, but the first shaky smile appeared on my face.

They were slapping me on the back now though it felt like I was being tossed around the room.

"You should have seen the look on your face," said one of the now undead guys, "Priceless!"

"Did you see the killing look she gave you Sarge, when you asked her about cleaning her gun? She was pissed; red face and all." The laughing continued.

"She stood her ground, protected her team and eliminated the threat," Said someone else.

I didn't know who the young cop was, who said those words, but I was thankful and started to relax.

The teasing and reruns of the action went on for about thirty minutes. All the while, everyone was introducing themselves. The "dead" guys I shot were not my co-workers, but ununiformed Sheriff Deputies from the county. They thanked everyone for the fun and were the first to leave.

Finally, Sgt. Spears called a stop to the ribbing and we left the house.

It wasn't until days later that I learned some of the finer points of my initiation into the department. The officers on the entry team with me had fake guns -- black painted wooden guns that had been used on every rookie at the department. The two bad guys that I "shot" were armed with toy cap guns, which I learned to hate at the academy.

Much later, I discovered that they held a long discussion about not doing the initiation because I was female. Sgt. Spears stood up for me. He told them to treat me as they would any other rookie. And I was glad they did.

It was an unspoken rule that this little exercise in fun, games and terror was not to be mentioned outside the department. I couldn't wait to have a newbie and get some of my own back.

Sgt. Spears and I returned to the department and he wrote my first daily review. He explained that I did a good job, but I wouldn't be part of an actual search warrant entry team for a while. My job during future search warrants would be covering the front or backyard of the house.

"A rookie's job is to provide security and not get killed. Is that understood Officer Ivy?"

"Yes sir."

My first day on the job was long and exhausting, but I left the office with a smile on my face. You could say the shit had literally hit the fan and I survived.

On my way home, I picked up my first box of Depends disposable underwear. I was forty-five years old, a little old to be starting a career as an officer but a little young to worry about leakage. I didn't care, after today's experience I knew I would need the added protection.

Chapter 3

That first day, after getting off duty, I stood in my house looking around. I realized my life would be guns by day and housewife by night. I had animals to feed and dinner to cook, it didn't matter that I was exhausted. I so needed to sit down with Norman, my husband, and come up with a two-person work schedule. We had been here before and I knew he would help. I just needed to make the first move because it wouldn't occur to him to change anything if I didn't point it out, MEN!

I decided to cook a casserole. While it was heating, I shined my boots, ironed my next day's uniform and prepared to clean my gun. Norman walked in as I was putting my gun cleaning supplies on some newspaper. He was holding a large bouquet of red roses and handed them to me with a kiss, "Happy first day of being a cop, Officer Ivy."

My heart melted and I decided to put off the talk about household chores to another day. We ate dinner and I told him the story of my first experiences while on duty.

He laughed asking, "Are you wearing the Depends? They sound kind of sexy."

It was nice getting old with someone who could appreciate it with me. I truly loved this man.

***

The rest of my first week was spent learning addresses and handling grievances. The temperature remained in the low thirties. No snow in sight as Christmas headed our way.

My major excitement was corralling Old Betty, a beefalo and the largest intact bull in town. A beefalo is a cross between a domestic bovine and a buffalo. Local ranchers breed them for their hardy adaptability to weather conditions, low-fat meat and foraging skills. Sgt. Spears gave me this explanation as we made our way to Old Betty's last known location. Prior to the call, I had no idea what a beefalo was.

We arrived at a sparsely populated area. There were only two houses on either side of the road with a large wood barn to the north. I shouldn't have been surprised to see the giant black outline of Old Betty standing in the middle of the road but I was. What was with this town and the blocking of city streets?

No one was in sight. I figured everyone was hiding safely inside. Sgt. Spears told me he would drop me off and then circle around behind the bull.

"Don't approach him. Just stay where I put you unless he charges, then run like hell. Bulls can't run in a tight circle so make sharp turns if you need to get away."

Was he out of his mind? I was not a cowboy and had no idea how to corral a bull and get him into a pen. Before getting out of the car, I looked around for a tree to climb. I didn't see a tree but I did see an old yellow dump truck parked about thirty yards from where I stood and I figured it was my safest route of escape. There was no way I was staying on the street making tight turns. I might be blonde but I'm not stupid.

I stepped out of the car and Sgt. Spears immediately drove away. I saw Old Betty looking mean and eyeing me closely. His front leg kicked back, pawing the ground. His head went down. I never turned tail and ran with bullets flying but that damn front leg attached to that enormous body was entirely different. I started at a sprint but a look backwards kicked me into high gear and I ran like hell as ordered.

The charge missed me by more than ten feet as I jumped on the hood of the dump truck. My radio sounded and I looked behind Old Mad Betty and saw Sgt. Spears a hundred yards away. He got out of his vehicle and approached slowly. My heart was thumping but as surprising as it sounds, I was having fun. It was an adrenaline rush.

Over my radio I heard, "Just stay where you are and I'll get closer. Keep his attention on you."

I began waving my arms, stomping my feet against the truck, and yelling, "Old Betty, come and get me." I didn't know what else to say to a one-ton devil with horns.

Sgt. Spears was within thirty yards when Old Betty turned and saw him. Sgt. Spears kept stepping closer. I noticed he had his Taser in his hand. I did not have one of these nifty devises and needed to take the required training before I could carry one. I wasn't sure what Sgt. Spears meant to do with the Taser and figured it would only piss the bull off.

"Get off the truck and be ready to make a run for the gate. It's about twenty yards to your right." Sgt. Spears said as his Taser made a popping sound and Old Betty backed up.

The problem was, he backed towards me. I jumped down from my position of safety. I was only ten feet from the bull but his butt was towards me and his horned head was facing my Sergeant.

"I'll get him going in the other direction." Sgt. Spears yelled.

He circled wide and somehow managed to get Old Betty to my left. As soon as the beefalo was no longer between us, I made a dash for the fence.

"He's almost on you, jump the fence." Sgt. Spears' yell was loud.

I didn't need to be told twice. I was over the four-foot enclosure with no problem. The six-foot wall at the academy prepared me for this exact circumstance, I think.

When I had the fence between me and Old Betty, I heard, "Now open the gate and bring it inward towards you, but keep the gate between you and Betty."

Sgt. Spears started hollering and popping his Taser as soon as I had the gate opened. Old Betty came my way. He ran past my position and I switched sides, shutting the gate behind me and closing Old Betty in. Sgt. Spears helped me to secure the enclosure with a loop of barbed wire made for that purpose.

"Is this his pasture?" I asked while trying to catch my breath.

"Nope, but we don't play around with loose horses and cattle. They go into the closest fenced area we can find. We'll get a complaint about it now and then but our job is to keep town folk from being trampled, so any fenced area will do. I'll have dispatch contact livestock to let them know where Old Betty is."

Being a country cop was turning out to be a lot different than my expectations. I now knew what a beefalo was, how to coral a bull and knew I needed to attend Taser class. In just one short week, I was learning just how much additional training I needed.

I was exhausted by the weekend, which started on Friday due to our four-day workweek. I cleaned house in the morning and then called my kids in the afternoon. My daughters were glad to hear from me but my son did not answer his phone and I left a message. I had no time to mourn my empty nest and was actually thankful my children had their own lives. That evening, Norman and I enjoyed a peaceful night and watched a rental movie.

I grocery shopped on Saturday and bought ingredients for a large dinner. I thought it would be relaxing to cook something complicated. In the middle of my meal preparations, I received a call from dispatch saying I was being asked to assist other officers on a vehicle traffic stop.

I asked Norman to take over the cooking. It took me ten minutes to gear up and run out the door. Dispatch gave me the address and said that Detective Alex Molinero was waiting. I had met the Detective twice before, once at the Thanksgiving potluck and also at my initiation search warrant. I managed to arrive five minutes after leaving my house with only one wrong turn. Detective Molinero and another officer had pulled a woman over and she was hiding something between her breasts. A K9 drug dog alerted on her vehicle and a large quantity of methamphetamines were found inside.

The detective smiled at me and said, "I did a safety search when I first took her into custody. I felt something in the front of her bra. I decided to take advantage of having a female officer at the department and had you called out. I hope you don't mind?"

I looked towards the woman then turned to him and smiled back. "I don't mind at all." I walked to the woman. She was handcuffed with her hands behind her back. I think there were only three teeth left in her mouth and those looked rotten. Her clothing was ratty and dirty. It's hard to describe her smell but I guess the word stale would cover it.

Detective Molinero handed me a pair of rubber gloves, which I was thankful for. I began my search the way I was trained. Part of that training was to never trust another officer's search. I held one of her wrists in my right hand, ran my left hand over and inside her pockets, then around her waist area, even slipping my hand under the waistband of her pants. I then ran my hands down the outside of her legs and then up the inner seem over her crotch area. I was checking for weapons or anything that felt out of the norm. I had her slip her shoes off and also searched her socks. She muttered unintelligible words as I proceeded. I next ran my hand under her arms and up her back. She was nothing but skin and bones, which was kind of creepy.

With my hand on the outside of her shirt, I pulled the back of her bra strap out and made sure there was nothing stuck in the stretchy material. My hand came around to the front bra area and I found the hard item stuck there. It was quite simple. I pulled her shirt forward, slipping my left hand a few inches under her shirt, and then pulled slightly forward on her bra with my right hand. A small metal pillbox fell into my left hand which was waiting below. I handed it to Detective Molinero.

He gave a nod of approval and said, "You can join me and take her to booking if you want?"

It was my first time as part of an arrest, so I decided to tag along. The other officer drove my personal vehicle back to the station while I joined Detective Molinero in his unmarked squad car.

The drive to the county jail is about two miles from the police department. When we arrived, Detective Molinero radioed, "We're 97 at the jail with one 10-15, please have them roll the east side."

Molinero made 10-codes sound super cool. The large steel door in front of us rolled upwards. We drove inside, got out of the vehicle and I followed the detective to some lockers where we stowed our guns. We removed our prisoner from the car after the large rolling door went back down.

I preceded the detective and our prisoner down a long hallway to a white metal door. The bolts made a loud clunk and unlocked as we approached. I pushed inward and was surprised at the heaviness. The door had to be solid steel. We entered a small room and moved to another door which unlocked as the first one closed behind us. I had never been inside a jail so it was a thrill to hear the doors locking clang as we stepped inside.

I was astonished that the jail didn't smell bad. It carried a faint odor of antiseptic and was decorated in institutional white concrete. I could see floor drains every twenty feet and figured a good hosing down kept things sanitary.

Our arrestee began getting mouthy. Detective Molinero ignored her, so I did the same.

After we entered the main booking area, I was told to remove her handcuffs and have her sit on a bench while we walked to where the booking papers were kept.

She kept up her unfriendly speech as I watched Detective Molinero fill out the paperwork, "You son a bitch, I thought you liked me? I hate you. You pig."

I didn't think this was bad as far as trash-talking went and I took my cue from the detective and continued to disregard her foul mouth.

When the paperwork was finished, we turned it in and went back to the Detective's car. We could still hear the woman yelling as we walked out.

After we retrieved our guns and drove outside, Detective Molinero told me about himself during the drive to the office. "I'm thirty years old, divorced and don't have any children. My mother has almost given up." With a killer grin he continued, "You're lucky you're married or she would be trying to fix us up."

I could feel my face redden. I bet all the girls in town were in love with his dark Hispanic good looks. Too bad I had fifteen years on him and of course, I WAS married.

He continued, "Sorry, but no more of this detective stuff while we're in a car together. My first name is Alex. I appreciate your help. I can see where it will be a huge plus having you on staff. I didn't want to put my hand in the places you did."

I had to laugh because I didn't blame him. I could tell I was going to like Alex and I was thankful for his willingness to have me called out. He dropped me at my vehicle and I drove home to enjoy the large dinner Norman had finished preparing.

On Sunday my son Roger called. We spoke for maybe five-minutes and then I gave the phone to his father. Their relationship was improving now that he was no longer living at home and I was happy to see it. With me going into a dangerous profession it put a wedge between our mother son connections but I hoped things would heal. I spent most of the day resting. Police work was exhausting.

Monday morning saw me back on the street. Sgt. Spears told me he would allow me to semi-handle a few minor calls. I was overjoyed to have a chance to actually use my budding skills.

My first opportunity came later that day when a woman's ex-boyfriend harassed her. He was texting her more than twenty times an hour. We headed to the ex's house.

Sgt. Spears stayed to the side of the door as I, standing in front of the door, knocked. A very large man, with muscles bulging out of his dirty gray wife beater tank top, answered. He had to be at least six foot three and probably weighed three hundred pounds.

"What do you want?" He had a deep voice with a not so nice tone.

"Hello, I'm Officer Ivy with Small Town PD. I need to speak with you about some text messages being sent to Molly Roth." I was polite and direct.

The door slammed in my face along with the angry words, "Come back with a warrant."

I looked at my Sergeant. "We're getting out of here now." He said.

He told me why as we headed to the patrol car. "When you have a situation like this, you clear out immediately. He's in the house, we don't know if he has weapons and this is a dangerous situation for officers. These circumstances require our retreat. Always think officer safety. Next time you approach a door, stand to the side. You don't want to be shot through the door."

I felt as if I didn't know anything. We parked around the corner and Sgt. Spears had me call Molly and have her text her ex and ask him to meet at her house in an hour. I didn't think it would work but I did as told.

"If the criminals were smart we wouldn't catch most of them." Sgt. Spears said as we ate lunch waiting for the hour to pass. We then went back and parked around the corner from the house. Fifteen minutes later, the ex-boyfriend got in his pickup truck and began driving away. We gave him some space and then followed.

Sgt. Spears gave me the rundown on what I would be doing next. "You're making an arrest for harassment. It's only a misdemeanor but Billy Bob needs to go to jail."

I looked questioningly at Sgt. Spears and he laughed, "Whenever I have a large stupid man, I call him Billy Bob."

Our red and blues were activated and we pulled Billy Bob's truck over. Sgt. Spears followed me as I approached the vehicle. He had his Taser down at his side.

"You need to step out of the vehicle." I said using my most commanding voice, nothing nice about it.

"You plan on making me?" He puffed up his bare shoulders as he spoke. It was only thirty degrees outside but he had neglected to put on a jacket. The better to see his muscles, I guessed.

"If I have to, I will. To be truthful, you'll look pretty stupid fighting a female along the side of the road, but if that's what you want…" I then used my best stern mother voice, "Get out of the truck."

Billy Bob stepped out. I had him place his arms behind his back and I placed one cuff on his huge wrist. I tried bringing his hands closer together but had no luck. The further end of the cuff wouldn't reach his other wrist. I had a dilemma and wasn't sure what to do. Sgt. Spears walked around and gave me another pair of cuffs. Billy Bob never uttered a sound as I fastened the two cuffs together and secured his arms behind him. Would I ever stop feeling so dumb? A note to self, order an additional pair of cuffs.

We took our prisoner to the jail and I filled out the booking packet this time. Billy Bob got to spend the night in county lockup courtesy of Small Town PD. I learned this "consideration" was called, "Three hots and a cot." Officers have their own names for everything.

That afternoon, Sgt. Spears wrote a good review on my daily appraisal. I was told I would transfer to nights the following week and work Tuesday through Friday from 1800 to 0400 hours. The department practiced shift rotations and this was Sgt. Spears' new assignment so I would be joining him.

My second week continued. I wrote two traffic tickets and about twenty warnings. It was frustrating being a traffic cop. Everyone in town ran stop signs and thought they had the right to do it. No one likes getting a ticket but these people were ridiculous.

One of my two tickets was to a young twerp who turned out to be the Mayor's son. I didn't know it was the Mayor's son until after I wrote him the citation. When we pulled away, Sgt. Spears started laughing and told me the bad news. I couldn't believe he hadn't informed me before I issued paper. He said it was because it didn't matter what your last name was, if you deserved a ticket, *you deserved a ticket*.

He continued with, "I've been watching you all week and you've done a good job of knowing when a warning will stop the behavior and when a citation is needed. The Mayor's son was driving recklessly and speeding. He's lucky he's not going to jail and he deserved at least a citation. A good lesson to learn with this experience is when you write a ticket to a prominent member of the community or to their family, you let me know. I will then let the chief know. This time you get to go with me to inform the Chief. It should be fun."

Wow, lucky me!

Chapter 4

After we arrived at the police department, we walked to the big office in the back of the building. Sgt. Spears informed Chief Lewis Varnett of the ticket I issued. It was obvious he was not happy. After combing his hand through his hair he said, "I don't need to be on the wrong side of the Mayor right now. Are you sure the ticket was warranted?"

I was alarmed. The last thing I wanted was to be on the bad side of the Police Chief. I realized both the Chief and Sergeant were waiting for my reply. I looked straight ahead and answered in the military style forced upon me at the academy, "I had no idea he was the Mayor's son but my first response was to take him to jail. He was driving erratically while speeding, and had no thought to the safety of the public. I believed him to be drunk when I first made the stop Sir."

I glanced slightly over to see how my words were being acknowledged. Sgt. Spears was smiling and the Chief just shook his head, "God save me from rookies. Bring her back when she learns she's not in the Marines and I'll have a decent conversation with her. In the meantime, I'll relay her words to the Mayor when he calls and he will call." He looked at me and then waved me away with his hand saying, "Dismissed."

I took two steps out the door when I heard him say, "Do something to get back in the Mayor's good graces Officer Ivy."

"Yes Sir." I managed to utter. I walked away and tried to get my trembling hands under control. I would never understand politics or this entire paramilitary thing.

Though I was terrified of Chief Varnett, I was brave enough to inform Sgt. Spears I didn't appreciate him throwing me to the wolves. He just laughed. "You handled that fine though maybe a little over the top with your soldierly bearing. You didn't pee your pants though and that's a good thing for a rookie.

"I did pee my pants but I'm wearing Depends so the leakage won't ruin my duty uniform."

Sgt. Spears laughed some more. He thought I was joking.

I decided to broach a subject I couldn't get out of my mind, "What will it take for me to be certified on a Taser?"

"I teach Taser training. The Sheriff's Department requested I certify two of their new deputies. The courthouse has a security guard that also needs the training. Are you planning on taking a ride?"

A "ride" is being Tased. "I don't think I have a choice. I don't have a problem with it and yes, I plan on taking a ride."

"Only half our department actually lined up to be Tased. It's up to you." He smiled at me. I would take a ride even if I didn't want to. It was part of being the first female officer. I had to appear tough at all times. The department was no different from the academy.

***

I had Christmas off. It was the first time in my life I wasn't into baking and shopping. I purchased my gifts while still in the city, before coming back to Small Town. Horror of horrors, I was buying Christmas dinner from our local Safeway. My kids would suffer tremendous mental anguish but that was life when mom's a cop. They were all over the age of consent so if they wanted something better they could cook for themselves.

Sgt. Spears told me this would be my last holiday off for the next few years. The newest officers always worked them and I was lucky I wasn't out on my own.

My kids came home and we had a nice family get together. Cassie, my youngest, and Letty, my oldest, wanted to hear all about my first two weeks on duty. Roger listened but didn't say much. He remained in a good mood though and I was thankful his behavior was improving. He suffered from middle child, spoiled rotten because he was the only boy, and my mother has no business being a cop syndrome. I'd take girls any day.

We sang Christmas carols, ate too much and then watched Christmas movies until late in the evening. I knew we wouldn't have many more years with everyone home and I enjoyed the day for the special celebration it was.

With the night shift to look forward to, I tried switching my sleep around slightly but had little success. I was a morning person. I knew I would have a few cranky days on the job before I got used to the new schedule.

Tuesday and 1800 hours finally rolled around. I went to the police department and began looking through all the forms needed to complete a police report. I never realized how much paperwork officers performed. I thought you just wrote a couple paragraphs for each call and then you were done. It wasn't that simple. Every call for service you took required a form to make life more complicated. There was a form for unlocking a vehicle, checking a business after hours, finding a dog running at large, a form for natural death, sudden infant death, and on it went. There were more than fifty in all. Thank god I was meticulous at paperwork. Now, it was easier to understand the amount of paperwork required at the academy.

Sgt. Spears arrived in a good mood. He stopped whistling long enough to say, "I love the night shift, especially in the winter. It's slow on the streets and I'm able to catch up on my administrative work." He then continued with his whistling.

Oh boy, I was thrilled for things to be slow, *not*. We headed out the door for a little patrol. The temperature was in the twenties and getting colder as the night continued. There was nothing happening. We pulled over a couple of drivers but I gave them warnings and we finally went back to the squad room. I was given some Officer Integrity Bulletins to read. It helped to pass the time. The quarterly issue gave decisions on officers facing the loss of their certifications, with a detailed description of their transgressions. The officers' names were A, B, C and so on. I learned that I never wanted to be referred to as a letter. None of the indiscretions were good things.

At 0200 hours the phone rang. I picked up and Sgt. Spears came and stood over my shoulder, I placed the call on speaker phone. Dispatch advised they had a woman on hold that wanted to report a death threat. I asked them to patch (police lingo) her through.

A timid female voice came on the phone, "I need to report that my brother threatened my life."

"How did he threaten you?" I took this very seriously and had my notebook on the desk and my pen at ready.

"He sent me a text saying I would not see tomorrow."

"This is on a text?"

"Yes."

"What is your brother's name, address and phone number?"

"Johnny Gibbons, space 32 at End of the Road Trailer Park, and 5657 is his phone number."

I need to explain telephone numbers in Small Town. There is only one prefix. No one gives it when giving their phone number. They only give the last four digits. It took me a while to get used to it when I first moved here but after six months, I only gave the last four digits of my number too. I may be from a big city, but I'm adaptable.

"I'll contact him right away and see what he has to say." I was all business, Officer Ivy to the rescue.

"Oh thank you, I'm really scared he might come after me tonight. His text sounded very threatening."

"I'll make contact with him as soon as we hang up. If you hear any noises outside, call 911. We'll be right there."

I finished taking her information and hung up the phone. I asked Sgt. Spears if we should go see the guy. To my disappointment, Sgt. Spears said to try calling first. I dialed the number and a sleepy Johnny Gibbons answered the phone.

"This is Officer Ivy with the Small Town Police Department. I've had a complaint that you threatened your sister."

"What?" said a very drowsy voice.

"I've had a complaint that you threatened your sister." I used my mean serious voice.

"What are you talking about?" A little more alert.

"Your sister called the police and said you sent her a text telling her she would not wake up tomorrow morning." My tone went deeper and meaner.

"Are you serious?" He only sounded confused.

"Johnny, I'm the police, I'm always serious." I thought this was quite official sounding.

"That crazy bitch! She sent me a text that woke me up over an hour ago. Hold on and I'll get my cell phone and read it to you."

I could hear shuffling noises as he reached for his cell phone. I didn't appreciate him calling his sister a crazy bitch. He was talking to the police and I think he should have been a little more circumspect.

He came back on the line, his voice fully alert and angry. "Here, listen to this, 'Be happy you have a good life and thank God it will be a wonderful day tomorrow. Send this to ten people you love and good things will come your way.' It's one of those damn chainmail text things for God sake. The text I sent back said, 'You better thank God tonight, because you may not be waking up in the morning.' That doesn't mean I'm going over to kill my sister, though the thought is sounding better and better. She knows I need to be at work at 6 am, I get up at 5, and I need sleep. She woke me up!" Johnny was pissed off.

My voice was now stumbling, "Ah, well, okay, I'm sorry to bother you. I'll call your sister back and tell her not to trouble you again tonight."

"You tell that bitch to never text me again, that hair brain, piece of shit, bit…"

I ended our conversation. Sgt. Spears began laughing and he couldn't stop. When he came up for air I asked, "What should I do?"

"This is your first big case involving death threats, harassment and possible domestic violence." I know you're fresh out of the academy but they must have taught you something. Figure it out." His laughing continued as he walked away.

I decided to call the chain texting crazy bitch back.

"Hello." She had obviously been sitting by the phone and answered on the first ring.

"This is Officer Ivy." I hesitated a moment and let that sink in. "I called your brother and he said you sent him a chain text and wanted him to send it to ten of his friends?"

"Well yes."

"Do you know what time he wakes up in the morning?"

"Yes, but I wanted him to have a good day."

"Well you ruined his good day because he's sleepy." Now I was using my serious mean voice on her.

"Well, he didn't need to threaten to kill me?"

My mean voice again, "I think it was rhetorical."

"What does that mean?"

"It means," I took a slow deep breath, "You will not text your brother again until he gives you permission. You will not send chain text messages to anyone after nine at night and if someone calls and complains about your messages, I'll cite you for harassment. That's what it means."

I could hear her sniff, sniff before she answered, "Okay, I'm sorry, I was just trying to assure he had a good day."

I hung up the phone.

Sometimes being a cop in Small Town was like being a cop in f-ing Mayberry R.F.D.

Chapter 5

My first week of working nights seemed to drag by. I was tired and had trouble sleeping during the day. By Thursday morning, I was so exhausted I didn't remember taking off my boots. I fell into bed and didn't get up until 1700, one hour before my shift started.

I showered and prepared myself for the long night. I said maybe two words to Norman and after a quick kiss, I was out the door.

Detective Alex Molinero was waiting for me when I arrived at the office. He told me that Sgt. Spears was not feeling well, and he was covering his shift. "The Sarg suffers from chronic headaches and blames it on new rookies." Alex didn't exactly smile when he said it and I wasn't sure if he was making this up or not.

He asked me what I was working on. I gave him a rundown of the "almost nothing happens at night" sob story.

He told me to follow him and we would find some "shit" to get into because he could not stand waiting for dispatch to call with *stupid people* complaints.

We were off. He was very different from what I was becoming accustomed to. Where Sgt. Spears was official and uptight, Alex had a spontaneous energy that was contagious. First on his list was checking out a house. I felt "cool" riding in Alex' unmarked Crown Victoria. He told me the entire town knew he drove it, but criminals could be stupid, and they looked for the light bars on police cars.

Someone gave him a tip that a drug drop would take place later at the house we were checking out. He also needed a description of the home in case we had to write a search warrant.

I was excited and felt I was finally doing real police work. We drove past the house. Alex had me write down the house, trim, and front door colors. We drove around town in a big loop and took another look and see. This time he had me get a license plate number off the vehicle parked out front.

After we left the area, Alex used his cell phone to call dispatch for a "28." There was Alex talking cool again. A "28" was the shortened ten-code for license plate check.

After he finished the call I asked, "Why did you use your cell phone and not the radio?"

"A lot of people in town have police scanners and when I read the license plate information over the air, the buzz starts. It quickly gets back to the person I'm after."

I decided right then and there I wanted to become a detective. I asked Alex how he got his position.

"I had a 'knack' and good detectives perform a different flavor of policing than patrol cops. Detectives are people persons, and like to talk. They listen and often see nuances that other guys can miss. One of the best cops at the department trained me. You'll train with him after your first two months with Sgt. Spears. Lucky you."

"Who is it?"

"Spike is what everyone calls him."

I'd met Spike at the Thanksgiving potluck. I wasn't very impressed. He was old, crabby and stood about 5'7". He'd reminded me of Peter Falk, from the seventies television show, *Columbo*. Only not as likable.

I told Alex about meeting Spike at the potluck.

"Don't let that old piece of shit fool you. He's the smartest guy at the department."

"Why isn't Spike a detective or supervisor"

"He doesn't conform, and doesn't follow orders very well. But his biggest problem is that he says what's on his mind. If the Chief does something wrong, Spike tells him and it never goes over well. He has more knowledge in his pinky than the Chief has in his entire body." Alex made sure I knew he didn't mean any disrespect to the Chief, but facts were facts.

"Take everything you learn from Spike and file it away. You will use it over and over and there will be times when Spike's words of wisdom save your life."

It would be five weeks before I partnered with Spike, so I was planning to learn everything I could from Alex tonight.

He asked if I wanted to eat at his house for dinner. I wasn't sure what to expect because of his single status, but I agreed.

It turned out Alex lived with his Mom and three of his brothers. His Mother could cook and it was a fantastic meal. Spanish was the language of the evening and I didn't have a clue what was going on around me. Every now and then Alex translated. I just sat and listened, smiled when they did, and laughed when it seemed appropriate. And I ate.

We got back in the car and Alex said his mother liked me. He told me she did not like skinny women or women that picked at their food. It was hard to be insulted because his mother understood why I was not skinny. I took a second helping of everything.

Alex said the drug buy would not go down until after midnight and asked what I wanted to do. I told him I was not overly comfortable with traffic stops and needed some help. He groaned and complained about the cold weather but started cruising town. Fifteen minutes later, we saw a large older model brown Cadillac swerving side to side on the road.

Alex looked over at me, "What do you want to do?"

"Pull it over. I haven't had a single drunk driver yet."

He activated the lights and mumbled a barely heard, "You'll be sorry.

It was too late for me to ask what he was talking about but I knew something was up. I ran the license plate through dispatch as soon as we stopped. I then approached the vehicle on the passenger side as I was taught to do by Sgt. Spears. The driver expects you on the driver's side and being opposite of where they think you are enables you to see what's in their hands before they have a chance to react. At least this is the theory.

I approached and saw an elderly lady behind the wheel. She was not looking towards me so I knocked on the closed window. She never turned her head but continued looking out the driver's side window.

I finally looked at Alex, "What should I do?"

"It's your stop, figure it out."

I decided to walk around and approach on the other side. I felt extremely foolish. The elderly woman rolled down her window and said, "I'm in a hurry and it's rude to interrupt someone while they're driving."

"Yes ma'am, I'm Officer Ivy, may I see your driver's license and registration?"

"What did you say? I can't hear. You'll need to speak up."

I tried speaking louder, "I'm Officer Ivy, may I see your driver's license and registration please?"

"What's wrong with you? I told you I can't hear. Are you deaf? I need to get home, my bowels aren't what they used to be and when it's time to go, it's time to go."

Dispatch came back on the air with the driver's information. Marie Lloyd was the registered owner and being a rookie I asked, "Are you Marie Lloyd?"

"Did you call me Marie? You're not my friend and I didn't say you could call me Marie. The young have no consideration for their elders anymore." Her indignation was palpable.

I looked at her and then looked to see Alex' grin. "Have a good evening Mrs. Lloyd." I turned and walked away.

I was learning fast. Alex held his laughter until the car was out of sight.

"You're such a jerk! Why couldn't you just warn me instead of putting me through that?"

Between laughs he said, "No one gives Mrs. Lloyd a ticket. She's sharp as a tack and has excellent hearing. She just can't see worth a damn and had her license revoked about three years ago. It's never stopped her from driving. She pulls this crap with everyone and never gets a ticket. I'm smarter than I look and won't be the first one to write her up."

I was pissed off. The woman didn't even have a driver's license. "I promise to be the first to give the old bat a ticket. Now I really want her. Let's go."

"She's probably home by now and I really don't want the hassle. The last rookie actually had her step out of the car and she mysteriously had her knee go out and fell to the ground. She threatened to sue the city and it's best to just let her drive."

I couldn't believe what I was hearing but realized this was just another sign of *The Mayberry Effect*.

We started cruising again and I looked for another traffic violator. It didn't take long and we pulled a man over for running a stop sign. I gave him a warning.

Alex critiqued my stop, telling me I needed to walk backwards and keep my eyes on the stopped vehicle when I returned to the cruiser."

I knew this, but it was easier said than done. I tried harder on the next stop and did a better job. I again wrote a warning.

Alex insisted on making the next stop, but he didn't tell me why. We pulled a man over for speeding down Main Street. I stood on the passenger side while Alex approached the driver's side. Alex told the guy that if he promised to slow down and his license and registration checked out, he would issue him a warning.

We walked backwards to the undercover vehicle, ran the driver's information and Alex filled out the warning slip. We then walked back to the stopped vehicle.

I was surprised when Alex said, "I'm sorry, everything checked out but I used my last warning slip and had to write you a traffic citation instead."

I saw Alex write the warning and had no idea what he was talking about.

The man didn't say anything for a minute but then exploded. "You've got to be kidding me, this is ridiculous. You should have told me in the beginning that you were writing me a ticket. I can't believe this."

Alex kept a straight face as he looked hard into the driver's eyes. Then he smiled, "Just kidding, this is your warning but slow down. Next time I promise it will be a ticket."

The driver laughed, appreciating the joke. They talked for a few minutes and the man promised to slow down. We walked back to Alex's vehicle.

This was my lesson for the night. Alex told me, "Be human and have fun. Let people know you're human and no better than them. It doesn't matter that you're fresh out of the academy. The citizens are judging you as a cop right now. Sgt. Spears is a great guy, but people don't relate to him. He's all cop and you need to be your own person. Take the best of what each of us teaches and file the rest away."

We drove back toward the drug house. I liked Alex. I liked the kind of cop he was. When I grow up to be a real cop, I want to be just like him.

Chapter 6

He pulled off the street and parked behind some trees around the corner from our target. Alex turned off his headlights so we could "sit on the house."

"We're going to be here for a while so tell me about becoming a police officer," said Alex.

That was all it took and I talked for the next thirty minutes. Alex was a good listener and didn't interrupt. I then began asking questions about his work.

"Many of the cases I work involve children and it would be great to have a female officer assist. Children need a soft touch. I think you could do it. Spike and I are the only two officers that handle sex crimes at the department. It's hard for Spike because he runs a patrol shift and sex crime cases take many hours to complete. They also tend to get to you after a while and I'm worried someday I'll reach across the table, grab a child molester by the throat and start choking. It will cost me my job, but sometimes I think it might be worth it. You have that grandmotherly touch. It's probably something you could be good at."

This gorgeous guy just called me grandmotherly. It sucks getting old, but maybe he had a point. I liked kids, couldn't think of anything worse than someone harming a child, and I wasn't exactly prudish when it came to sex. It was worth thinking about.

We continued talking until just after 0100 hours and saw some lights moving up the street. A vehicle stopped in front of our target and Alex told me we were not going to approach, just watch. Two men exited a black SUV. They didn't look around which surprised me. On television, they always look around, but these guys acted self-assured, like they owned the house. They knocked on the front door and went inside when it opened. Alex pulled out of our hiding spot and drove by the house, so I could write down the SUV's plate number. It was dark inside our car and I wrote blind on my time log in big numbers and letters. We then circled the block before returning to our post.

Five minutes later, the two men came out, got in their SUV and drove away.

We waited five minutes and then Alex told me to get out of the car and follow him.

As we walked over to the house, Alex said, "Let me do the talking. Keep your eyes and ears open but most of all don't do anything stupid."

I was getting the feeling that everyone thought rookies had no intelligence at all.

Alex knocked on the door and a tall skinny guy answered. As soon as he saw Alex, he knew he was in trouble. His eyes opened wide and his hands started shaking.

Alex said in a cool matter of fact voice, "I know you got the drugs tonight, we need to talk."

A quivering hand opened the door wider and he stepped back. "I don't want no trouble, and I don't got no drugs."

Alex read off the SUV plate number and told the guy that officers were pulling the vehicle over right now.

You gotta love a cop that can bluff like that.

"They're going to think you're ratting them out, and I'm gonna let them think just that."

"Please Molinero: I don't need no more trouble, what you want?"

"Who's making the buy off you?"

"No please, I can't tell you."

"My vehicle's hidden around the corner and I can just wait in here until they come."

I didn't know if we could wait in there or not. We hadn't actually seen any drugs, and according to the fourth Amendment, I didn't think we could stay if he told us to leave. We didn't have a warrant. I was confident in what I learned at the academy, but wasn't sure what I should do, so I kept my mouth closed as Alex suggested. I also looked around.

The place smelled rank and it was a mess. There were paper plates and opened cans of food on every surface. There was also a pornographic movie playing on the TV, but I couldn't hear any loud moaning so I figured the volume was turned off.

"Okay man, but you gonna get me killed, it's JJ. He's pickin' up and he should be here any time." Even his voice was quaking now.

"I'll leave, but not a word out of you or the SUV guys will think you gave em up." Alex took out his cell phone and made a call. He said, "Just give them a warning and tell them to use their blinker next time." He hung up.

"We're outta here so keep it cool Jose," and then he shook Jose's trembling hand.

We left the house and ran back across the street to our vehicle. I wasn't sure what just happened so I asked. Before Alex answered, we jumped in his car and drove away. We ended up at the park about a mile from Jose's house.

"I'm after Jeff Jackson, known as JJ. I've wanted him for a long time and I already knew the answer to my questions before I asked Jose. It's all about playing the game Ivy. Shit bags always give up other shit bags."

"Why aren't we going after the guys in the SUV?"

"They may not have more drugs. We want to catch them heading into town with a load and not after they've made their drop. Don't worry, we'll get 'em eventually."

"Who did you call and tell to release the vehicle?"

"I called Sgt. Spears' home phone, which he never answers. I left the message on his machine and he'll get it in the morning. I've used Sgt. Spears' phone for bogus messages before. He's used to it."

I was on a roll, "What about the constitution and staying in the house if we were told to leave?"

Alex looked at me for a long time. I'll never forget what he said, "Most crooks are stupid. I'm not teaching anyone their rights if they're not smart enough to know them. If he told us to leave we would have taken him out of the house and written a search warrant. I was ready for that, but he never told us to leave. Criminals get the upper hand when it comes to the court system. They don't need our help."

"Why do you want JJ?"

"Jeff Jackson beat up an old girlfriend of his. He broke her leg and busted her cheek bone. He scraped by with only six months in jail. He's midway up the crime chain here in town and I've been after him for a long time. He might recognize this vehicle. We're going to stay away from Jose's place and try to stay out of JJ's sight. He lives around the corner from the park and his car was still in front of his house when we drove past. I want to get him with the drugs after he picks them up. Jose's a pretty good snitch if you lean on him. He spent time in prison about ten years ago. I use him a lot and try not to give him a hard time. I got this info from another source. Jose is getting in deep again and he'll probably end up back in prison. I'll let another one of the cops handle it when it's time. I've got to protect my name on the streets."

I sat there absorbing everything I was told.

Alex radioed dispatch and told them we were Code-7 at Paychecks. This meant we were eating a meal at the restaurant. He explained he gave this information to dispatch because JJ had a scanner and now thought we were eating dinner.

The Paycheck restaurant was a favorite of the cops in Small Town. They had quick, semi-healthy food and Alex told me they didn't hire the dirt bags that we put in jail, so we didn't need to worry about spit in our food. They got their name because they were busiest on paycheck Thursdays and Fridays. Alex was just full of lovely information. Spit in food was never covered at the police academy.

A few minutes later, I saw vehicle lights down the street near JJ's place. Alex waited for the vehicle to pull completely out onto Main Street before he followed. A few minutes later we saw JJ turn down Jose's street, but Alex didn't follow. He said we would wait around the corner and pick up JJ when he got back on Main Street.

Ten minutes later, JJ pulled in front of us and we followed. Alex was giving me directions on how this would go down. First we had to have a legitimate reason to make the stop. If we got that, I was to stand on the passenger side of the vehicle with my gun drawn but down at my side. Alex told me to put my gun away and go for my Taser if JJ wasn't armed and decided to fight.

"He likes using his fists, especially on women. Keep that in mind."

"Umm, I don't have a Taser."

Alex smiled, "Okay, I'll tase him if he needs it. You good with that?"

"Yep."

When JJ turned down the street by the park, he didn't use a turn signal. We hit our red and blues and made the stop. I followed directions and moved to the passenger side.

Alex approached on the driver's side and said, "What's up JJ, you know why I stopped you?"

"Because you're a piece of shit and like hassling me."

"Hey, I was being nice to you." Alex's voice was friendly and personable like they were old friends. "What are you doing out this late?"

"It's a free country and I can be out whatever time I want." JJ's voice was not friendly.

"Well, you can, but you need to use your signal when you make a turn."

"That's bullshit and you know it, what you gonna do, write me a ticket for not using my turn signal?"

"Yes, I am. Do you have any weapons, drugs or other illegal items in your vehicle?"

"Hell no, you know I can't have no guns. I'm not stupid."

"Well, you don't mind if I take a look do you?"

"Yes I mind, that's bullshit. All I gotta do is give you my license and registration." With that JJ handed those items over.

"Officer Ivy, keep an eye on JJ's hands and I'll be right back."

Until that moment I don't thing JJ knew I was there. He glanced at me and then looked away. I stood there for ten minutes watching JJ and waiting for Alex.

At the five minute mark, JJ started cussing, "This is fuckin bullshit, that's what this is." JJ's language got more colorful but it's not worth repeating. He wasn't very inventive only repetitive.

Another vehicle pulled up at our stop and a plain clothes officer got out. I couldn't remember his name, but he was our K-9 handler. He took his dog out of the back of his unit.

My hand was still at my side with my gun in it. Alex came back over and told JJ to stay in his vehicle and keep his hands inside. JJ grumbled, but did as requested. Alex and I walked back to our patrol vehicle as the dog went to work around the car. Alex gave a nod towards my gun and I figured he wanted me to holster it. I must have guessed right because he ignored me after that and kept his eyes on the car and the dog. When the K9 alerted his handler, by whining and sitting at attention, I heard the officer say, "Show me the drugs." The dog placed its front paws on the back window and began barking with her tail wagging away.

Alex walked back to JJ's car and asked him to step out. I was behind Alex as JJ climbed out of the vehicle. He was peaceful one minute but went ballistic the next, swinging his arms and cussing. Alex and I moved back and Alex drew his Taser. I put my hand to my gun as Alex switched his Taser on and pointed the laser dead center on JJ's chest. He calmed down immediately. It had the same effect on him that it had on the Beefalo. *Don't mess with the Taser.*

"Officer Ivy move around to the front of this gentleman while I check him for weapons."

I moved to stand in front of JJ, but stayed out of arms' reach. Alex had JJ in handcuffs almost before I could blink. He then had JJ walk back to the K9 officer's patrol vehicle and told him to spread his legs wide. He grabbed JJ's shirt and pulled him slightly back and off balance, just like I learned at the academy.

Alex started patting JJ's pockets and obviously found something because he asked, "What's this?"

"Figure it out your own fucking self, asshole."

Alex did just that and pulled a glass pipe from JJ's pocket. "Looks like paraphernalia to me."

Alex then began emptying JJ's pockets placing everything on the front hood of the patrol vehicle. Alex hit pay dirt when he began pulling extra small zip lock baggies with white powder from the inner jacket pocket.

"What do we have here?"

"This is fuckin bullshit." JJ didn't have a very big vocabulary.

Alex walked him to his unmarked vehicle and placed him in the back seat. He handed me a camera and told me to get pictures of the drugs and items emptied from JJ's pockets. I did as instructed.

It took about an hour to completely search the vehicle. A couple of marijuana roaches were found in the ashtray but no additional drugs. Alex had me call a tow truck.

After the tow truck did its business, we got back in with JJ and headed to the PD. JJ didn't say a word. We took him into our interview room and Alex read him his Miranda rights. JJ wanted his lawyer and wouldn't answer questions. I filled out the booking paperwork while Alex called JJ's Probation Officer. We then dropped him at the jail.

Poor Alex and all my questions. "Why didn't the dog attack JJ when he flipped out?"

"Astro is a drug dog, whose primary function is finding drugs. He has no training as a police attack dog, they're two different things. An attack dog needs a lot of liability insurance and we don't have the money in our budget though we really need one."

"Why did you write JJ a warning for not using his turn signal? Why didn't you give him a ticket?"

"If I had not found drugs on him, I would have written him the citation. Because I found the drugs, I wrote the warning to show I had a legitimate reason for pulling him over. Cases are thrown out all the time because they're ruled illegal stops. Doesn't matter how many drugs you find, if you had no reason to pull the person over, you're screwed in court."

"So you can't pull someone over because you know they have drugs?"

"Not unless you saw the drugs go into the vehicle or you want to write a warrant on the vehicle first and use your snitch's information. By the time that's done the drugs are usually out of the car and somewhere else. Good drug dealers know to check their headlight, taillights, use blinkers and go the speed limit. JJ is a dumb shit and plays the game, but doesn't know the rules. That's lucky for us and this job takes a lot of luck."

My questions continued until the end of our shift. Alex's patience astounded me and I felt smarter than I did when I aced a test at the academy.

Before we left, Alex gave the next shift a rundown of our evening. I got slapped on the back for pulling over Marie Lloyd. I was also told Alex was a "shit magnet" and to be prepared when I went out with him.

I started home for my weekend off and some much needed sleep. This had been my best night of policing yet. I couldn't wait to tell Norman about the fun I'd had.

Chapter 7

No call outs over the weekend. I was disappointed but enjoyed the time with my husband. A department meeting was scheduled for Tuesday at 1500 hours. It was my first. The department secretary called me and said that rookies were required to bring donuts to their first meeting.

Yes, I know… cops and donuts. I could give you the short history that donut shops were the only place open late at night and thus drew the cops but I'd be delaying the inevitable, cops like donuts. I had received a t-shirt from my best friend Veronica at my police academy graduation. It reads, "Throw your donut in the opposite direction and the cops won't get you." I love wearing that t-shirt.

Everyone was in attendance at the meeting. Sgt. Spears pointed me to the empty chair next to him. I sat. Chief Varnett began by introducing me to the men.

"This is our new department member Officer Suzie Ivy. She's field training with Sergeant Spears and doing well from everything I've heard. Welcome to Small Town PD." He said this last part as he looked at me, then without a blink went into his next recitation, "Now I've had it with whoever has the shitting squirts and is spraying all over the toilet. For God's sake, clean up after yourself or eat something that gives you a firmer bowel movement. I don't want to bring this up again, understood?"

We all shook our heads in agreement and I heard a few, "Yes Chief." My brief introduction and then the shitting squirts, I knew just where I fit in.

Chief Varnett went over the stats from the previous weeks; tickets, arrests, etc. There had been multiple burglaries reported to the day shift and he wanted the night shift to keep our eyes open. There were four of us on nights and I drove with someone so it only gave us three officers to cover the entire town throughout the week. He gave one of our officers a pat on the back for getting a letter of appreciation from the grade school for reading to the classroom. He also told us that Mike and Benito, he nodded his head in their direction, were back from advanced high-risk stop training and the following week would give us a rundown on what they learned.

He admonished an officer for being rude during a traffic stop and held up his hand when the officer tried to rebut. He didn't care about the officer's side, the officer was perceived as rude and that's what mattered. He told us we had better be "selling" our tickets.

The floor was then handed over to Sgt. Spears. He complained about speeders on Main Street during the high school lunch hour. I wasn't a detective, but I guessed it was high school kids speeding. He also complained that the squad room was a mess and no one emptied the trash cans at their desk.

"I am not your mother! Clean up after yourself or you'll have bathroom cleaning duty for a month and I myself will have the shitting squirts. Is that understood?"

Again everyone nodded in agreement. Alex spoke next. He reviewed a few cases he was working and gave information on a couple of people he was looking for. I envied him his job. Plain clothes, no set hours, and interesting cases. Maybe someday I would get a chance to walk in his shoes. I knew I had a few years in front of me before that happened, but it was nice to dream.

Spike was up next, and began a colorful recital, "What the fuck's wrong with you assholes. At every meeting, your messes are brought up. Your mommies don't work at the police department. You're grown men and you wear a badge. Clean up your own shit or I'll call you in while you're sleeping and make you do it."

No one said a word. Spike may not have a title of authority, but he definitely had a voice. I was impressed. I think I was looking forward to working and training under him. It would definitely not be dull.

After everyone had a chance to say something the meeting broke up. The donuts were gone. I had brought three dozen.

The officers started cleaning their desks and emptying their trash cans. I figured this was done after every meeting and not thought of again. Did men ever change?

I headed home to put my uniform on and prepare for my shift.

When it was time, I met up with Sgt. Spears. We drove around for more than an hour. It didn't seem like it was going to be an exciting evening, but then we got a call of a domestic in progress. Sgt. Spears was familiar with the unloving couple and he turned on the emergency lights but no siren.

Like he did with all our calls, he went over the rules as he drove to the scene, "You don't want to use your siren when going to a domestic. These are some of the most dangerous calls we face and we don't want the bad guy to know we arrive until we get to the door.

Sgt. Spears parked two houses down and we approached slowly on foot. There were no cars in the driveway. We stood to either side of the door and he knocked loudly.

A woman answered. She was holding a bloody cloth to her face.

"Hi Rachel, is Charles still here?"

"No, he left when I called the cops." She opened the door to let us inside. She was not crying she just had a resigned look on her face.

We entered the room, it was a mess. Sgt. Spears looked around, "What happened?"

"Charles got mad while we were at the bar. He said I was giving signals to the guy at the next table. We left the bar and drove home. He just started hitting me like he always does. I try not to make him mad but when he drinks, I can't stop him."

Rachel sat down on the couch and Sgt. Spears sat beside her. He gently took the cloth from her hand, peering at her face. He asked me to grab a camera from his patrol vehicle. Rachel began crying softly.

I studied domestic violence at the academy and aced the DV scenarios. Reality was incredibly different. I knew the odds of her leaving her husband were slim. I knew the odds of him beating her again were high. I didn't feel disgust for her, I felt pity. What would bring a woman to value herself so little?

I was lucky to have two grown daughters who had been taught to respect themselves above anything else.

I went back inside and heard Sgt. Spears talking, "You know he will eventually kill you. We can't help if you continue to take him back."

"Is he going to jail?"

"Yes, as soon as we find him."

She didn't want an ambulance, but Sgt. Spears talked her into going to her sister's house for the evening. I started by taking pictures of the room and then asked to photograph her injuries. She didn't object. I don't think she had the mindset to object to anyone.

Sgt. Spears stepped outside and I asked her if she had any other injuries. She showed me a long scratch on her breast which was bruising badly. She had a cut on her face and a bloodied and swollen nose. She told me Charles broke a kitchen chair and hit her with the leg. I took pictures of the chair pieces.

After she collected a few of her things, we drove Rachel to her sister's house and then returned to the police department. I was angry because I wanted to hunt for Charles but Sgt. Spears was more the "let them come to you" type. So, I held in my frustration.

He called dispatch and put out an attempt to locate (ATL) with a description of what Charles was wearing and the license plate number for the vehicle he was driving. He placed the ATL in all surrounding areas.

We finally headed back out to the street, but had no success in locating our dirt bag. I went home with unfulfilled thoughts of pepper spraying my bad guy.

I had slept an hour when I got a call from Alex. The sun was just coming up. He told me he thought he had located Charles and asked if I wanted join him in the apprehension.

I was ready in less than ten minutes. Alex picked me up at my door. Norman was still sleeping and I left him a note.

Alex explained that he received a call from one of his informants who gave him a heads up on Charles' location. I was learning that Alex had connections.

"I don't have paid informants, but I can swing favors now and then when someone gives me a useful tip. On the street your word means everything. I have a reputation as being fair. I'm not going to let someone get away with a major crime, but there are times I can give people a break. I work with the County Attorney's Office and frequently get their help. Sometimes you don't need to pound a person that's doing more for you on the street by giving up information."

We drove to a small house on the east side of town. Alex told me it belonged to our suspect's mom. The vehicle we were looking for was not there but Alex felt his information was good. He asked me to go around to the back and keep an eye on the windows.

I slowly made my way through high weeds. There was no fence and I stood at the corner of the house keeping an eye on the back and side windows. A phone rang loudly and it was coming from my chest pocket. I quickly silenced it and seeing the call was from Norman, I didn't answer. Another note to self; turn cell phone to silent when you're trying to be sneaky.

I heard Alex knocking on the front door and then talking. The voices faded and I began getting impatient when Alex started yelling at me over the radio. 1510 was my call number and Alex's voice was panicked as he called me into the house. I heard something about a gun and I ran like hell, trampling the vegetation under my boots.

A small older woman was standing inside the front door, she pointed down the hallway. I rounded the corner and Alex was standing inside a bathroom. A man, I guessed to be Charles, was kneeling in the bathtub, fully clothed. The shower curtain was torn down and Alex was yelling at him to keep his hands in the air.

I finally took a breath. My heart was pounding and I was surprised no one could hear it. My gun was in my hand. I didn't even remember taking it from the holster.

Alex had our guy step out of the tub with his hands up. He told me to watch the hallway and make sure we had no other problems coming at us. I did as told.

Alex told Mrs. Santos thank you as we walked our guy out to Alex's vehicle.

She watched, with the same sad eyes as Rachel, as her son walked past her.

As we helped Charles into the back of the car, I noticed blood on his white tennis shoes. I told Alex and he made Charles take his shoes off.

"Those are new shoes and I want them back."

"They're evidence now and the only person who can release them is the judge. You should take better care of new shoes. Blood is hard to wash off."

Charles didn't say another word.

We drove to the jail and Alex asked what I wanted the charges to be. I told him aggravated assault because he used the table leg to beat up his wife. Alex added disorderly conduct, and kidnapping. All the charges carried domestic violence as an aggravating circumstance.

I didn't ask about the kidnapping until we got back to the car.

"When you limit someone's movements with force, it's kidnapping according to Arizona statute. The County Attorney's Office will probably drop the charge, but Charles won't get out of jail in the next twenty-four hours. Maybe Rachel will have a chance to recover."

"A judge would actually let him out tomorrow?" My disgust was evident in my voice.

"You'll learn that almost everyone gets out within a few days. You need at least a class two felony to assure someone stays in jail for any length of time. In a small town like this, everyone knows everyone. Bail is designed to guarantee someone shows up for their court appearance. Charles is a shit bag but he always shows up. The judge knows this, considers it, and lets him out. I'm just buying Rachel a few days. She'll be back with him before her bruises completely disappear. He'll be the perfect husband for a while and then things will start getting bad again. Let's hope he doesn't kill her anytime soon."

Charles *would* eventually kill Rachel and I had trouble grasping the disillusion I was feeling. It was one thing to learn and train for domestic violence cases. It was quite another to be faced with the reality. I thought I would feel better after making the arrest. I didn't. Maybe it would have helped if I'd used the pepper spray. Alex drove me home.

"You did well today Ivy. We got another piece of scum off the street for a short time and that's always a positive in this job. Get some sleep.

It was easier said than done. I tossed and turned thinking about what it would be like to be beaten with a table leg.

Chapter 8

The nights seemed to run together. Sgt. Spears was a great teacher and he was methodical. The one thing he tried to teach me was to slow down.

He repeated his favorite lecture almost nightly, "Cops are adrenaline junkies. They make mistakes because they go too fast. They run to the problem and leave key items behind, like notebooks, pens and flashlights."

I was becoming addicted to adrenaline highs. It was difficult for me when an urgent call finally came in, after nights of pretty much nothing, and Sgt. Spears took his time.

Alex did a great imitation of the Sergeant one evening. It went something like this...

Call comes in "Bank robbery in progress."

Sgt. Spears picks up his cell phone, his cup, his jacket, and his radio. He then walks slowly towards the squad room door. He stops near the bathroom and looks in. He walks back to his office, lays down his cell phone, his cup, his jacket, and his radio. He then walks into the bathroom. He comes out and heads to his office again and slowly methodically recollects the items. He then walks back to the squad room door, stops, thinks for a minute, then walks out.

Alex actually does the entire scenario in pantomime. It's priceless.

I hated waiting for Sgt. Spears to finally get out the door. But, he controlled the car keys so I had no choice.

It was finally the last week I would spend with Sgt. Spears and it was the most boring time since I started field training. We received no calls for service and Sgt. Spears was busy writing performance reviews. All caught up on my reports, I needed to do something in order to stay awake.

I begged Sgt. Spears to go out patrolling. He finally gave in. At 0130 hours, we hit the streets. The town itself was dead. It was nine degrees according to Small Town's outside digital thermometer.

Sgt. Spears let me drive. I decided to go through the poorer section of town just as Alex had shown me.

I noticed, out of the corner of my eye, flames in a small trailer park. I turned around and headed back in that direction. I could see the remains of a large plastic garbage bin and a wooden fence on fire. We called for a fire truck and then ran up to the front door of the closest trailer and began pounding. Sgt. Spears sent me to the next trailer to wake up anyone inside. If more than the fence ignited we were in for a large fire and trailers went up fast.

The fire department showed up and got the flames under control. The guy we talked to blamed his wife for poring hot coals into the plastic garbage can.

We left at around 0330 hours smelling like smoke. We were cold and tired.

"You did really well and probably saved lives. No one understands our job, but a lot of it is just being observant."

I went home feeling proud and slept like a baby. It was finally my last night with Sgt. Spears. We spent the evening patrolling as he quizzed me about all I had learned. "You'll make a good cop after five more years of practice." For him, this was a compliment.

I was in the driver's seat and we made a few traffic stops. As luck would have it, I saw a large brown Cadillac putting along. The caddy made a right turn using no turn signal. It was fate.

Sgt. Spears asked me if I was sure I wanted to do it. With a huge grin, I activated our overhead lights. I called in the plate number and the location of my stop.

I walked up to the vehicle and knocked on the window. Marie Lloyd rolled it down. I asked for her driver's license and registration.

Every word uttered by Mrs. Lloyd was said condescendingly between clenched teeth. I remained firm but polite.

"Do you know who I am young lady?"

"My name is Officer Ivy and you are Marie Lloyd."

"I'm headed home and I would already be there if you weren't so rude. Who was I hurting?"

"I stopped you because you didn't use your turn signal and you don't have a driver's license."

"I've been driving longer than you've been alive. I can drive better than you ever will and I don't need some card to say I can drive."

"In the state of Arizona you need a driver's license to give you the right to drive. I have one of those "cards" and you don't. It doesn't matter who can drive better. I'm writing you a ticket and towing your vehicle. Is there someone I can call to pick you up and take you home?"

"Just write me the ticket and I'll drive straight home."

"You won't have a car to drive, it's being towed. I can give you a ride in the back of my patrol vehicle or I can call someone for you. The decision is yours."

"Are you threatening me? I'll have your job young lady."

"My name is Officer Ivy. Do you want to call someone or do you want a ride?"

"I WILL HAVE YOUR JOB!"

"That may be, I'm still towing your car and writing you a ticket. People go to jail for driving on a suspended license. I'm actually giving you a break."

Mrs. Lloyd seemed to deflate, "What if you just took me home and didn't give me the ticket?"

"Sorry, but I can't do that. I won't be responsible for your getting into a future accident. Why don't you step out of the vehicle and come with me to my patrol car?"

The tears started then, but she walked with me back to my vehicle. I stayed close to her side in case she tried the falling thing on me. I called the tow truck and started filling out the tow sheet. I left Mrs. Lloyd in the back of the patrol vehicle sobbing as I walked back to her car to begin an inventory. The tow truck arrived and we watched the old Cadillac get loaded and then driven away.

I joined Sgt. Spears back in the squad car. Mrs. Lloyd stopped crying and her anger returned.

"You will not have a job after this. The police in this town don't treat their citizens this way. Shame on you."

"No, shame on you." I said in a soft voice looking her directly in the eyes. She looked away first.

We arrived at Mrs. Lloyd's house and I opened the car door for her. She huffed up to her front door and walked inside. The door slammed shut.

Sgt. Spears was beside himself. He couldn't believe I actually did it. He had not said a word during the entire stop.

"Suzie, I have a feeling we will wonder how we ever got along in this town without you. Good job. I'm glad I got to see this."

The following day, I received a call, at home, from Sandy, the Chief's assistant. Mrs. Lloyd's daughter left a message thanking me for bringing her mom home. She asked that I give her a call. It was my day off but I called the phone number Sandy provided.

Melody was her name.

"Thank you for taking my mom's car." said Melody. We've been worried about her for years. No one would do anything and we really didn't blame them. She's a lot to handle when she gets going. We're getting the car back, but it's going to my brother's house. Did you really threaten to arrest her?"

"No I didn't. I wouldn't have arrested her but I told her I could and that she was lucky."

Melody laughed. "You will be our family hero for a while. Can we call you if she starts acting up again? It would serve her right."

"I don't think I want to be involved if she's not breaking the law. I'm not her favorite person."

I hung up the phone and surprisingly felt sad. Mrs. Lloyd was obviously independent. Getting old and having your means of freedom taken away must be rough, though Mrs. Lloyd was lucky. She had a family that obviously loved her. They just lived in fear of her. I wondered if I could pull that off when I was her age.

I decided it was time for housework, the never ending chore. One year ago, I was lying in bed with a broken hip. Now, I had been a police officer for eight weeks. Even without the broken hip, I wouldn't go back to my old life for anything. I was glad Norman was so accepting. I knew he worried, but he knew I was trained to take care of myself. He made a joke one day while we were shopping at our local grocery store, and I discreetly pointed out a guy I had arrested.

"If anything goes down," said my loving husband, "I'm throwing you in front of me."

I laughed and realized I wanted to be thrown in front of him. Norman was a tough man, a great father and husband. It didn't bother him to have an independent wife. I always had a strong personality, but never considered myself dangerous until the police academy taught me to be that way. It felt great to have confidence in myself and the job I did. I couldn't believe what I'd learned during my first two months.

When I finished the housework, I grabbed some old newspaper from a shelf in the pantry. I laid it out on the family room coffee table. Next, I took out my firearm cleaning kit and then my gun. Slowly and methodically, I unloaded the magazine and ejected the round in the chamber of my Glock 35. I then disassembled it and began cleaning.

It was calming as I ran the small white swatches through the chamber and cleaned every crevice to get out the dust particles. I used only two drops of oil as I was taught then put the pieces of the pistol back together. I pulled back on the slide, pointed my gun at the wall and pulled the trigger. I repeated these steps as the oil worked into the slide. I made sure everything felt right in my hand. It was soothing and reassuring.

Yes, my life had definitely changed.

Chapter 9

To work with Spike, I switched to mid-shift, noon to 2200 hours. Alex thought Spike was great but I had my doubts. He had no patience and was abrupt and crass. He was Sgt. Spears' polar opposite.

Spike immediately began teaching me his way of policing.

"Forget everything Sgt. Spears taught you." he said. "I have nothing against him, but he's not street cop material, and it's my job to see that you know what you're doing on patrol. In a large department, Sgt. Spears would be a desk Sergeant. Being under him for two months, you probably learned how to fill out every form perfectly, but that doesn't impress me. This job is more than paperwork. It's about observation, keeping your head in the game and not fucking up. Fucking up will get you killed. Even good cops die. Every day you need to be at your best. If not, you're dead." Spike's voice was sharp, gruff and no nonsense.

I couldn't argue with him. Spike was right, but I didn't need to like it, or him. I was trying to remember why Alex thought so highly of this ogre, but nothing came to mind. I was not impressed and didn't think I would enjoy my next four weeks.

Spike issued me the keys to my own patrol vehicle and made me sign the paperwork. I was given car number three. I would later learn that the earlier the number, the older the vehicle. We walked outside and I headed toward my very own patrol unit. Spike stopped me.

"I don't like women cops and I like women drivers even less. Get your ass on the passenger side of my car and shut up. You'll get to drive your own unit soon enough but it won't be with me sitting beside you."

I was fuming. I now understood why Spike never made a supervisory position, he was an ass.

We drove around for a while and I didn't say a word. Most of my time spent on field training was monotonous and it's hard to remember everything said to me during my first months. During that third month I remember every syllable that came out of Spike's mouth.

After about fifteen minutes of silence, he finally spoke up again, "So are your panties still in a wad or do you want to start learning something?"

I didn't even hesitate, "I'm not wearing panties."

Spike laughed, "Alex told me you could stick up for yourself and you weren't a pushover. I terrorize most new officers. Just know I won't put up with any shit. I don't care if you don't have a set of balls. I expect you to do your job. Crying won't get you anywhere with me so don't even try."

I wondered if it would be worth having to go home and clean my gun again. Putting a bullet between Spike's eyes was sounding better and better.

Spike then began his litany. "You will learn the rules of policing during your month with me. Today it's the first rule. Cops are sharks they eat their own."

I thought I might be losing my mind as he went on.

"In this business you will have very few friends. Most cops will turn on you for a dime. They will always save their butt first unless there's shooting involved. We are type "A" personalities. We are better than everyone else and that includes each other. At the same time we are a family, incredibly dysfunctional, but a family none the less. We will lay down our lives for another cop, but we will not stand behind each other if we make a mistake. Now tell me the first rule of policing."

I looked at him and tried not to roll my eyes, "Cops are sharks they eat their own."

He told me he expected me to remember it the next time he asked. I then made the mistake of asking what the number two rule was.

"I don't want to tax your rookie brain. I say when you get the rules. Learn the first one."

I gritted my teeth and kept quiet.

One thing I did notice while driving in the car with Spike was people waved, flagged him down, or stopped to talk when we got out of the vehicle. Everyone knew Spike and he knew everyone's name. He introduced me to the citizens of Small Town as Officer Ivy.

After we drove away from yet another person needing Spike's attention, I asked what he wanted me to call him when we were on a call. I didn't even know Spike's last name. Everyone just referred to him as Spike.

"Call me Spike or I won't know who you're talking to. I will always refer to you as Officer Ivy. This town has never had a female cop and they don't need to feel familiar with you just yet. They need to know you have authority. Respect is a different matter and that you may or may not earn. It's up to you."

Since this conversation did not end with me wanting to kill him, I broached the subject of why he didn't like female cops.

He looked me over slowly, "I've worked with two types of female cops. The ones that think they need to fight all the time in order to prove themselves and the type that hide behind their male counterparts if things get hairy. Which one are you?"

"I'm the kind that doesn't particularly want to fight and if it means saving your ass, I see myself just standing back and letting the chips fall."

He laughed again, "We'll see what you have over the next few weeks. It only took me five minutes to figure out you have a smart-ass mouth."

Our first night was rather uneventful but Spike told stories of his glory days. I only believed half of them but they were entertaining.

Spike is one of those people that remembered every name, first and last, from the time he was a toddler. I noticed this when he greeted people on the street. I guessed Spike was around sixty-years old, but he surprised me by telling me he was fifty.

The shock must have shown on my face because he said it was hard being a cop and it showed when it came to aging. This only caused me more shock because I wasn't that much younger than he and didn't want to look anything like that when the big Five-O hit.

Spike continued telling his stories and told me a few about Alex's rookie days.

One of Alex's first cases was the theft of a tricycle. The tri-wheeled wonder belonged to a three-year-old boy who was crying when Alex arrived at the scene. The mother said the tricycle was left on their front porch the night before and it was now missing.

She described the trike as red with white tassels on the handlebars.

Alex left the scene and went around the block. He noticed a small girl riding a tricycle that matched the description of the missing one.

He stopped his patrol car, got out, and approached the toddler. The child immediately began screaming. Alex stopped and looked around. He saw the mother walking towards him and she didn't seem very happy that her daughter was crying.

Alex told her he had a report of a missing tricycle and asked if the one her daughter was riding could be the lost bike.

The mother lost her mind and asked Alex if he planned to arrest her two-year-old, and place her in handcuffs, if it was the missing trike.

The little girl heard the anger in her mother's voice and began screaming at the top of her lungs. The woman grabbed her daughter and the tricycle and told Alex to go pick on someone his own size.

The story probably would have ended there, but the mother made a complaint to the Police Chief. She claimed her daughter was afraid to ride her tricycle because of her fear of the mean police officer.

For the next month, every officer seeing a kid on a tricycle would notify Alex to go check it out in case it was his stolen bike.

Spike could tell a great story and I could picture everything he was saying in my head. Poor Alex, I wondered what my biggest rookie mistake would be. Knowing fate, I was sure it would rival Alex's.

We made several traffic stops. They lasted forever. Spike carried on long conversations with everyone he pulled over. They all liked him and it seemed Spike's traffic stops were more a social hour than anything else. I didn't mind, but wasn't sure what to do about Spike's no paper policy. He didn't write warnings and gave few citations. I was taught by Sgt. Spears to always "cut paper." He said we needed to account for our time on the street and the stats helped. I made the mistake of asking Spike about it.

"I don't give a shit what Sgt. Spears taught you. You're in my car now and under my authority. I'm not filling out a piece of paper for every stop I make. If the driver needs paper it's because he needs a ticket. I don't care about stats or other police bullshit. Do we understand each other?"

I understood Spike perfectly. Rules were made for other cops and not him. I wondered why they even used Spike as a field training officer. Alex was such a smart guy. What the heck could he possibly see in this egotistical dickhead?

We took a call for a vehicle accident with no injuries. Spike made me do all the work and griped about how long I took. Sgt. Spears would at least grab the camera and start taking pictures while I took driver's information and ran plate numbers. Spike was no help but was quite good at criticizing.

After I took my first few pictures, he said, "You always take pictures of the license plates first. That way you know when your accident pictures start. Do everything in the same order every time and you won't fuck up as much."

The only thing I was thankful for was both drivers were too far away to hear. I continued taking pictures.

"Do you plan on spending your entire shift here? If you have more than one gear, then shift it. I'm hungry and getting cranky."

I took my time. It was very petty of me but if he wouldn't help then I would do it my way. He did have a point with the order of the pictures and I would do it his way from now on, but I refused to be hurried. I was not one of his previous rookies that he could browbeat. I was thinking Spike was a lot like Sgt. Dickens from the academy. I had learned to respect Sgt. Dickens but I never liked him.

I finished processing the scene and we headed to Paychecks for dinner. Everyone there knew Spike. He talked, joked and laughed with them all, but only introduced me if he had to. I ate my food slowly. I figured we would be there for a while.

We finally received a call for cattle in the road and left the restaurant. I'd taken plenty of cattle calls with Sgt. Spears. Spike handled them as well as the sergeant. I was thankful that he at least assisted me. I didn't speak cow and had wondered how I would ever get a large herd into a fenced area by myself, because I would have refused to ask Spike. He was making me as grumpy as he was.

By the end of my shift, I was exhausted. Spike followed me home while I drove my patrol car. I got back in with him and we went back to the station so I could pick up my personal vehicle. Tomorrow would be my first day of driving a patrol vehicle to work or being in one alone. The sad fact was that I no longer cared. I only wanted to get my four weeks with Spike out of the way without getting fired, or going to prison for the rest of my life.

Chapter 10

The next night started much like the one before. Spike gave me the second Rule of Law Enforcement. "If you realize you need to pull your gun, it should already be in your hand."

This one at least made more sense than the first rule.

I repeated rule one and two whenever Spike asked. He knew it irritated me so he asked often. We were about three hours into our shift when we received a call from dispatch saying they had a woman on the line reporting her twelve-year-old son had been "improperly touched."

Spike had them patch the call through to his cell phone. He asked the Mom to meet us at the police department. We then drove in that direction.

"Ivy, I don't want you to say a word unless I ask. Sit back and listen, see if I miss anything."

I did as he said.

Laura Thidwell brought her son Darin to the police department. The kid looked scared to death. I sat in the lobby making small talk with the boy while his mother went back to the interview room and spoke with Spike.

Darin didn't really say anything to me as I asked him about school and what he got for Christmas. He looked much younger than his twelve years and I was hoping things had not gone far enough to leave lasting scars.

Spike walked back in the lobby, with the mother, and I could tell she wasn't happy. She sat down and Spike asked Darin and me to follow him back to the interview room.

Darin never looked at his mom. He followed the two of us.

When we entered the small interview room, Spike engaged in the same small talk I'd begun. It didn't seem to be working, Darin had tears in his eyes and would not look at him.

Spike started asking questions about a woman named Angela. Darin would not look up, he just shook his head no, when asked if anything happened with her. This gentle questioning went on for about fifteen minutes, but Spike got nowhere.

As I listened to the questions Spike asked, I began piecing together the story.

Angela was Laura's friend and needed a place to stay after losing her job. She had been living with Laura and her son for three months. During that time, Angela had been getting a little too close to Darin.

I was not sure of the extent of "the touching," but obviously Darin's mother thought it was inappropriate.

Spike finally said he was going to step out of the room and speak with me. Darin nodded his head up and down slightly and I followed Spike out.

After closing the door to the interview room, Spike asked if I thought I could get anywhere with the boy. He said, because the molester was female, Darin might relate more to me. I wasn't sure if being a woman would help, but I was willing to try. Spike told me he'd monitor the interview from the other room and would not go back in the interview room.

"Whatever he says, don't show any type of shock at his words. He'll stop talking immediately. Can you do that? You need to get very specific with him, exactly what they did together, where and when things happened."

I told him I would try and then walked back into the room.

I sat down, but this time sat a little closer to Darin. I told him Spike was going to go and speak to his mother and I would just stay in the interview room to keep him company.

I asked Darin if Angela was a nice person. He nodded his head. I then asked if he liked her. The small head went up and down again. My next question was very gentle, "Do you love her?"

Darin looked up at me. He started crying softly and covered his eyes with his hands.

I placed my hand on his back and told him it was never a bad thing to love someone.

Darin continued crying, but said through his tears, "I want to marry   her."
I gently told Darin he was too young to marry anyone right now. I asked how Angela felt about him.

"She says she loves me and she'll wait until I'm old enough to get married."

I asked how old Angela was and Darin told me she was thirty-two.

I don't know what made me ask the next question, but it was what popped into my head.

"Have you thought about what would happen if Angela got pregnant?"

Darin looked up at me. "I think she is. That's why I'm so scared. She told me if anyone knew it was my baby she would go to prison and if she goes, it would be my fault."

My heart broke. I knew I needed details of what had been going on, but all I could think of was stomping Angela into the ground. In my mind, child molesters were big creepy men not grown women.

I asked if Angela had any children. Darin told me she had a ten-year-old daughter but she lived with Angela's ex-husband and they never saw each other.

I said, "The sadness from not seeing her daughter must make her feel that you are really special?"

"She loves me but not like a child and she loves me more than she ever loved her ex-husband."

"I know these are things that are probably hard to talk about but I need to ask you some questions." Darin had stopped crying and was now looking at me.

"I know this is going to be a stupid question, but do you know how babies are made?" I said this with a small smile on my face.

Darin's face turned slightly red and he said yes, timidly smiling back.

"Thank goodness, I didn't want to have to tell you about the birds and the bees. It was bad enough with my own kids." This I said with a laugh.

Darin laughed too.

"Okay, so did you do something with Angela that would make babies because it's important that we find out if she's pregnant?"

Darin looked down again but said he did.

I told Darin I needed to know what he did to get her pregnant.

Darin just looked at me like he didn't understand.

I said, "I need to know everything you can tell me. I think you're old enough to talk to me about sex." I had decided to talk to him like an adult since what we were talking about was an adult situation he had experienced.

Darin said, "I put my thing in her."

I asked Darin what his thing was called. He whispered "penis" very quietly.

I asked him where he put his penis and he told me it was in her thing. I asked if he knew what her thing was called and he said "pussy".

I remembered Spike's words and did not show shock at his use of "that" word. He probably heard it from his friends and even possibly Angela herself. I then told Darin, it was not as easy to get pregnant as some people thought, and many times if people had sex it did not cause pregnancy. I then asked how many times he did this with Angela.

Again I didn't show shock at his answer. He said, "Maybe a hundred."

"When do you have sex?"

"Before school, after my mom goes to work. Angela likes to crawl in my bed and that's when we 'do it' and sometimes after school before my mom gets home."

I asked if they ever did it anywhere else besides his bed and he told me they had done it on the couch and also in Angela's car.

I then began asking questions about calendar dates when the sex took place. He told me about specific times. There was the two weeks he was off school for Christmas break and other times when Angela took him for long drives. The hardest for me was when he told me about Christmas Eve and Angela sneaking into his bedroom to give him a "special" present.

We talked for over an hour. Once Darin began speaking, he didn't want to stop.

When he was done he looked me right in the eye, "Is Angela going to jail?

I couldn't lie to him. "Yes, it's against the law to have sex with someone your age."

"Am I going to jail?" He looked petrified.

"No, you haven't done anything wrong. There is no reason to take you to jail."

"What if Angela is pregnant?"

"Then you'll be a daddy. The baby won't be in trouble either."

"Will I get to see the baby?"

I didn't know how to answer so I said the only thing I could think of, "You will be the baby's father and nothing can change that."

Darin seemed satisfied with my answer and I told him I needed to speak with Spike. I asked if he would be okay in the room by himself. He told me he was.

I walked out and joined Spike. I was trying to keep my tears in. Spike looked at me with a big smile and said, "It might not feel good right now, but when we pick up that bitch, put her in handcuffs and lock her up, it will be one of the best feelings you've ever had. You did great. That's why Alex said he thought you would be good as a detective. You knew exactly what to say."

I wanted to feel happy, but I couldn't. We walked into the waiting room and spoke with Darin's mother. She cried and said, "If you don't find Angela before me, I'll kill her." I would have felt the same way if Darin was my son. Neither Spike nor I commented.

I asked Laura if she wanted to go into the interview room and speak with her son. I also told her Darin thought Angela might be pregnant and he felt responsible. I said, "Right now the thing he needs most is for his mother to love him and not blame or judge him."

Laura followed me back into the room. Darin did not look up at his mother. I told him his mom knew everything. He still didn't look up. I closed the door and walked away.

Spike and I started checking addresses of the homes of Angela's friends. Some of them were in our computer database.

Laura and Darin walked out of the interview room ten minutes later. They had both been crying. Laura had her arm around her son. She asked us to call her when we found Angela.

Spike asked Laura not to speak to anyone until Angela was in custody because she might run. Laura agreed.

He had me write down the addresses of Angela's friends. He spoke about other child molestation cases he had worked. There were a lot of them. He told me it was rare for women to be suspects. He said the boys usually only told their friends and it was purely for bragging rights.

"Even juries have trouble with a boy Darin's age being molested. To me, a child molester is a child molester. It doesn't matter what sex the suspects or victims are. A child is a child and that's why the law is written and a young juvenile can't give consent. The bad thing is we'll be lucky if Angela spends five years in prison for this."

I was floored. Darin was forever changed. He thought he loved Angela and in his young mind, he did. He would live with the guilt of Angela going to prison for many years and all she would get was five. A life sentence was not long enough in my opinion.

Spike and I left the police department with my list in hand. We began our hunt for Angela Garza.

Chapter 11

Spike said once we started knocking on doors, the word would get out and Angela would hide. He called Alex to see if he was available to help. Unfortunately, Alex was not in town and Spike was stuck with me.

We were looking for a white four door 1996 Corsica. Laura had told Spike that Angela's vehicle was run down and would not get her very far.

We drove by the addresses I had in my notebook. Most of the "homes" were trailers spread around town. We had a list of six friends but only had four addresses. We found the car at the fourth house.

I wasn't sure what would happen at this point, but I was sure I'd be placing Angela into the back of our car in handcuffs. I was wrong.

Spike spoke to her professionally, "Hi Angela, I'd like to speak with you about a problem and I really need you to come to the police department. It shouldn't take very long and it is important."

It was obvious she wasn't happy and I was surprised when she followed us out to Spike's vehicle.

While we were searching for Angela, Spike told me that I would not be in the room while he interviewed her. He wanted me to monitor the interview and take notes. He said the most important thing when interviewing a suspect was not to let them know what you really thought of them. I was guessing he didn't think I could keep my anger under control. He may have been right.

Spike and Angela entered the interview room and I went into the viewing room. I was just getting comfortable when Spike asked Angela if she wanted a coke or some water to drink. She didn't. He then began making small talk about the job she no longer had. She told him the owner at the deli said she missed too many hours at work and that's why he let her go. Angela said she hadn't missed very much time, but the owner's wife had it in for her.

Spike asked Angela about her parents whom he apparently knew. He then went on about her sister who left town years ago. Angela just sat and talked to him. This unrelated conversation went on for twenty minutes.

Spike finally mentioned he needed to read Angela her Miranda rights. He took a card out of his pocket and read from it. She nodded her head yes when he asked if she understood her rights.

Spike said, "You nodded your head up and down, does that mean, 'yes?'"

Angela said, "Yes," out loud this time.

"Do you know why you're in here speaking with me?"

"I don't have any idea."

"You must have some idea. What's going on in your life recently that would involve the police?" Spike kept speaking in a pleasant tone of voice.

Angela sighed, "Laura is mad at me and she's probably making up rumors to get me in trouble."

"Why would Laura be mad at you?"

"She thinks something is going on with me and her son."

"Why would she think that?"

"I don't know, I told her she was crazy. That lady is nuts."

"Did Laura see something she might have misunderstood?"

"I think that's exactly what happened and she's jealous because Darin enjoys spending time with me and he doesn't really like his mother."

Spike asked a variety of questions about Darin's relationship with his mother.

"Laura is always at the bar. She doesn't care about Darin, he just seems to be in her way. It's hard to be a party girl with a kid. Darin thinks of me as his mother and Laura is just someone who comes home drunk."

I felt sick.

Spike let Angela talk for a while and then asked what Darin would say about her.

"Darin loves me. Like I said, I'm his mother as far as he's concerned."

"Darin is worried that you may be pregnant." Spike said in a gentle voice.

"I don't know why he would think that. I'm not pregnant."

Spike went on, "I understand how it must have been being alone with Darin. Boys that age can be a handful. They also have sexual fantasies and many times they fantasize about older women. I know how I was at that age. I was in love with my sixth grade teacher and the fantasies I had about her would make a sex therapist blush." Spike laughed and went on, "Those fantasies are not your fault. Darin is a growing boy on the verge of being a man. He's probably the most popular guy around his friends. I know what these young boys talk about."

"Darin wouldn't talk about me to his friends. He loves me and our relationship is special."

"So you think Darin hasn't bragged to his friends about what the two of you have been doing?"

"He wouldn't do that."

Even without admitting what was going on Angela was telling us. I was amazed.

"Why don't you explain to me about your 'special' relationship with Darin?"

"I love him and he loves me. He's too young and nothing has happened that he would brag to his friends about." Her voice was becoming shaky.

Even I could see she was clinging to this last branch before she drowned. Angela was holding on for dear life but she was in way over her head.

"Angela, Darin told me about the relationship the two of you have. He's worried you're pregnant and he told me he does love you. He's a very upset young man right now and you could help him by telling me what's happened between the two of you."

Angela began to cry.

Spike continued, "It's important we understand what happened and understand your side of things."

Angela continued to cry and was no longer looking at Spike. He kept pushing, "Darin thinks the baby is his."

"There is no baby." She said in a whisper.

"Why would he think it was his?" Spikes voice was just as quiet.

"We did some things…but not that."

"Okay, why don't you tell me about the things you did?"

"We just touched each other. It was no big deal, but Darin needs to feel loved, he needs to feel a woman's arms around him."

"What kind of touching are we talking about?"

"You know, I was just rubbing his back and I think he accidently touched my breast. It was purely innocent but I could tell he liked it and I didn't think it would matter. It's not against the law if he touches me, only if I touch him."

Spike didn't correct her about the law. Some people are so incredibly stupid.

"Did he touch you anywhere else?"

"Not that time, but he has touched me in other places at different times."

"Tell me about those times?"

Angela started telling the story of how everything happened. She placed all the blame on Darin, a twelve-year-old boy. As the story unfolded I was astounded by the fact that Angela obviously wanted to talk with someone and tell them what was going on.

By the time Angela finished, she had told Spike the intimate details of her relationship with Darin. She fully admitted to being a child molester, but I realized she didn't think it was wrong. The notes I was taking had more to do with my own questions for Spike.

When she finished, Spike continued talking to her and asking questions. He finally told her she was going to jail.

Angela began crying harder but it appeared faked. She looked up at Spike to see how her crying affected him and said, "Can Darin visit me? He needs to know I'm okay."

"That isn't up to me. It will be up to the court."

I knew there wasn't a chance in hell that she would see Darin while in jail, and I added Spike's response to my list of questions.

I wondered what kind of person could sit across from a child molester and keep his cool, speak respectfully, and not lose his mind. At the same time I was wondering if I could do it. If calm acceptance got a molester to tell the truth, I thought I might be able to.

Spike came out of the room and gave me a fist bump. He was smiling as he told me to grab a booking packet, fill it out in the interview room with Angela and then place her in handcuffs. Angela answered my questions for the booking paperwork. Other than that, she did not talk, and her tears dried up. She seemed more resigned than anything.

We transported her to jail and took her inside. Spike told her the people at the jail would take care of her, he then shook her hand and we left.

When we got back out to the car, Spike gave me a high five and said, "Good job."

He was smiling and so was I. My questions started immediately.

"Why did you shake her hand?"

"Let me tell you something Ivy, you will arrest a lot of criminals in your career. You will be surprised at how many get out of jail the next day and you run into them in town or out of town. When you have the upper hand always treat them with respect. We won. Angela will go to prison for years. What other questions do you have?"

"Why didn't you arrest her right away?"

"You will find that when you make people think they have a choice they will respond better. The law says we must read Miranda rights. It doesn't say we can't do a little sweet talking beforehand. Technically, as long as Angela was free to leave that room, I didn't need to read her Miranda, but it's a good habit to always read them their rights. A jury believes more in television law than the real thing. If I placed her in handcuffs and read her Miranda immediately, chances are she would have lawyered up and I wouldn't have had a chance to get her confession. By making her think she was the good guy for coming with us, and letting her think she might not go to jail, I increased my odds of getting a confession."

"Why did you read her Miranda from a card?" I had to memorize Miranda when I was at the police academy.

"You haven't been on the witness stand yet. When it happens you'll be nervous and your mind will go blank on the easiest of questions. When a defense attorney asks me if I read Miranda to his client, I tell him yes. I am sitting on the witness stand nervous, and sweating. It doesn't matter how many years you do this job, if you're not nervous over a case, it's time to stop being a cop. If the defense attorney asks you to recite Miranda, you tell them you always read it from a card. That way you never mess up while under pressure. It really pisses an attorney off when you tell them you'll be glad to read Miranda and you take out your card. I had to memorize Miranda in the academy just like you. It doesn't matter. We read from the card every time. The cops that don't are stupid."

"Why did Angela admit what she did?"

"Everyone essentially wants to tell the truth. Angela knew what she was doing was wrong. The thing is, even the guilty don't want to be thought of as bad. You just need to give them something to blame their crime on. Angela is like every other choe-mo (child molester in cop speak), if there was a chance this was not her fault, she wanted to grab onto it. She expects us to believe it was a twelve year old boy's fault because then she's not the bad guy. You did great tonight Ivy. I'm not the best at interviewing kids. Give me a bad guy to interview any time. I don't really like questioning victims at all and when the victim's a child it's just that much harder. For your good job I'm going to give you a present."

I think I held my breath. Spike was making me feel really good.

"I'm giving you the third rule of policing, one day early."

I groaned.

"Just because a guy wears a badge it doesn't make him your friend. Now tell me what the third rule is."

I repeated the rule.

I went home that night thinking Spike was a total and complete jerk, but a brilliant one.

Chapter 12

The third and fourth days with Spike went quickly. Spike gave the fourth and fifth Rules of Law Enforcement and then tested me on what he'd pounded into my head. Again all eye-rolling was done while looking away from him. Here's the rundown of Spike's rules:

Rule #1 – Cops are sharks they eat their own.

Rule #2 – If you realize you need to pull your gun it should already be in your hand.

Rule #3 – Just because a guy wears a badge it doesn't make him your friend.

Rule #4 – This job will weed you out.

Rule #5 – Two things will get you fired in this job; your dick and her pussy. (I recited this one with gritted teeth)

I wasn't sure about all of Spike's rules but number four was already coming true. We lost one third of our academy class before graduation. Now, I had just received news that two officers from my class did not survive field training. One quit (as unbelievable as that was) and one "washed" out due to poor performance with his agency.

After all we had been through at the academy, I could not believe someone would willingly leave this job.

The text messages and phone calls I received from fellow cadets were starting to slow down. A few friends like Rocco and P-Rod stayed in contact. P-Rod would never change. He was the youngest cadet we had. He turned twenty-one while at the academy. Our classmates teased him incessantly, but he always took it in stride and displayed a great sense of humor. He loved his job. Every time we spoke he was more excited than the time before. I was so happy for him. He was now engaged to a young woman he fell in love with while at the academy.

Rocco was doing more work as a fireman than as a cop but he was content. He went to the academy to become a SWAT medic. His dream was coming true but first and foremost he loved the fire department.

Spike said, "There are only a few men left from my academy class and no one has retired. All left because they lost their certification or quit from burnout. Male cops cannot keep their dicks in their pants and it's the biggest reason they don't make it."

"I don't think I'll have any trouble keeping my dick in my pants."

Spike laughed, "I won't be surprised if you really have a dick."

I think he meant it as a compliment, but with Spike it's hard to tell.

He gave the child molest case to me, which meant I had to type the initial report while he typed the supplemental report.

It took me practically an entire shift to finish it. I listened to the recorded interview about a thousand times as I typed.

Spike reviewed my report and rejected it. "This is a child molest case. You need to portray the child's feelings. Describe the instances when Darin would not look at you, when he cried and when he conveyed his feelings of guilt. The words you use are important because the taped video can be thrown out. It doesn't matter how good you think your case is, crazy things happen at trial and sometimes testimony like Darin's is thought to be too prejudicial to the defendant. Paint a picture with your words and convey the picture in your report."

I figured out why Spike gave me the lead on the case. He enjoyed making me do most of the work.

My finished product was very good. I learned more in writing this report than the entire report writing class at the academy. It was a great feeling to finally have it pass Spike's inspection.

My days off were Wednesday, Thursday and Fridays. Spike told me we would be in court on Wednesday for a preliminary hearing. My weekend off would be a short one. This was the bane of a cop's existence. True days off were a luxury.

I wore my class "A" uniform to court. It was the same uniform I wore when graduating from the academy. Spike showed up in a suit and tie. He had a clip-on badge and his gun in a belt holster. I didn't yet own a clip-on badge or belt holster. I added them to the list of things I needed. Most of my list consisted of items that would make me appear cool, and less of a rookie, if that was possible.

I arrived at the courthouse with my report in hand and scared to death. Spike told me not to worry, because Angela's attorney would "waive" the preliminary hearing, and have it taken upstairs to the superior court.

None of this made any sense to me so I asked him to explain.

He gave me an exasperated look but said it like this, "The prosecution needs to show probable cause to have the case heard in superior court. This proceeding is similar to a grand jury. If the defense and defendant do not want the case heard by the lower court first, they can forgo the prelim."

I kind of, sort of, understood, but like many things I figured I would learn more just by doing. We waited in court for two hours as I repeatedly reviewed my report. We were finally released when the defense waived the prelim.

On the plus side, I received two hours of overtime pay. On the minus side, I wasted the first part of my day off and didn't gain any courtroom experience.

I returned home and cleaned my house. I thought it would remain cleaner after my kids moved out but in reality it still needed dusting, sweeping, mopping and vacuuming. I then cooked a nice meal for Norman. Weeks before we came to an agreement and he was helping more with household chores. When I was disturbed, I cooked and cleaned. I realized I was still thinking of Darin as I scrubbed the shower. My job would enable Norman to get the better part of our agreement on occasion, and I was fine with that.

After dinner, Norman wanted to go see a movie. He was not a big movie goer, but it was something I always loved to do. I think he was worried because, when I wasn't working, I rarely left the house. I had always enjoyed entertaining or going out with him and another couple. Over the past months, I turned down every opportunity presented. I found myself just wanting to unwind at home and wasn't sure why, but knew I craved down time.

We went to the movie and he was right, I did need to get out more. The only disagreement we had was over my insistence that I bring my gun. I was told to never go anywhere without it. Norman didn't like it, but eventually gave in.

This was only one small issue, but being a police officer, meant a big change in our lives. I put my gun in my purse and knew I needed to get an off duty holster ordered. It would probably have been easier to conk someone over the head with my bag than to actually draw the gun and fire. No one recognized me as their arresting officer so we made it home safely. And I was relieved that I never had to resort to assault by loaded purse.

I was back on the street at 1400 hours on Saturday. For some reason, crime decided to peak that week, and we made more than our average number of trips to the county jail. This also meant my next Wednesday "off" would see me sitting in court again.

Spike talked, a lot, about the "color" of the law opposed to the "intent" of the law. He practiced what he preached. I was surprised at the people he let walk out the door when I felt they should go to jail. Spike tried to explain it to me, but believed it was something you could only learn with time. Again, he was right.

The incident that bothered me most that week was a domestic violence call. Spike made the decision to arrest both the husband and wife. I, on the other hand, felt only the husband should go to jail.

"I've dealt with this couple repeatedly and I'm sick of it. The kids witness their parent's behavior time and time again. I promised the unhappy duo that if I was the responding officer they would both get locked up for the night. Being a cop is like raising kids. When you promise a punishment, you follow through."

I called Child Protection Services to pick up the children. CPS was no more pleased than I was. They wanted Spike to release the mother and just send dad to jail. Spike stuck to his guns and refused. The children didn't cry or object when strangers took them away. For me, this was the saddest part of all because the children had obviously been through it before. For them, it was just another day.

There were so many different types of calls during my field training that I sometimes felt overwhelmed. I didn't think I would ever know how to deal with the entire range of situations that occurred.

Spike told me there were never two situations alike and I needed to think on my feet and go with the flow. His secret, "You will sometimes make the wrong decision but only you will know. Make sure the people you're dealing with think you know what you're doing."

Spike had a special "wisdom" for everything. He also had a joke for everything. The jokes were usually crass, politically incorrect and sometimes just plain vulgar, but it was hard not to laugh, even when he told me the same joke five times on different days.

"Why does my wife have two black eyes? Because, she should have listened the first time."

Like I said, off color, extremely inappropriate but I was learning this was how Spike relieved stress.

Whenever Spike needed additional backup, he called Alex, who was usually available to join us. These were the only times I truly enjoyed being around Spike.

I respected Alex. Spike, with all his crotchety ways, respected Alex too. I know Spike wondered many times what Alex liked about me.

By the end of the week, Spike and I made six arrests and I had pulled and pointed my gun at four bad guys.

At the end of every shift, Spike always asked me about the Rules of Law Enforcement. Today he thought I was ready for number six.

"How many times could you have died today?" he asked.

There was only one answer he wanted. "Each and every time."

He drilled it into my head. "This is a dangerous job and cops are killed on the job every day of the year. Rural police officers are in as much or more danger because they think they know everyone and they grow lax. When that happens, officers die."

Spike was not what I would call cheerful with his lessons and I wondered if like Sgt. Dickens, this was his way of weeding out officers that would not make it on the job. He was not nearly as tough as Sgt. Dickens, and if he thought he could scare me away, he was wrong.

On Tuesday, the last day before my weekend, we served a search warrant on a drug house. What affected me most was that the house was around the corner from my own home.

A relative that lived out of town, asked us to perform a welfare check on the occupants. The relative was concerned because her fifteen year old daughter was visiting and she had not heard from her in two days.

Spike and I went to the house, but no one answered the door. We walked around and tried looking in the windows, but they were all covered. We called back the relative and found out the occupants only had one vehicle. We could see it parked in the driveway.

Spike checked the hood of the vehicle. It was cold. He tried the front door and found it unlocked. He said the house was a known drug hangout, but anytime he knocked someone answered the door. He told me we were entering because we had reason to believe the occupants were in danger. I didn't argue. I followed Spike inside with my gun drawn.

Spike yelled the entire time as we walked into the house and down the hallway. In the first room I could see a woman lying in the bed. She was not moving. As he entered the room, Spike pointed out drug paraphernalia on the dresser. He told me to keep an eye on his back as he approached the bed.

At this point, I thought the woman in the bed was dead. Adrenaline was pumping through my system.

Spike walked to the bed and tried yelling at the woman. She didn't move. He used his left hand, while holding his gun at his side in his right hand, to check her pulse.

He told me she was alive but in a "meth stupor." He took out a pair of handcuffs and placed them on the woman's wrists. She never moved. We then continued our search and found our fifteen year old girl and a man in the master bedroom bed, asleep. It didn't appear either had clothes on. Spike was able to get the man to respond.

"What the fuck, you fuckin' pigs. Get the fuck outa my face. Fuck you!" Like many criminals I dealt with, he had a very limited vocabulary.

The fifteen year old barely opened her eyes. She didn't say anything.

Spike placed them both in cuffs. He took covers off the bed to drape around the girl's naked body. Spike could have cared less about the naked man. I got an eyeful and knew my face was red but for safety reasons, my eyes weren't leaving him. I wondered if I would ever get lucky and see a naked body builder, I thought not.

Spike called an ambulance for the girl and took the cuffs off as soon as the EMS crew arrived. He also had them check out the woman in the other room who was slowly coming around.

The ambulance took the girl to the closest hospital and we notified her mother. We took the two adults to jail and booked them for contributing to the delinquency of a minor, sexual conduct with a minor and drug paraphernalia. We then drove to the police department and began writing a warrant. Alex wasn't available so

Spike requested another officer watch the house until we came back with an order signed by the judge.

About two hours later, we were ready. It took us another two hours to complete the search. I went through at least twenty pairs of rubber gloves. The house was disgusting. There was garbage and spoiled food everywhere. I was just happy to have something to protect me.

We managed to find an "eight ball" of methamphetamine with a thousand dollar street value. Spike explained that after a meth high, which lasts a few days and makes it impossible to sleep, the users come down hard and fast and will then sleep around the clock.

We left the drug house and went back to the jail to add more charges. The amount of meth and other items found showed signs of distribution so Spike added charges for selling.

We received word that the young girl was fine, but tested positive for meth. It was definitely a productive night for us. I went home feeling dirty and tired. I'd lived down the street from that house for ten years and never knew what happened in my own back yard. This was not the town I thought it was. I called P-Rod, my friend from the academy, and we compared naked-meth-head stories. We both laughed and the adrenaline finally wore off. I fell asleep smiling.

Chapter 13

Wednesday was another trip to court and I had my reports in hand. The prosecutor called Spike to the stand on the case of the sleeping meth heads. I was able to sit back and watch.

He answered questions from the prosecution and on the retelling, it sounded as if we saved the life of a teenage girl, who was being exploited for sex. I hadn't thought of it in that way but it was true. Spike's description of the filth in the house was exceptional. I was impressed and I was learning. The case was moved up to Superior Court. The husband and wife were each given a $25,000 bond.

I felt shock that the two of them were married. The woman was the girl's aunt and knew her husband was having sex with her niece. I guess, when drugs are involved, anything goes. My brain was getting a wakeup call to what went on in the criminal world and it started around the corner from where I lived.

I went home feeling baffled but good and wasn't even upset that part of my day off was spent at court.

I decided to spend some time with my horse, Biz. I had neglected her since my return from the academy. It was cold outside but cleaning her hooves and brushing her down were another of the luxuries that put me at peace. I loved the horsy smell and she was a sweetheart who appreciated whatever time I gave to her. Norman and I rented a movie and went to bed early. He was leaving first thing in the morning and would be gone on business until the following week.

The next morning, after seeing Norman off, I decided to go outside and shovel snow from our walkway. I had not been exercising as I should and needed to get my heart pumping.

I didn't head out until it warmed up to twenty degrees Fahrenheit. It was still quite chilly even with the sun shining. I used a snow shovel to move the snow off our walkway and parts of the driveway. It felt great to use my muscles.

I heard a vehicle drive by and looked up as it passed. The vehicle looked familiar, but I didn't think too much of it. I looked up again as it turned around at the end of the road and headed back my way. It stopped at the cross streets closest to my house, about twenty yards from our property line.

The vehicle didn't move. I was openly staring at it, but the occupants did not get out. It suddenly clicked in my head that this was the vehicle parked in front of my neighbor's drug house.

I was standing outside about fifteen feet from my front door, and did not even have my cell phone. I wasn't sure what I should do, but I was getting angry. This was my house, my domain and I wasn't going to be bullied. I placed my right hand behind me trying to make it appear that I had a gun at the small of my back (it was one of those super cool moments from TV). I then began approaching the vehicle in a fast stride.

When I was about ten yards away, the vehicle sped off with the front two occupants giving me the bird. I could see the outline of another passenger in the back seat.

When they were completely out of sight, I went inside and grabbed my cell phone. I didn't call Sgt. Spears or Alex, my fingers had a life of their own and dialed Spike.

He told me he would call the jail and check to see if the couple had bonded out. He also proceeded to yell at me for not having my gun or my cell phone with me. He hung up and I waited for his return call.

Fifteen minutes later, Alex pulled up in his unmarked car. Spike had called him and Alex wanted to make sure I was okay.

I told him the story and he was also concerned that I didn't have my gun with me while working outside. I thought it was stupid that I approached the vehicle, but Alex said it was exactly the right thing to do.

"You can't let the lowlife scumbags know you're intimidated. I know you don't want to hear this Ivy, but they did it because you're a female. It's never happened to me or any of the other officers that I know of. They don't know what to make of you. They need to know you're one of us and a cop is a cop. It doesn't matter what sex you are. Wear your gun every time you go out and keep it close while you're inside your house. I know it doesn't seem fair, but I'd rather you be inconvenienced than dead."

I wasn't going to argue. I calmed down as I realized this was another example of the changes I had to expect as a police officer.

Alex went on, "Both parties, from your bust, were bonded out this morning. A drug buddy put up the money. When does your husband get home?"

"Not until Friday."

"I'll get the night guys to drive by and keep an eye on your house. Are you going to be okay?"

"I'm angry more than anything. This is my house, my space, and no one has the right to try and intimidate me here."

Alex left and I finished my shoveling with a fanny pack on. My duty weapon was inside along with my cell phone. When I was done, I went inside and made lunch.

That evening, Spike called to check on me. I told him I was fine and he proceeded to give me a ten minute lecture for not having my gun with me at all times. I wasn't angry with him. It made me realize he and Alex cared.

Norman was another matter. When I spoke to him, on the phone, he was pissed off. He wanted to come home immediately. He got angrier when I asked him what he could have done had he been home. This was the worst thing to say to his manly ego but I wasn't thinking. I told him I was stupid for not having my gun. He wasn't thrilled when he hung up and I had a feeling, he probably didn't get any more sleep than I did.

The next morning, I had one thought on my mind and I was impatient as I waited for ten o'clock to roll around. I went jogging in the snow. I jogged right by the drug house. The front curtain was open and I saw someone look out.

I was probably lucky I didn't fall, because I wasn't looking where I was going. I gave the good old "stare down" to the house. I don't know why this made me feel better but it did. I jogged around the block and then went home. It wasn't very comfortable jogging with my fanny pack and the weight of my gun pulling it downward, but I would never again go anywhere without it.

When I returned home, I got online and ordered two holsters. One was for concealed carry and the other a belt holster for court. I also started looking for a smaller back up gun. I would need to ask Alex and Spike for suggestions.

As I thought about it that evening, I couldn't imagine what I would have done a year before. I know I would have been intimidated. I would never have approached the vehicle or jogged by the house.

I knew Norman would have a rough time adjusting to the new me, but I also knew he loved and supported me. We would learn to adapt.

I went back to work on Saturday with Spike. He lectured me again and I laughed. "Your words sunk in during the second lecture and you're now wasting your breath.

This made him angrier, "Why the hell didn't it sink in the first time."

I smiled and winked, "I just knew it would piss your off more if I said it wasn't until the second lecture."

Spike stormed away and stewed for thirty minutes. I refrained from asking if his panties were in a wad. I was learning that with Spike, I had to be on my toes and never let him push me around. I could see by his treatment of other officers, that they feared him and he had little respect for weakness.

Being older was helpful in many ways since I wasn't easily intimidated. Raising three kids was another bonus and the third bonus was the hell I went through at the academy. So far, nothing being thrown at me from the department could measure up to the discipline we faced daily during that eighteen weeks.

My dislike of Sgt. Dickens was also changing. I was learning that his harsh expectations made me stronger and I needed all the strength I could get. Maybe someday, I would be able to let go of enough resentment to send him a thank you letter. Then again, maybe not.

Because of the number of arrests made the week before, Spike and I spent a lot of time doing follow up interviews and typing reports. The interviews were interesting, but the report writing was monotonous. I wanted to be out on the street making more arrests.

When I complained, Spike said, "You're just like Alex, he's always looking for trouble when he should be appreciating a quiet week. Take the down times slowly!"

I knew he was right, but I was craving that adrenaline rush and I wanted to feel it again soon. Spike was at the point in his career when even intense situations didn't give him the rush they used to. I felt bad for him because I knew he had been quite the officer back in his day. He might compare me to Alex, but I knew Spike in his early years was probably worse than Alex and I combined.

I was just finishing a victim's rights form when a domestic violence call came in. I recognized the address. It was Rachel and Charles Fellows. Spike and I took off running for the door.

Charles' vehicle was still there when we arrived. We could hear the yelling as we ran to the front door. Rachel was screaming for help. Spike checked the door, but it was locked. He didn't wait any longer and squared up with the door and kicked close to the knob. It took two kicks and it flew open. Spike entered first. We both had our guns drawn. Rachel was on the floor. She wasn't moving or making a sound. Charles attacked Spike. I struggled, to return my gun to my holster, wasting valuable seconds.

Charles had his arm around Spike's throat. I ran at him with everything I had. I broke his grip on Spike and Spike threw a punch that landed straight into Charles' gut. He bent double. I tried to grab his arm and get it behind him but he threw his arm and shoulder toward me. I was then hit upside the face with what my ringing brain thought was his fist. It was a good shot, but the adrenaline kept me from feeling pain.

Spike jumped on Charles and began beating the shit out of him. I kept looking at Rachel to make sure she didn't come at us, but she remained still.

With my head spinning, I began yelling, "Spike, Spike. He's down."

"Fucking son of a bitch! Mother fucking, woman beating, son of a bitch! How does it feel?" Spike gave one last punch and he was through. His breathing was ragged.

Before Spike could catch his breath, he grabbed Charles' wrists and cranked the cuffs on. I checked Rachel. Her face was a mess. I knew who she was but didn't recognize her. I looked around for a weapon. I didn't see anything. Rachel was lucky. If it had been something besides his fist, like the table leg from the last beating, she would be dead. I called the ambulance.

"Ivy, sit down before you fall."

"I'm fine." I touched my face. My hand came away with blood.

"Sit down, it's an order." I sat.

The ambulance crew arrived and we had them check Rachel first. They took her immediately to the hospital and called for a second ambulance. There was no way I was going to the hospital, but Spike had different ideas. Arguing didn't help. I was loaded up and driven away. I was pissed off because I wanted to book Charles into jail.

I needed two stitches on my cheekbone. The numbing shot hurt like hell and they also loaded me up with all kinds of antibiotics and a tetanus shot. I was not happy, and when I looked at myself in the mirror, I knew my entire face would be black and blue by the next day. I didn't care about facing the guys at work. I didn't want to face Norman and I was feeling really sorry for myself.

Alex arrived and whistled when he saw me.

"You are one ugly bitch."

"Shut up asshole. If I could feel my face it would hurt to smile. What are you doing here?"

"I came to drive you home. You get the next two days off, but longer if you need it."

"I don't need any time off. I don't have a concussion and didn't hurt my gun hand. I know my eyes are swollen, but I can still see."

"That's all fine and dandy, but it's not up to you. Come on and take the time off like a man. Tomorrow morning the guys are going to be so jealous about you getting to fight, they won't want to see your face."

I laughed. It was true, I couldn't wait to call Rocco and P-Rod and tell them about my domestic fight. I would wait until the bruising was at its worst and send them a picture. Battle wounds were great.

"Are you going to have a scar?" Alex was looking at my stitches with concern.

"The doctor said I wouldn't. Darn, nothing to show my grandchildren, but pictures."

Alex laughed and stepped aside as the doctor came in and had me sign the release forms. He wrote down that I could return to work after twenty-four hours and asked if I needed a prescription for pain. I said no and he left. I told Alex I wanted to check on Rachel but discovered she was flown to a city hospital. The nurse quietly told me Rachel might have a skull fracture. Alex and I left and he drove me home. He said one of the guys would drive my squad car to me. I gave him my spare key.

I fell asleep fairly easily, but woke a few hours later with a splitting headache. I got up and made an icepack, took some Ibuprofen, and headed back to bed after looking in the mirror. I was sorry I did. The clown effect was starting to set in and I knew it would look worse the next day.

Chapter 14

I managed to sleep until noon, make coffee and drink a cup before I looked at myself in the mirror. It wasn't easy to absorb my new aspect of loveliness. I could barely see past my swollen eyelids. I made another icepack and sat in front of the television. At 1300 hours, I took a shower, put on a pair of jeans and a t-shirt, and then drove to the department. I couldn't stay away.

Sgt. Spears was the first to see me. He whistled like Alex had. "Have a seat. It looks like you were run over by a truck. You were supposed to stay home, but since you're here we can start filling out the workman's comp paperwork. We charged Charles with aggravated assault on a police officer. We need to get pictures of your injuries. I'll have one of the guys grab a camera and take some shots."

It was stupid. I know trust goes both ways, but couldn't help it. I wanted Sergeant Spears, Alex or even Spike photographing my injuries. I did not feel comfortable enough with the other guys at the department yet.

"Could you take the pictures?"

Sgt. Spears didn't object. He got the camera and started with a full body shot explaining to his trainee/victim the reason for each shot as he went along.

"The first picture I take is to show you are who we say you are. This is so a defense attorney can't argue. A close-up of your injury does not attach the emotion to a real person. I start with your full body and then move in closer."

It was uncomfortable and surprisingly emotional to be under the scrutiny of the lens. I didn't cry, but I wasn't yet ready to appreciate that I would now understand a victim's feelings when I asked them for pictures of their injuries.

When the photo session was over, we started filling out the paperwork.

Spike walked in just before I got up to leave. "Wow, look at you. Battle scars and everything, I bet you think you're hot shit now?"

"Go to hell, you'd still be fighting if I hadn't jumped in."

You were more like a fly on a horse's ass, irritating at best."

My hand made a fist. The guy knew how to push my buttons. "I'll show you a fly on a horse's ass and you'll look as pretty as I do in a second."

Spike laughed, "Black and blue looks good on you and brings out your blue eyes. You're something else Ivy, especially for an old lady."

Alex walked in next and everyone in the building lined up behind him. He was the one who spoke. "We can hear you bitching all the way up front. You can't be hurt too badly."

I'm not hurt at all. I'm just ugly."

Everyone laughed. Spike began his rendition of the events embellishing to make me sound like super woman, even with my "You're so full of it," throughout most of his story. Chief Varnett came into the office and asked how I was doing and then told me to go home. He said he didn't want to see me for the next two days. I was bummed, but couldn't argue with the Chief.

Before heading home, I called the hospital to ask about Rachel. She would spend a few days in the hospital, but they didn't think she had any lasting injuries. She was awake and talking, with only a minor skull fracture. I didn't know skull fractures came in the "minor" variety.

I spent the rest of the day reading and watching television. I called my daughters and talked to them about their lives, brushing aside any questions they had about my police work. Norman came home from his trip that night and took the condition of my face better than I thought he would. Being my hero, he took an extra day off from his job and his presence was the only thing that kept me from going stir crazy.

Returning from my two days of medical leave, I only had one day of work before my scheduled weekend. I had court again on Wednesday, but the defense waived the "prelim" (preliminary) hearing and the case was moved to superior court. I was finally getting the hang of courtroom jargon.

I was back on the streets Saturday for my normal shift. Things went smoothly and the week ended with no major difficulties. I was anxious to get my stitches out on Monday. They itched like crazy and made me look like I had a bug on my face. The swelling of my eyes was gone but I now sported a lovely combination of yellow and purple bruises. I couldn't wait to look normal again.

My time with Spike was coming to an end and I was surprised to realize I would miss him. After Spike, I would spend two additional weeks with Sgt. Spears. I would then get an evaluation to see where I needed help and be given a chance to train with the officer that could help the most.

My organizational and writing skills were high on my "doing good" list but I continued to struggle with traffic stops and couldn't figure out why. I began dreading anytime Spike pulled someone over because I would immediately become flustered. It was beyond frustrating. It wasn't something that should have been hard. I just seemed to have a psychological block about traffic stops.

Spike didn't have a lot of patience to begin with but my inability to get this right was testing him beyond his limit. On one of my last nights with him, I flubbed so bad his patience ran out.

"What the fuck Ivy? You couldn't possibly have learned anything at the academy. If the guy in the car had shot you, we would be looking for the wrong vehicle because you screwed up the plate number."

I hadn't even realized I misread the plate. I had been more worried about our location and reciting the correct address to dispatch. Things didn't improve as the night continued.

I thought Spike would actually have a heart attack when we pulled over a lifted truck for speeding. There were a couple of young guys inside, but because of my height, I wasn't able to see into the window of the cab and get a view of what they were doing with their hands. I should have had the driver step out. But I didn't think of it until we cleared the stop and I was back in our vehicle with Spike yelling in my ear.

"What's rule number six, Ivy?"

I had one through five down pat, but my mind could not bring up rule six. I just sat there looking straight ahead not saying a word.

"How many times could you fucking die today?" was yelled in my ear.

It was a good hint and I replied, "Every time."

Spike was seething, "I'm pulling over every car I see. You better have a reason for the traffic stop, recite the correct plate, and know where the hell you are when I make it. Understood?"

Sometimes I had no clue why Spike pulled over a vehicle. I told one driver that something flew from the back of his car. I ran his license then checked his insurance and registration. Everything came back normal so I let the perplexed driver go.

Spike refused to speak the entire time, but I will admit I was better at traffic stops when the shift was over. I was also thoroughly sick of Spike. He wasn't exactly thrilled with me either. Exhaustion took over after I drove home and fell into bed.

Two hours later, I was called out and sleepily got into my clothes and gear. I found myself sitting in my car and not remembering what dispatch told me when they called. I was hoping I was still dreaming and my phone never rang.

I wasn't that lucky. Winkler's, our local grocery store, had been robbed. The suspect was a short Hispanic male armed with a gun. This was almost unheard of in Small Town. For us, the occasional shoplifter was the norm. Our bad guy had put a gun to the clerk's head and threatened his life. He left the store after hitting the clerk upside the head with the handgun and the unlucky cashier was on his way to the hospital by the time I arrived on scene.

Chief Varnett was there, along with everyone but Sgt. Spears who was out of town. I was to assist Spike.

Before the semi-conscious store clerk, Shawn, was taken away, he told the responding officers that the suspect had opened the drawer with ungloved hands. Spike explained that meant we would have to take the drawer as evidence and send it off for finger prints and DNA analysis. We needed an accurate count of all change, checks and bills left in the cash drawer so the store would be able to give us an idea of how much money was stolen. And, we had to count the money first because once the drawer was bagged it wouldn't be touched until it arrived at the state lab. I gloved up and began helping.

"We're going to get this scumbag." Spike said, "No one comes into my town and hurts one of our own. Shawn is a good guy and there was no reason to assault him. He could be dead right now."

Alex walked over and told us he followed footprints around the side of the building and thought they were possibly from "our guy," the suspect. Shawn had given a description of the suspect and mentioned white tennis shoes. Shawn also said he noticed the suspect in the store a few times over the past week.

Spike told me to go with Alex to check it out and we walked to the back store office.

"The store manager is on his way over to run the video equipment. I can't figure out how this stuff works. Do you have a clue?"

I figured it couldn't be any harder than the television remote control I had to teach Norman to use. "Give me ten minutes."

"Take your time. The manager won't be here for an hour."

Four minutes later, we were watching the robbery on digital video. After viewing the crime, I took us back a week. Alex told me to look for the same shoes and jacket. We found our guy twice. We were hoping to see him arrive in a vehicle but our suspect appeared to be on foot, which meant he probably lived close by. Using his camera, Alex took still shots after I stopped the frame.

The store manager arrived and made copies of the video with the dates and times I'd logged. When we left the back room, I didn't see Spike. Alex told me I was staying with him. We went to the police department where everyone was waiting. The still pictures were downloaded and copies were passed out.

Chief Varnett briefed us. "You will be working in pairs. We will find this guy but I don't want any dead heroes. You will all be going home to your families when this is finished. Don't take any chances. Are we all clear?"

Everyone answered yes and assignments were given. With all officers in pairs, it left me as odd man out. I looked at Spike who was speaking to Alex. He told me to go with Alex and then walked away.

I was floored but knew I needed to focus on what was happening. Alex told me to jump in his car and we headed to the housing near the location of the robbery. I was handed copies of our suspect's pictures and told to put them in my pocket. My hands needed to remain free in order to pull my gun.

We were only five homes into our search, when we got a hit on our suspect. A sleepy mom said she had seen him walking in the area over the past few days. Sometimes he was walking south towards Winkler's, the grocery store that was robbed, and other times he was headed   north.
We began a door to door of all the homes north of the apartment

complex. Alex walked along the road looking at footprints. He had a picture of the print he found at the store.

His cellphone rang and he listened for a few minutes before hanging up.

"How are you feeling? Are you too tired to get this scumbag?"

"I'm doing okay but I could use a cup of coffee."

We stopped by Winkler's for a caffeine infusion and then Alex drove to a house in another section of town. It was nowhere near Winkler's.

As we pulled up to the decrepit house, he explained, "I got a tip that the vatos here might know our suspect. Let me do the talking but keep your eyes open for our guy and any weapons. He's not supposed to be here but we may get lucky."

I had no idea what "vatos" were but figured now was not the time to ask. We walked up to the door. I stood to the right and Alex stood to the left and knocked. The door was finally opened by a Hispanic man in his early twenties.

Alex introduced himself in Spanish and asked if we could come inside. The man said something back and then the door shut. Alex put his finger over his mouth in the universal sign for quiet.

We could hear the shuffling of feet inside. It sounded like there were three or four people running around. I looked at Alex and he smiled.

The door finally opened and we were invited inside. Alex didn't waste any time and said in English, "You know who I'm looking for and where he is. I can smell marijuana and I'd be happy to come back with a warrant. I don't give a shit about your pot, I only want the guy that robbed Winkler's."

My eyes were traveling around the area. Only two guys were in the front room but I knew there had to be more people in the back. Chances were they were armed. This wasn't a good situation. I slowly pushed down the lever on my holster, ready to draw my gun.

The man who had opened the door said something to Alex in Spanish. His tone was belligerent and I heard the word "puta" as he nodded towards me.

The words barely had time to register when Alex moved. He wrenched the guy's right arm behind his back. "The only person in this room that's a puta is you and you'll be everyone's puta in jail. I'm not asking again, where's my guy?"

I didn't think the man being manhandled would answer and wondered what Alex would do next. I knew Alex's conduct had probably crossed a line and he would have a tough time articulating a perceived threat to justify it. Being called a whore was on the low level as far as cop threats went.

One of the other guys in the room spoke up.

"We don't want no trouble. Carlos isn't here and we haven't seen him since yesterday. We told him not to bring any shit down on us. He has a girlfriend named Amanda at the trailer park. He hangs there when he's in trouble."

Alex released the man with a push. The guy said something under his breath, but didn't look at Alex or me. After giving instructions to call us if Carlos showed up, we left. There may have been a threat or two in the conversation but most of it was in Spanish and I wouldn't be able to testify for or against Alex if any threats of bodily harm were mentioned.

Adrenaline had jacked my body up pretty high and when we got in the car, I took a long, deep breath. Alex started laughing.

"If you could have seen the look on your face when I grabbed Juan, it was priceless." He continued to laugh.

"Juan is my second cousin and he's the one that called me. He said his friends had been talking about the robbery but he himself didn't really know the guy we were looking for. These guys understand aggression, they're from Mexico and they expect it from the police. I didn't want anything coming back on my cousin. He hangs with some, not so nice guys, and has a marijuana problem, but he's cool. Now we have a name I can use without Juan being tagged as my snitch."

The laughter disappeared from Alex' voice, "Let's go find Carlos."

Chapter 15

Small Town's largest trailer park is run by a 6'6", three hundred and fifty pound ex-convict named Cherry, who also sports a shaved head and an abundance of tats.

As a cop, I was becoming familiar with tats - the blue, poorly drawn, and usually ugly prison artwork that helps kill time behind bars and connects you to your prison homeboy group. Beauty was not Cherry's strong suit, but he had a great smile which he displayed when he saw us walk up. Alex assured me he was cop friendly.

Alex asked Cherry about Amanda and her boyfriend Carlos, our suspect. We learned that Amanda was in space fifty three, but Carlos was not allowed on the property. No reason was given for the trespassing ban on Carlos. And I wondered if Carlos was brave enough to ignore it.

Amanda answered the door when Alex knocked. I was ready for Carlos and stood to the side with my gun out of my holster and down by my leg. Amanda answered, took one look at Alex and started complaining.

"That no good piece of shit, he in the shit, I knew it. I'm gonna kill him."

Alex asked if we could come inside and search. Amanda stepped back and let us in. The small trailer was extremely neat and clean. I was told to watch Amanda as Alex went into the bedroom and then the bathroom to look for Carlos. Amanda looked at me with sad eyes. I noticed her hand on her stomach and the small round bump visible under it.

When Alex finished his search, he said to Amanda, "We need to find Carlos, he's in a lot of trouble and I don't want to see him dead."

"He was here early this morning and he told me he had to leave for a while." Amanda now had tears running down her face and her hand shook as she wiped them away.

"I need you to call him and make him talk to me. We know he's armed and if he fights us he'll be dead." There was no sympathy in Alex' voice.

Without hesitation, Amanda made the call. "You son of a bitch, the police are here and Molinero wants to talk to you." The phone was handed to Alex.

He got straight to the point, "I don't care where you're hiding; I can find you. I will bust all your friends. I'll bust your old lady for the drug paraphernalia I see on her nightstand and I'll bust your Momma when I find her. Do everyone a favor and turn yourself in. I'll be cool with you but you only get one chance."

I couldn't hear what Carlos replied but Alex shot back with, "You have five minutes to call Amanda's phone or she's going to jail." The look on Alex' face told me he would do it.

Amanda sat down, looked at me and asked what Carlos had done. I told her the truth and she cried harder. She never questioned that she was going to jail; she just sat quietly and cried. Four minutes later, Carlos called back. Alex spoke to him and then hung up.

"I'll return your phone after we have him in custody." We walked out the door.

Alex used his own cell phone to call dispatch and tell them to send all available units to the old Calley Bar. I knew from my previous weeks of field training, that the bar closed down five years ago after a fire in the kitchen. It was barely standing, but from what I remembered seeing, there were a few rooms someone could hide in. The bar is located on the edge of town right before you get to the city limit sign.

Alex didn't use lights or sirens but he drove faster than usual through town, giving me directions on what we would do when we got there.

We were the first to arrive. Alex parked to the side about fifty feet back and we both positioned ourselves in the "V" of our doors after opening them. Our guns were drawn as we waited for backup. A few minutes later, two more squad cars arrived and fanned slightly to the right and left of us and parked.

Alex got on the radio speaker microphone and called out "Carlos, this is Detective Molinero. I want your hands in the air and I want you to follow every command I give. If you follow every direction exactly, no one will get hurt."

Within ten seconds, Carlos walked out slowly with his hands up.

Alex' voice was firm and controlled, "Use one hand and pull up your shirt from the neckline and then slowly turn around."

Carlos followed his directions and we could see, as he turned, that he did not have any weapons hidden in his waistband.

"Now you need to walk slowly back towards us, keep your hands high in the air."

When Carlos was about ten feet in front of our fanned out vehicles, an officer in the next vehicle said he could take control when Carlos was closer.

"You want this Ivy?"

"Yes." My heartbeat was fast but my hands were steady on my gun. High risk stops were something we practiced in the academy and also during my field training. I knew what I was doing.

"Ivy's got control." Alex relayed to the other officer.

When Carlos was closer to the vehicles, Alex had him stop so I could take over.

"Carlos," I said. "This is Officer Ivy. You will follow my commands now. Do you understand?"

When he said he would, I gave my instructions, "Get on your knees." Carlos dropped to his knees. "Put your hands behind your head and interlock your fingers. Don't make any sudden moves." Carlos had long sleeves and I knew it was easy to conceal a knife. I put my gun back in my holster and removed my handcuffs. I approached, cuffed his right hand, then grabbed his left hand and brought it behind him.

"Stand up and walk slowly backwards with me." I then walked Carlos to the back of Alex' vehicle. Things could not have gone more police academy perfect.

I began searching him and asking questions; remembering my search techniques and making sure every inch of him was weaponless. "Is there anyone else inside the bar?"

"No, I'm alone."

"Where is your gun?"

"Inside, next to the door."

I shouted the information to Alex. He used his radio to call out to the bar, telling anyone inside that they needed to come out. He waited but nothing moved. Carlos thought we were stupid and told me again no one was inside.

I ignored him and placed him inside the back of Alex' patrol car. I drew my gun and got back into my door position. I could hear Spike's words in my head, "Never trust the bad guys. If there's one person, there are two. If there's one gun, you can bet your ass, there are two."

After a few minutes, Alex and the other officers approached the building, entered and cleared it of threats, while I covered their backs.

Carlos was telling the truth. The gun was found next to the door and no one else was inside. What we didn't find was money.

After we cleared the bar and drove to the police department, we sat Carlos inside the interview room. We stepped out and Alex told me he wanted me in the interview room with him, but like always he wanted me to keep my mouth shut.

He took Carlos' cuffs from behind his back and placed them back on with his hands to the front. Alex then read him his Miranda rights and the questions began.

Alex was being nice and doing the "good cop," routine. I was doing the silent rookie cop routine. Carlos decided to be an ass and told Alex he didn't know what he was talking about. The interview went on for thirty minutes, but Carlos wouldn't budge. He didn't know what Alex was talking about and knew nothing about any money. I couldn't figure out why he didn't just ask for a lawyer.

Alex began to let his frustration show as he went into more of a bad cop routine. Alex suddenly threw back his chair and told Carlos he wouldn't listen to anymore lies. Alex didn't look at me as he opened the door and left the room. The door slammed behind him.

Oh boy, I was alone with Carlos. I looked at him and he asked me what I was staring at. The room is small and it has white walls, I wasn't sure where to put my eyes and I didn't feel comfortable taking them off Carlos. I continued looking at him for a few moments and then, because I'm not one to keep my mouth shut when I'm nervous, I said with my best soft mom voice and face, "I'm trying to figure out what Amanda will tell your son when he's born and his dad's in prison."

Carlos' dark brown eyes stared into mine. He wouldn't look away. But suddenly his eyes began to well up. The tears slipped down his face, one by one, and he turned his head toward the wall. After a minute, he put his head down and placed his hands over his face.

I could barely hear his mumble, "It doesn't matter what I say. I'm still going to jail."

This was no different than dealing with my own son when he did something stupid.

"It does matter." I said. "There must be a reason why this happened. I don't think you're a bad guy and its obvious Amanda loves you. She was so scared when we talked to her. Amanda needs to know why this happened. She's the one that will tell your son the story."

Carlos pulled his hands away from his face and looked at me. "I needed money for the baby. I didn't know what to do. I didn't want to hurt anybody and I wasn't going to shoot the guy at the store. I don't know why I hit him. It just made me angry that I was stealing the money"

"Well, you got lucky, he has a bump on his head and a concussion, but he'll be okay."

"Will you tell Amanda I'm sorry?"

"Yes, I promise I'll tell her. Who does the drug stuff at her place belong to?"

"It's mine. I was there this morning after I bagged the store."

"Does Amanda have the money?"

Carlos just looked at me.

"Okay, I might be able to get Amanda out of some of the trouble but there will only be one chance. Did she help you with plans to rob the store?"

"Hell no, she didn't know anything about it."

"If Amanda has the money, I'm sure I can talk her into handing it over and working with us. She's scared and doesn't want to go to jail."

"She's got the money, but you have to promise me she won't go to jail."

"I can't make promises. It will depend on her cooperation. I think she will. She seems to care a lot for your baby. I think she was feeling guilty when we were there this morning, but she loves you and doesn't want you in more trouble."

"She didn't want to take the money and I wouldn't tell her where it came from. I made her. She was so pissed at me. She told me not to come back."

"I'll do everything I can to help her. I have three kids of my own and I don't want anything worse to happen while she's pregnant. I'm going to get Alex and I need you to tell him everything we talked about."

I got up and walked out. Alex came around the corner and gave me a high five. He had been monitoring my conversation with Carlos and had a huge smile on his face, but it probably wasn't as huge as mine.

We both put our serious faces back on and went into the room again.

"Officer Ivy tells me you want to talk."

Carlos went through the robbery step by step. Alex knew all the right questions to ask for a stronger conviction. I learned from everything he said. He assured Carlos we would try to keep Amanda out of trouble but we couldn't promise because she had already lied to us.

Spike had taught me to be cautious when making promises to bad guys and Alex was careful too. The County Attorney's Office would make the decision about Amanda. If she turned over the money I was hoping she would be in less trouble. Even knowing she lied to us, I couldn't help but feel sympathy for her.

Alex asked another officer to fill out the booking paperwork and then transport Carlos to jail.

It was time to find the money.

Chapter 16

Before we could get out the door, everyone converged on us, laughing and giving high fives. Alex said, "I told you guys she could do it. It's that mother thing she has going. She could guilt anybody to admitting anything."

The guys told me how shocked they were when Alex left the interview room. They had seen him go on for hours, with a suspect, and never miss a beat. After leaving Carlos with me, Alex walked into the viewing room and said for them to wait and see what happened.

Everyone was speaking at once as they told the story. I noticed Spike standing at the back of the room. When I looked at him he winked. I knew the other officers were trying their best to accept me but Alex and Spike already did. They didn't care that I was a woman and older than everyone else. They didn't care that I was not what most officers felt was "cop material." They looked at my good points, encouraged me, yelled at me (Spike) and wanted me to succeed. Spike pissed me off almost every day but I knew why Alex thought Spike was so wonderful. He was a crotchety old cop, but a great one, and had seen and done just about everything in his career.

Alex had publicly shown faith in me twice today, when he had me handcuff Carlos at the bar and when he allowed me to interview Carlos. I was flying high, but our case was not over. The other guys continued talking as Alex and I left to get the money from Amanda.

In the car, Alex told me how proud he was. He said I kept my mouth shut during the interview but he could tell it was killing me not to be involved in the questioning. "I don't know what it is about you, but you have that knack. I have it too, but yours is something more. You get into that mothering role and the bad guy doesn't have a chance. Spike sees it too. He thinks of you as his protégé. In a couple of years you're going to be better at this than Spike and I will ever be."

That was going a little far, but I loved Alex for making me feel good about the job I did. Now if I could just get over my dread of traffic stops and citations.

We arrived at Amanda's, and she came to the door immediately. Alex told her we needed to talk. She backed up and allowed us inside.

"We have Carlos. No one was hurt."

Amanda had the same dejected look when she said, "You want the money don't you? I was afraid he would come back and if I didn't have the money he would be angry. I'm sorry for lying to you. I didn't know what else to do." Amanda cried softly as she explained.

She got up and we both followed her into the small bedroom. The money was hidden inside a pillow on the bed. "Am I going to jail?"

"I'm not taking you to jail, but it will ultimately be up to the County Attorney's Office. I have questions for you and being honest is the best thing you can do to help yourself at this point."

We walked back into the small kitchen area and sat down.

Alex glanced at me with a look on his face that I was beginning to understand. I read Amanda her rights and began asking questions.

"Tell us everything that's happened during the past twenty-four hours." My voice was soft and coaxing but also firm like I would hear Alex use.

Amanda continued to cry but managed to get the story out. "Carlos has been upset because he can't get a job. He's had a few but he loses them because of his temper. He yelled at Cherry when Cherry came to collect the rent. Because Carlos wasn't on the rental agreement, Cherry kicked him out of the park. He sneaks in whenever he can but he knows I need money. He always talks about getting a bigger place for the baby. I thought he was looking for a job, I had no idea he would rob a store. I was so scared when he brought me the money." Her tears continued and it appeared that she was telling us everything.

I looked around at the small trailer and the life Amanda led. She was bringing a baby into the world and by the time he or she arrived, dad would be in prison. It was hard not to feel sympathy for her but at the same time, I had little for Carlos. I might have felt differently if he hadn't hit the clerk. Amanda had spoken about Carlos' problems with anger and the Winkler's store clerk had felt it first-hand. I wondered if Carlos would have killed him if he resisted. I was thankful it hadn't happened but realized Carlos put himself into circumstances that could have ended in the death of an innocent person and now an innocent baby would pay too.

Alex promised Amanda we would come arrest her if we discovered she was lying. We went back to the department to place the $302.00 into evidence. We didn't have an accurate count from the store yet. I was hoping the money we just confiscated matched the amount that was missing from Winkler's.

I was finally able to go home and get some sleep. It didn't matter how tired I was, I lay awake for over an hour rehashing everything that happened. I had to be back at work in five hours. I set my alarm and unwillingly fell asleep.

I should have been exhausted when I woke up, but wasn't. Norman made dinner and I was able to eat before leaving. While we ate, I told him about my previous shift. He was worried about my lack of sleep, but otherwise took it in stride as part of my job. I think it helped that I shared everything with him. He got nervous sometimes about things I told him but accepted my explanations and seemed to understand.

I went to work and waited for Spike to arrive. Mike and Benito were there. Naturally, we talked about the arrest and confession.

"You did a great job Suzie. You seem to be picking up what you need to learn really fast. That's a bonus in this job."

"Yeah, bull shitting just comes easy for me but some things…like traffic stops are driving me crazy."

They were both looking at me with smiles. Benito spoke first, "I'm kind of considered the road hound here. I love 'running traffic', it's in my blood. If you can get permission from Sgt. Spears, you can come out and work some DUI task force with me."

"If you spend one night with Benny here, it will be like spending a month with Sgt. Spears and Spike combined." Mike went on to say.

I was finally fitting in. I knew they felt uncomfortable around me, and were uncertain how to talk and include me in their male world, but the walls were slowly coming down.

Benito said in a teasing voice, "I could see tears in your eyes on the monitor while Carlos was feeding you his sob story."

I knew I hadn't come close to crying but it felt good to be treated like one of them and I took the teasing in stride.

He continued, "We'll make sure you always have a box of Kleenex in the interview room from here on out."

The box of Kleenex appeared the next day. The box reminds me that suspects are human. They have feelings and regrets just as I do. And, if I push the right buttons; they're mine.

Spike arrived as we were laughing, "Don't get too cocky because you can't write a traffic citation for shit."

Mike and Benito gave me a look of sympathy as I walked out of the squad room on Spike's heels.

We continued with traffic stops that night and for a while I was doing better. I then became so tired I could barely keep my eyes open. Spike took me to Winkler's for a cup of coffee. The two night clerks wanted to talk about the robbery and I was surprised when Spike gave me credit for bagging Carlos and getting the confession.

After we left, Spike told me, "The town is just beginning to respect you and they need to know you're a damn good cop, even if I'm not sure about it. I won't tell them about your problem with traffic tickets. If you can't get your traffic stops down, I will send your ass back to phase-one of field training." So much for Spike's kind words inside the store.

That night Spike was also too tired to go after speeders and we went back to the office so I could begin writing my report on the robbery. I typed for several more hours and then Spike called it quits two hours early. He told me to go home and sleep. I didn't argue.

Spike was off the following evening and Alex was my training guide during my shift. We stayed at the office and typed until we finished our reports. He said we would be in court the following Wednesday for a pretrial conference. He looked over my report and asked me to make a few corrections. He was satisfied after that and left both our reports in Sgt. Spear's box for approval.

We headed out to get some food but when we got to the restaurant, dispatch radioed us about a neighbor dispute.

Alex said, "Consider these calls similar to family domestic violence calls. When people live in close proximity things can get violent."

Like eighty percent of our calls, this one turned out to be easily settled. The neighbors were arguing because neighbor number one's dog, knocked over neighbor number two's garbage can, and then tore it to shreds. Apparently it had gone on for years but neighbor number two held his feelings in until he couldn't take it anymore. We didn't have to arrest anyone and the two men shook hands before we left.

Paychecks was now closed and we headed to Winkler's to get a burrito. They were in the frozen section and had to be heated in the microwave. I realized I had better find more time to exercise or I wouldn't fit in my uniform much longer. We were warned at the academy that it is especially hard to maintain a workout schedule on night shifts.

Department policy stated once I was off field training; I could work out during my shift if someone else was on duty and covered calls. We got thirty minutes for lunch and could take the same for workout time and use the hour to stay in shape. Alex told me there was a physical therapy place in town that encouraged the night shift to use the facility to exercise. He had me drive to the location and used his key to show me around. There was a treadmill and different machines for weights.

"When you get your key, just bring a towel and some workout clothes."

I was beginning to hate field training almost as much as I disliked the academy. I was ready to be on my own. The thought was no longer as scary as it was that first day of duty.

A week later, I came to work an hour early for my field training review. The Chief, Sgt. Spears, and Spike were waiting for me. It was obvious they had talked for quite some time.

Sgt. Spears started, "How do you feel about your progress?"

"Good, but I know I have a few things to work on."

"Explain."

"I'm improving with my traffic stops but I don't feel entirely comfortable yet. I think I will do better alone, with no one looking over my shoulder, but I won't know until I do it."

"We don't have a lot of concerns with the job you're doing but sometimes you need to be a bit firmer and control situations. Nice will not always work and you need to be prepared to prove who's in charge. Other than that and traffic stops, we feel you're doing an excellent job."

"Thank you."

"You'll be with me for the next two weeks and then we're putting you with Benito for a week. If everything goes well you'll go to your last two weeks of field training where you get a little more freedom."

This would mean I would be by myself, though Sgt. Spears would be keeping a close eye on me.

"Do you think you're ready?" This from my chief.

It was an easy reply, "Yes Sir, I do."

The meeting ended.

My last few days with Spike were actually fun. He told stories about his field training and his rookie year as a cop. He called it the good old days.

"Back then police work was not a lawsuit waiting to happen and we got away with a lot more. If someone threw a punch at you and you laid them out on the ground, needing medical attention, you wrote a short form. None of this bullshit pile of paperwork we have now."

I don't know about the good old days, but Spike was right, we wrote reports for everything.

I was ready to move on. My next two weeks with Sgt. Spears couldn't be avoided, but every day put me one day closer to being on my own.

Chapter 17

Sgt. Spears hadn't changed. He was more concerned with his piles of paperwork than patrolling the street. The two weeks dragged by. I knew the Sergeant had to work on admin stuff but it didn't make things easier. I missed Spike, even if I frequently wanted to strangle him.

The two weeks finally came to an end, and it was time to work with Benito. He worked the same time schedule as I, but on different nights of the week. This only gave me one day off before I was on shift again.

"So Ivy, you ready to see how real police work is done?"

I held back my groan and said "As ready as I'll ever be." I was discovering that almost every officer thought their way, of doing things, was the only way. The only person outside this "cop norm" was Alex.

To my surprise, we didn't head out to stop vehicles. The next two hours were spent going over officer safety during traffic stops. He used one of our unmarked vehicles to show me what the driver could see or not see. I could tell Benito loved being a traffic hound and he knew his stuff. He spoke about what a driver expected from a cop and what a cop should always expect from a driver.

It was simple in his mind and like Spike's discouraging warning, expect death. He didn't have a numbered list of rules like Spike but he knew danger was a part of every stop. We went over safety until he finally felt I was ready to hit the road.

He had me pull over vehicles for every infraction imaginable; not using a turn signal, not stopping completely at a stop sign, and the traffic cops' favorite, no license plate light. I wasn't even sure if my personal vehicle had a license plate light. I had never checked.

Benito told me, when he had time, he stopped multiple vehicles for not having their license plate lit up. Many of his DUI's were discovered this way. He explained that defense attorney's loved calling it a BS excuse to pull someone over. Benito said he just recited the traffic code and explained, to a judge or jury, that he pulled many driver's over for the same reason and they were not drunk.

I learned a lot during my three days with him. It was nice to get to know another officer. He gave me the inside "guy" take on sending women to the academy.

"You should have seen the uproar over two women going to the academy for our department. And you, being an old lady." He cast a sidewise glance in my direction so I could see his smile and continued, "Most of us have never worked alongside women and we didn't know what to expect. We were worried you would carry a purse with your uniform or something."

I didn't feel slighted by his words. I knew he wouldn't be telling me this if he was having a problem with me.

"How do you feel about working with a woman now?" I couldn't help but ask.

"It took me a few weeks to figure it out, but you're not much different than the guys. I thought I would feel this sense of protectiveness, but what I feel is that you can handle yourself. You don't panic, you keep your cool and you can shoot your gun. I don't know if I would have felt the same way about the hot chick."

I laughed, the "hot chick" only made it through the first day of the academy. I survived eighteen and a half weeks. "You're a dork."

"As you approached graduation, the entire department should have been put on antidepressants. We were scared shitless. There was a fifty dollar pool. Alex and I were the only ones to bet on your side. It was funny that the two "Mexicans" thought a forty-five year old woman could make it. We split the money, so thanks for surviving."

We both laughed.

My lessons continued and I was gaining confidence under Benito's tutelage. He was married and had two small children, a boy and a girl. His wife worked at the courthouse and he wanted to introduce us. I thought I remembered her from the Thanksgiving party but wasn't sure. I looked forward to meeting her.

Benito was proud of how well I was doing but worried, because he scheduled the following day off, and I would be working with Jared Stephens.

"Watch yourself. None of us are real fond of Stephens but his father sits on the City Council and we walk softly around him. He thinks very highly of himself and was the most outspoken about hiring a female officer."

I wasn't told what Stephens said but I understood the warning. It was the first time I was told anything bad about a fellow officer. I didn't remember actually disliking anyone at the academy besides Sgt. Dickens. I figured I got along with most people and I would do okay with Officer Stephens too.

***

I arrived twenty minutes early for my shift the following evening. Officer Stephens was waiting and told me I would be driving his vehicle. This seemed strange, but I got in and adjusted both the seat and mirror, before I pulled out. I was told to stop and pull back into the department parking lot.

"What did you do wrong?" He asked in a condescending voice.

I was at a loss.

He gave me the "you are incredibly stupid" look and then let me have it. "When you get in your vehicle, at the beginning of your shift, you walk around the outside, check the turn signals, lights and tires. When you've done your safety inspection you search the back seat for items left behind by arrestees."

I was trained to do this, but I performed my inspection before coming to work, while I was in my driveway. Dumb me; I thought Stephens would perform his own check, on his own vehicle. I did as I was told and discovered a pocket knife in the crease of the back seat. It was planted for me to find. He seemed very proud of himself for proving his point but not proud of me for finding it.

I then waited while he spent the next five minutes writing on my evaluation form. I was then told to clear the station. It was going to be a rough night.

My first traffic stop was on a vehicle that ran a stop sign. The older woman was nice and courteous and I planned to write a warning. Stephens had other ideas and told me I was writing a ticket.

Since beginning my field training, I had been able to make my own decisions on whether to issue a warning or citation. Stephens was starting to piss me off.

I later pulled over a young girl for driving fifty-two in a thirty-five. She was chewing her gum and being a complete spoiled brat. When I got back to my patrol unit, to check her license, Stephens told me to write a warning and he would issue it. I wrote the warning and he approached her on the driver's side and proceeded to flirt. I should have heeded Benito's warning a little more and called in sick.

I made several additional stops and they were no different. If you were a pretty young girl, you got a warning. If not, you were given a citation. I was so pissed that I became careless and forgot my officer safety training. I completely screwed up a stop and "Don Juan the Devil" was making my night a living hell.

Our shift continued, and I thought I would make it when I saw a red Mustang clocking a speed fifteen miles over the speed limit. Oh boy, I knew that car. Stephens told me to make the stop.

I walked around to the driver's side and my best friend Veronica charged out the door and threw her arms around me while jumping up and down.

"Oh my God, you look so cop and official like. Are you going to write me a ticket? Will it be your first one?"

Veronica is the person who helped me get in shape in preparation for the police academy. She kicked my ass daily and never doubted I would make it. She was in her late thirties, gorgeous and like the "before me" had no clue that drugs, child molests and wife beatings went on in Small Town. I could see Stephens out of the corner of my eye. I whispered to Veronica, "Dick on the right will give you a ticket if you don't stick out your boobs."

She was quick on the uptake. "So who is your good looking cop friend over here?" She said as she looked his way. I made introductions.

"Hello, you know you were going a little fast there." Stephens' chest was pumped up and he looked ridiculous.

"Yes and I'm so sorry. I was on my way home from my high school reunion committee meeting and didn't realize I was going quite so fast." Her chest was extended as far as it would reach.

"Well," I swear, he leered. "Slow down and I'll just have Officer Ivy write you a warning this time."

"Oh thank you Officer, you're as kind as you are good looking."

Could I barf now? Veronica could chew Stephens up and spit him out just for kicks. It was fun to watch her in action. She was born with a silver spoon in her mouth, served on every charity committee in the entire county and did not take no for an answer. If it got her donations she would show breasts and would even do the honors to avoid a speeding ticket. I loved this woman. Stephens was out of her league and she wouldn't be caught dead with him. It was kind of sad to see the hope on his scumbag face.

We left the scene and Stephens asked me if Veronica was married. I told him the truth, which was no. If he made a move on her, she would be at his door soliciting money from his wife. When that didn't work, she would make sure he saw her speaking with his wife. He would be donating the money. God, I loved that woman.

I couldn't wait for the night to be over. I knew Stephens and I would never be friends. I wasn't the right age or body type for him. He wasn't even good looking, but he had no trouble telling me he was the world's greatest lover. I really needed a bag for my vomit.

After our run-in with Veronica, he told me his wife rarely had sex with him for religious reasons. I had trouble keeping a straight face, with this information, and gave his wife points for originality. Stephens told me he was forced to seek his comfort elsewhere. I couldn't believe he got away with it much less had the nerve to brag.

About thirty minutes before the end of our shift he said, "You know, I have no choice but to fail you on your performance evaluation tonight."

"I'm aware of my mistakes." I left it at that.

It took him a minute and then he said, "Well, I would be willing to give you a good score under one condition." I kept looking straight ahead and he continued, "If you give me a blow job, I'll give you a pass."

I don't think two seconds passed before I had the car pulled over. I was so angry I was shaking. I turned to him, "I'm old enough to be your mother, I'm happily married and if you ever put your dick anywhere near my mouth I'll bite it off. Are we clear?!"

"Hey, hey, hey, I was only joking. I wanted to see how you would react and if we needed to worry about you with the other guys. It was a test and you passed but you didn't pass your evaluation for the night and there's nothing I can do about that." His hands were shaking, the scumbag.

I pulled back into traffic and headed for the police station. We did not speak another word. My evaluation was beyond bad and it took me hours to calm down. I should have had my brain washed out with soap with all the derogatory words I had running through it.

The next day was the start of my weekend but the department secretary called me in. Sgt. Spears led me into his office. He read my evaluation form, out loud, from the previous evening. He actually laughed as he read the words, "Officer Ivy should be discontinued as an officer and sent back to the academy or told she is too old to be in law enforcement."

I didn't see the humor but appreciated that Sgt. Spears seemed to hold little regard for Officer Stephens' words. He told me if I had received a glowing report, he and everyone else would have assumed I slept with Stephens. I just looked at Sgt. Spears.

"Is there something you want to tell me about your shift last night?"

"No, but I'm not looking forward to working with him."

"None of us ever are but he wears a badge and we put up with him. Are you sure you don't want to tell me anything?"

"I'm sure."

"Well then, regardless or maybe in spite of this less than glowing report, you will be on your own from now on. Find yourself three self-initiated incidents over the next two weeks and I'll release you from field training. You've done an excellent job and we need you on your own to give the rest of us a break. Never hesitate to come to my office with a problem. We all need help from time to time so don't think you're too good to ask."

"I won't sir, I promise."

"Now get out of my office and enjoy your time off."

I went home and took a nap. All I could think about was Jared Stephens, that rotten son of a bitch. It made little sense to me that a jerk like that was a cop. I didn't care who his father was, Stephens was scary, and I planned to stay out of his way.

I was going back to the day shift and I had four days off before it was time to work again. That night was the first time I didn't share everything that happened at work with my husband. If I wanted to kill Stephens I was sure Norman would carry through. This just made me angrier at the bastard.

The following evening, Norman and I played pool and I got good and drunk. It was something I never did when my kids were in the house. I might have a glass of wine or two but I never overindulged. I told Norman we were celebrating the, almost, end of my field training, but didn't tell him I was actually drowning my need to kill a fellow officer. My hangover the following morning didn't help my disposition and I regretted my unwise decision to take those last two shots of tequila.

Chapter 18

My last two weeks of field training began. I was driving my patrol vehicle alone. It felt good and somewhat strange. I was part of the call rotation but a fellow officer had to oversee me at the scene. That part wasn't much different from my earlier field training but it was nice to roll up on a scene by myself.

The first day was uneventful, but I did manage to pull over a drunk driver. This was the first of my three required self-initiated police actions.

The unlucky driver was Harry Skilt.

"May I see your driver's license and registration?" I smelled the alcohol as soon as the window was rolled down. I waited until the requested items were handed over and read the name, "Mr. Skilt, how much have you had to drink this evening?"

"Two beers." He said with a slur in his voice.

"I need you to stay in your vehicle while I run your information." Mr. Skilt was attempting to open his door and get out of his car.

"Could you just take me to jail? I'm drunk and I think I just need to go to jail."

"I need you to sit here, while I run your license, and then I'll decide what I will do next. Do you understand Mr. Skilt?"

"Yeah, but I really think you need to take me to jail."

I kept Mr. Skilt in my sights as I headed back to my patrol car. He had a valid license, registration and current insurance. Too bad he was drunk.

I left his information in my patrol car and walked back to his car. "I need you to step out of your vehicle." I moved back to allow him to open his car door and get out. Nothing happened.

"Are you taking me to jail?"

"I'm going to do field sobriety tests, so I need you to get out of the vehicle."

"I want to go straight to jail and don't want to do field 'sobrevity' tests."

I would use his word 'sobrevity' in my report. "That's not up to you Mr. Skilt. Step out of the vehicle." My stern mother voice was back in play.

"Okay, but I think you just need to take me to jail."

"Just how much did you say you had to drink?"

"Two sixpacksofbeer I'm really drunk butyoucancallmeHarry." His words were slurred and run together. It was difficult to understand him but I knew I heard "two beers" not "two six packs" when I asked the first time.

Sgt. Spears arrived and chose not to interfere. I moved Harry, out of the way of traffic, in case he fell over. "I'm going to give you some instructions and I need you to wait to start until I give you the go ahead. Do you understand?"

"When do you wantmetostart?"

"I'm planning to show you. First you will do the walk and turn. Don't start until I tell you. When I tell you, the first thing you will do is place your feet together like this." I placed my feet together and watched Harry do the same. First clue…did not wait for my go ahead.

"Next, when I tell you, I want you to tip your head slightly back, like this." Of course Harry tipped his head back. "I then want you to place one foot in front of the other and take ten steps, counting them out loud. No don't start yet, let me show you what I want you to do." I showed Harry what I wanted.

"Then, when you are finished with the ten steps, I want you to pivot on your right foot and take ten steps back to me. Do you understand?"

Harry didn't answer my question, he just began his count. It went like this, "One, two, two, three, six, seveneightten."

At least he made it without falling. I spoke too quickly, Harry fell over when he performed his version of the pivot.

Sgt. Spears decided to help as I began pulling Harry off the ground.

"I think Harry was right and he needs to go straight to jail. Get a BAC on him when you get there and book him in if he's not too drunk."

BAC is breath alcohol content. If Harry was over a .25, the jail would not take him without a medical evaluation. It was 30-minutes to the nearest hospital and due to Small Town's budget constraints, I did not expect to receive permission to make the trip. This meant I would need to find a family member willing to babysit Harry at home. I would then file a long form and he would spend his night in jail at a later date.

It was a miracle but I managed to get Harry booked into jail. His BAC was .22. It was my first chance to speak with the detention officers alone. They were friendly and what I liked most was their courteous treatment of Harry. I always imagined jail guards as being big mean gorillas. This group disproved my theory.

After I left the jail, I went home for lunch. It was nice to have a break and enjoy a meal without looking over my shoulder. I learned, in the first few days of field training, that as an officer you always sit facing a restaurant door. As the rookie, I usually sat with my side or back to the door depending on how many of us there were.

About halfway through my lunch, I was called to a traffic accident. It ended up as a 961 (accident no injuries) but accidents generate a lot of paperwork. This one, thank goodness, didn't require mathematical equations to determine who was at fault. The guilty man was upfront and apologetic.

After clearing the scene, I decided to go back to the department to begin working on my driving under the influence (DUI) and accident reports. With a DUI there are two sides to the case, civil, which you agree to when you get a driver's license, and criminal, which happens when you make the decision to drive drunk. The driver's license needed to be mailed to the Department of Motor Vehicles along with Admin Per Se, which is your agreement as a driver to take a blood, breath or a urine test. I must read the Admin Per Se form to the suspected drunk driver and have him sign it.

Drivers get an Admin Per Se hearing within two weeks of being charged with DUI if the driver requests it in writing. If they win the hearing they don't lose their license for the mandatory 30-day suspension on a first DUI offense. If the driver requests the hearing, I'm required to testify and support my charge.

Then there's the criminal aspect of DUI, which required me to be in court the following Wednesday. I figured Harry would be released from jail the next morning but I was still required to have my report finished in forty-eight hours.

The traffic accident required me to fill out multiple pages of accident forms. Everything from insurance, vehicle description and road conditions were covered, including information that didn't seem pertinent to me. My job was not to question why, it was only to fill out the damn paperwork.

About an hour before I went off duty, I was dispatched to the home of Sarah Evans. Her house was located in Cherry's Trailer Park at space 15. When I pulled up I saw a woman, who looked to be in her sixties, sitting on the front steps of a large fifth wheel trailer. She introduced herself as Connie, Sarah's mother.

"Sarah is off her meds again. She does this at least once a year. I can't control her when she's like this."

As she spoke, Sgt. Spears pulled up and joined me. I asked about weapons inside the home and then entered to speak with Sarah.

The fifth wheel was compact and I didn't see her in the small living and kitchen area. I called her name and announced who I was. I heard a faint voice saying she was in the back. I walked past the bathroom and entered a room that was wall to wall bed. Sarah was lying on her stomach. She did not have a stitch of clothing on her body.

I introduced myself and Sarah rolled over. I could see that both her hands were empty. Her nudity made me uncomfortable but I was trained to keep my eyes on the problem. I asked if she wanted to put some clothes on and talk to me.

"Go ahead and talk, I'm not doing anything wrong and this is my house. My mom's crazy, she tries to put garbage on me and I won't let her."

I was a little startled, "Garbage?"

"She wants me to wear garbage and she takes it out of the garbage can."

"Did you put clothes in the garbage can?"

"No, not clothes, she wants me to wear garbage."

I just looked at her as I tried to figure out where to go from here. "I'm not sure what you're telling me. I'm new here, why don't you explain."

"It's garbage, bread, bags, old milk. I can't wear those, they stink like shit. I need you to tell my mom to leave me alone. I'm not a little baby."

"I'm going to go out and speak with your mom. Will you be okay?" She rolled over and ignored me.

Connie explained she was trying to get Sarah to put on some clothes but she refused. Connie had no idea where "garbage" came into the story and explained that Sarah talked crazy when she was off her meds.

I asked if Sarah had a counselor or therapist. Connie said she called and the therapist should arrive shortly. I decided to go back in and speak with Sarah until help arrived.

I entered the back bedroom calling out to Sarah again as I walked in. I asked if I could sit on the side of the bed and speak with her for a while. I rambled about work, children and animals. She answered any questions I posed and finally looked over at me. She didn't seem to be upset that I was in her room and she was naked. When I mentioned animals, she perked up.

"I love cats and feed the neighbor's. They're wild but they like me."

I could see the front door from where I sat and a man finally stepped into the fifth wheel. I left the room to greet him. His name was Allan.

Sarah is not wearing clothes." I whispered.

Allan called to the bedroom, "Sarah, I need you to put clothes on so I can talk to you."

Before I realized what was happening Sarah shoved me out of the way and threw herself at Allan. His arms went around her in reflex but his face was bright red as he gently tried to push her away. "Ah, you need to have clothes on. Get dressed so we can talk."

She cheerfully walked back into her room.

Allan quietly explained he would try to get Sarah to go inpatient to the closest facility. He had been her councilor for the past two years and this was the third time she stopped taking her medication. Allan asked if I would stay while he spoke with her.

Sarah came back out wearing only panties and a backwards t-shirt. Allan urged her to go to the hospital but she refused and began telling Allan about her mother trying to get her to wear garbage.

"Sarah, you know your mom would never do that. She's worried about you and wants you to feel better."

"My mom hates me and I want her to leave. I won't wear her filthy garbage."

Allan's reasoning did nothing to convince Sarah to get treatment. "When's the last time you ate?"

"I don't know but I'm not hungry."

"Where is your medication?"

"I flushed it down the toilet."

Their discussion went on for twenty minutes before Allan and I went outside. He spoke to Connie and told Sgt. Spears and I that we could leave. He said he was sure we would be seeing each other again if Sarah continued to refuse her meds.

We went to our vehicles and cleared the scene.

I went home after filling out a short form about the incident with Sarah.

The next two days were slower and I cited a man, who did not have his dog on a leash at the park. I was with Alex a few weeks earlier when he warned the man about the leash law. This was my second self-initiated incident and I needed one more to complete my field training.

It was my Friday and seemed to be as slow as the past two days when I received a call from Dispatch that there was a naked woman walking down the road. It didn't take much to figure out it was Sarah.

I drove around the corner and sure enough she was strolling down the street completely naked. I pulled up beside her but she continued walking. I then pulled my car ahead of her, turned on my overhead lights, and got out of the car to see what I could do.

Sarah wouldn't stop walking and ignored me. She said, "Here kitty kitty," as she walked.

I gently placed my hand on her shoulder and said her name. All hell broke loose. Sarah started fighting me. She swung and connected with my jaw before I could fight back. I yelled into my radio for backup. Usually another officer was already on scene with me. I tackled Sarah and got her on the ground but she continued kicking and swinging her arms. I managed to get one of her hands in cuffs, but was unable to get control of the other. I kept a death grip on the hand with the cuff. I didn't want her swinging it and using the clunky metal as a weapon. I was lying fully on top of her body and that's what Sgt. Spears saw when he pulled up.

He calmly walked up beside me. "Do you have everything under control?"

The smart ass. "I think I need a little help." I was gasping for breath as I tried to keep hold of Sarah's hand as she wiggled and fought. Another squad car pulled up. This was turning into a party. It was a younger officer named Robert Swells. Everyone called him Roberts. He helped me get Sarah into the other handcuff.

She began spitting on both of us. "You bitch, you fucking bitch." There was spittle running down her chin.

I managed to get her into the back of my vehicle. She continued fighting and began kicking the side window. Roberts pulled his Taser, took off the pronged end and threatened her with a drive stun. A drive stun was acceptable if someone was in handcuffs. It caused a sharp electrical shock when you touched the person with the end of the Taser. Sarah stopped suddenly after the Taser was popped, but continued to call me every name she could think of. It was a fun ride to the jail.

I asked Dispatch to notify Allan and he arrived at the jail. I told him I was willing to release Sarah if she would go to the hospital. Allan spoke to her and she agreed. I also told him I wouldn't file charges if she got back on her meds. Sarah left jail in an ambulance

When I walked into the police department, I was met with loud clapping and wolf whistles. Everyone was laughing. My vehicle has in-car-video. When my fight with the naked Sarah started we were in front of my vehicle, so everything was caught on tape. The only thing that would have made it more entertaining for the guys was if we had added mud to the altercation. Learning that the video of the fight would be used as a "training lesson" only added insult to injury. The single lesson I learned was to fight naked women behind my car and not in front.

My jaw was sore, but luckily only red and not bruised.

It was true, no two calls were ever the same. But just how many different situations could there be? The number seemed endless.

Chapter 19

I was thankful to have three days off and the chance to enjoy some time with my husband. We made a turnaround trip to Phoenix and took our daughter Cassie to an early dinner. Cassie wanted to know all about my first few months on the streets and I ended the stories with my naked girl fight. We laughed and it felt good to be away from town.

My weekend ended and another work week began. I was looking for my last self-initiated report but had no luck the first day. I handled petty calls and caught up on paperwork. I had to fill out a use of force form for my fight with Sarah. I was surprised we didn't have a form for using the restroom, but I knew better than to bring it up or someone would find one for me.

The naked girl fight jokes continued and I should have realized Spike would want to get his own interpretation in. I heard shouting from the Sergeant's office. I couldn't help but head that way. I saw everyone standing outside the office door and they parted like the Red Sea. Spike was standing on the Sergeant's desk in men's swim trunks and a bikini top, dancing to music as the guys clapped and shouted.

Spike saw me. "There she is. Come get some baby. I'll put up a good fight if you want."

His hairy chest and potbelly were almost more than I could take, but I jumped up on the desk. "I don't need a fight. Did you bring the baby oil?"

Everyone laughed and clapped more as I danced with Spike and we performed a few dirty dancing moves. The noise level dropped suddenly and I didn't want to look. It didn't stop Spike.

"Hi Chief, we can make room for you."

I'm sure my face was bright red. The Chief shook his head and muttered, "I don't even want to know," and walked out of the room.

Spike and I jumped off the desk and he gave me a big hug. "You're all right Ivy."

I received pats on the back and good natured calls as I went to my desk.

On the second day of my shift, I was cruising through town and saw a guy leaving an abandoned house. He appeared to come from the backyard and started running when he saw me. I radioed my location and pulled my car up beside the house. I got out and approached the front door. I looked in the dirty windows but could barely see in. I tried the front door knob but it was locked.

Out of the corner of my eye, I saw Alex arrive and went over to give him a heads up on what I did or didn't have. Alex and I approached the back of the house. He looked in the back door and said he thought someone was inside. He tried the back door and it opened. We drew our guns then heard a baby crying.

"Shit," said Alex and we entered the house.

Beer bottles and trash were everywhere, though the rooms were bare of furniture. Alex whispered for me to cover his back.

He cleared the first bedroom and then entered the next one.

"Son of a bitch," His voice was angry.

A few moments later, he came partway out of the room holding a baby that looked to be about six months old. The child had stopped crying.

"Call for additional backup and when it arrives, get Child Protective Services on the phone. Mom's passed out on the floor. I can see drug paraphernalia next to her. Be sure to keep an eye on the back door for papa."

Sergeant Spears arrived and covered the back door. I made my phone call and went into the bedroom with Alex. He was holding the baby as it slept on his shoulder. The front of Alex's uniform was wet.

He spoke softly, "There are no diapers and I don't even see a fucking bottle. I wonder how long he's been here."

I looked at Mom, hoping she was only unconscious. I couldn't help asking, "Is she dead?"

Alex shook his head, "It looks like meth and she's probably coming down so hard nothing will wake her. I checked her pulse before I picked up the baby. Did you call CPS?"

"I asked dispatch to get them and patch me through. Do you want me to take him?" I was guessing the baby was a boy but wasn't sure.

"No, there's no use in both of us getting pee on our uniforms."

A man who didn't wilt under baby pee...He needed a good woman and a couple of children. I'd have to join his mother in looking around for a good match.

CPS finally arrived and took the baby off our hands. He had slept the entire time we waited. Our next move was to get Mom up and out to our car. It wasn't easy. When she finally came to, she started screaming about her baby, asking what we did with him. She started to fight Alex and refused to put her hands behind her back. Alex had a hard time grabbing her arms, I finally grabbed the only thing available and that was her hair.

"Let go bitch." She said as she tried to slap me. I got hold of her arm and put it in one of the holds I learned at the academy. It didn't stop her. Drugs seem to give people extra strength and increase their stupidity.

"Let go of her and push off." Alex yelled.

I trusted him and did what he said, giving her a hard shove away from me. Alex's Taser went off. Her earlier screaming was nothing compared to what we heard as she fell to the ground.

It was hard to keep the grin off my face. Alex didn't even try.

"Officer Ivy is going to place you in handcuffs. If you don't cooperate, I'll give you another taste of the Taser. Do you understand?"

"Yeah, yeah, don't do it again!"

I got the handcuffs on without a problem. I then removed the Taser prongs and we assisted her to my car.

At the police department, she told us that her boyfriend, who was not the baby's father, was supposed to watch the baby. She had no excuse for the absence of diapers or food. She was booked into jail for child endangerment and drug paraphernalia. I dropped her off and went back to the department.

Alex was there filling out his use of force report.

"Sorry about Tasing her Ivy, if I had helped and put my hands on her, I don't know what I would have done. I wanted to break her neck."

"It's okay I know how you feel. How can she care so little about her child while getting high, then pretend the child is the most important thing in her life when she's getting arrested?"

"That poor baby doesn't have a chance. He'll go to foster care for a while and then Mom will get him back."

"Do you want me to start looking for the boyfriend?"

"No, he'll show up soon enough. I know who he is and we can get an arrest warrant. You got your third self-initiated incident. Congratulations, you should be on your own starting next week. You ready?" Alex had a grin on his face.

"I'm ready but at the same time scared to death. Please don't tell the guys."

"I won't, I remember feeling the same way. You've worked hard and I'm glad you're here."

I looked at Alex, with his peed on uniform and that smile. "Go home and change. You stink!"

Alex left and I began writing my report. I described, in minute detail, the condition of the house and the bedroom, where we found the baby. I then called CPS. They said the child was a year old and couldn't yet crawl. They asked when I expected to complete my report and I told them it was done and just waiting for approval.

I walked out of the squad room and saw Sandy at her desk, directly outside the chief's office door. She waved me over.

Sandy was friendly but never went out of her way to converse with me. The guys had a healthy respect for her, and repeatedly told me to stay on her good side. She had the chief's ear. I walked into her domain.

"How are things going?" She asked.

"Good, I think. I just got the last report I needed to get off field training."

"That's great, want to go celebrate after work?"

Maybe I heard wrong. "I need to call my husband and make sure he doesn't have plans but if I'm free I would love to."

"I know a place in the next town and if we need a ride home my brother will transport us."

I knew the rules of no drinking in town. It was a bad idea to get drunk or tipsy and have a run-in with someone you've arrested.

"Sounds great, let me call Norman." I used my cell phone and Norman said he was tired and had to get up early. He told me not to wake him when I came in. It was a joke because he slept like the dead and he was the one that usually woke me. I laughed and said I would be quiet.

Sandy overheard the conversation and told me to go home and make myself presentable and to try and not look, "Cop like."

I went home and with Norman watching me, proceeded to get dolled up. I cleaned up pretty good for an old lady. I put on my favorite pair of jeans and a sheer beige blouse with a camisole underneath. I took my hair down and then straightened it. Norman loved when I straightened my hair.

"Who did you say you were going out with? What was his name?" Norman was teasing.

"Her name is Sandy and she's the chief's administrative assistant."

"Is this a good idea?"

"I think it would be worse to say no. The guys are afraid of her. She's friendly enough but aloof."

"Okay but don't say I didn't warn you!"

Sandy picked me up. She cleaned up nicely too, and it looked like we were headed for a fun girl's night out.

It was a thirty minute drive to the next town. We made small talk about work and she told me a few stories about the department. She had worked there for twelve years.

I thought Sandy was around thirty years old but had never been sure. It turned out she was thirty-eight but looked much younger.

We got to the restaurant/bar and found a back table. A few people said hello to Sandy, but she didn't introduce me, just walked to the corner.

The waitress came over and greeted Sandy by name. She ordered a gin and tonic. I ordered a margarita. The restaurant served everything from steak to Mexican food. Norman and I had not eaten there yet.

"My sister owns this place," said Sandy.

"That's great. Do I get to meet her?"

"Probably not, she works the day shift and has kids to go home to at night."

"Do you have kids?"

"Yes, two boys. One's in junior high and one's in his first year of high school. It's nice to not need a babysitter. My husband is making sure they stay out of trouble tonight."

Our drinks came and a slow evening of inebriety began. We ate and I stopped counting drinks after the fourth. Sandy told me great stories about all the guys. Mostly about their love lives and what she called the "badge bunnies" in town.

I about spit out my drink when out of the blue she said, "So did Stephens ask you for a blow job?"

I began laughing. I was feeling no pain and my mouth was loose, "Yeah, he did, that son of a bitch."

"Why didn't you make a complaint?"

"I'm new, he has connections, and I didn't think he would lose his job over it. Was I wrong?"

"No, everyone knows he's an SOB but he does have connections. Someday his daddy won't be there to help him. Do me a favor and write down what happened. Make sure you put the date and time. I've written everything down and someday it will be enough."

"What did he do to you?"

"The same thing, I screwed up on a major project and was running around like a chicken with my head cut off. He said he would help me fix the error for a price."

"Does everyone know what happened the night he was with me on patrol?"

"They suspect, but actually respect you more because you kept your mouth shut. Cops are a strange breed. They haven't fully accepted you and even though Stephens is a jerk, he's one of theirs. I hope someday it will be different and I know Alex and Spike like you. Spike isn't easy to make friends with but he's probably the best friend you can have when your back is against the wall. Alex will be Chief some day and he's also a great guy and a good guy to have on your side."

Politics, they happen everywhere. I just hoped I could remember all the words of wisdom Sandy was imparting. My head was spinning like crazy.

Sandy continued to talk. She told me the chief hired her because she used to be a dispatcher for the county and made a formal complaint against him. "Though he was only a deputy back then." She said he disliked her for a long time but when he took over the Chief's position, the old chief's administrative assistant retired. He wanted someone he could trust and who would stand up to him so Sandy got the job.

I was learning more about inside office politics than I had learned since starting at the department. I hated to admit it but Sandy drank me under the table. Her brother picked us up and drove us home. Poor guy, by this time we were laughing for the sake of laughing. Sandy told me she would see me at work the next morning.

Oh God, I had to get up and go to work. I just hoped I could puke in the next hour or so.

Chapter 20

I'm not sure how I made it through the next two days. Note to self: Don't get into a drinking contest with Sandy. She looked great the next morning. I, on the other hand, looked like a big-rig truck ran over me. Somehow I survived until my weekend and was able to recuperate.

The big day arrived and I was finally out of training. Less than a year ago, I was lying in bed with a broken hip. I never dreamed life would bring me here. Now I would be on my own. Getting dressed that morning was almost like putting on my uniform for the first time. I felt like a cop.

I walked out to my squad car, started the engine, and radioed dispatch that I was 10-8 (ready for duty). The dispatcher said good morning and told me to stand by for traffic (a pending call). This would be my first call with no one looking over my shoulder or checking up on me. I held my breath as I waited for the information.

The radio squealed and I was told there was a large suspicious case in the garbage can at the Circle K. An officer was being requested immediately.

Several things went through my head upon hearing "suspicious package." My first thought was bomb and my second was body parts. I'd definitely watched too many serial killer and terrorist movies. Either scenario would require me to contact a supervisor. I decided taking a look first was my best course of action.

***

I arrived at Circle K and saw three women standing at the large dumpster on the side of the building. I approached and they all turned, looking at me with expectation. The manager spoke up, "There's a large suitcase in the dumpster with blond curly hair sticking out the side. I think it's a dog but I'm not sure."

I walked up to the dumpster and looked at the suitcase. It was about two feet wide, two and a half feet high, and eight inches deep. I could see the hair in question and it did look like it belonged to a dog.

In my most professional cop voice, I said, "I need you ladies to stand back and let me take a look inside the suitcase."

Everyone moved further back with a few "ewes and awes" cast my way. Yes, I was one professional cop.

My radio chirped and Spike asked me what was going on.

"What do you have 1510?" came Spike's sharp deep voice.

This is where my professionalism bit the dust.

"I have a 962 (accident with injuries)." Of course, in my mind I thought I said 931(dead dog).

"How bad is it?"

"Well sir he's dead."

"I'll be right there."

The next thing I heard over the radio is an ambulance being dispatched, but I wasn't paying close attention because I was wrestling to open the suitcase and trying not to gag as the smell overwhelmed me.

Dispatch radioed me and asked if I needed more than one ambulance.

It started to sink in then and I realized I told Spike my call was a 962 (accident with injuries) and I had further stated my subject was dead (which is a 963). I immediately radioed and said I miss-spoke the code and I actually had a 932. Dispatch questioned what I said and I repeated 932. There is no such code. Why this unknown code came out of my mouth, I don't know. I was on a roll.

As this was going on, I was getting my first look at the fluffy blond, very dead, forty-pound dog that was crammed inside the suitcase.

Spike pulled up, jumped out of his car, and began yelling. "What the hell are you doing? If you don't know a code, use English."

He was pissed. His face was red. My face was even redder. Everyone was staring.

"What the hell is a 932?" he demanded.

This is when I realized I had blown it again when I radioed my correction. I don't usually hold back, even when I'm wrong. So I very sarcastically responded, "A 932 is a dead dog in a suitcase. Didn't you learn than at the academy?"

I thought Spike would lose his mind. His face went from red to purple. I was afraid he might shoot me, but he took a deep breath, turned his back on me and marched to his patrol car. As he was driving away, his words to dispatch came over my radio, "Please make a note that a 932 is a dead dog in a suitcase, and if 1510 ever has another one, you need to know the proper code."

I closed the suitcase and slunk to my vehicle, leaving behind fluffy and my audience. Laughter sounded in the background of my radio communication as I cleared the scene.

Later that day, I had to call dispatch by phone. As soon and they heard my voice, the dispatchers started laughing. I apologized for my mix up, but they said it was okay. They had never enjoyed a call so much in their lives. And to prove it, they posted a special sheet on the wall for other codes I felt I needed to add. Their laughter was infectious and I began to see the humor in my blunder. But I had no doubt that I would never quite live it down.

My bad luck day continued with my traffic court appearance at two. It was my first time alone in court and on the stand and I forgot to point out that I wrote the ticket in the jurisdiction of the court. It was a stupid reason to lose a traffic case but again everything at this point was a learning lesson.

After court, I drove to the office and entered the squad room. There was a small suitcase lying on top of my desk. I knew it was someone's idea of a joke. I also knew I had to take whatever came my way.

I opened the suitcase and a yellow stuffed animal, yes a dog, was lying inside. She was rather cute and I named her 932 and placed her on a shelf over my desk. I heard laughter behind me. The secretaries and a couple of officers were standing there.

"I feel so dumb so go ahead and laugh. Thanks for the present." This started an abundance of rookie stories and Sgt. Spears joined in. He had a knack for remembering every detail of all mistakes made on his watch by fellow officers. Hearing all the stories was fun. I stopped feeling quite so stupid and started feeling a sense of family.

***

It wasn't until several months later, that I added a new code to my list at dispatch, but this one was out of necessity. The call came at eight, on a rainy morning. I was informed a mother needed help with her incorrigible child. I arrived and spoke with Tina Warren. Her son Max was giving her problems and missed his school bus. Tina didn't want Max arrested, she just wanted me to give Max a ride to school as punishment.

"Is there a reason you can't take Max to school?" I was trying to keep the dismay out of my voice.

"Well, Max missed the bus because he wouldn't wake up, and I think he deserves to be driven to the school by a cop."

I stared and I'm sure my mouth hung open as she continued. "I don't know what to do with him. He's bigger than me, and I can't hit him."

I looked over at Max, who looked sullenly back at me. "Max, how old are you?"

"Eleven." He looked down at his feet.

"When's the last time your Mom gave you a spanking?"

"I don't know."

"Do you remember?"

"No."

"Well then I guess you need a spanking."

Max's big eyes looked up at me.

"You didn't get out of bed when your mother told you to, you missed the bus, and now a very busy police officer is here at your house dealing with you."

Max continued to look my way.

"You can't spank my son!" Tina's voice was belligerent and challenging.

"No, but you can. I don't care if he's six feet tall and weighs three hundred pounds, if he needs a spanking, you his mother, can give him one."

"Well, I don't think he needs a spanking for not getting out of bed."

"That may be, but maybe you need a citation for erroneous reporting to law enforcement (I made this charge up on the fly)."

Tina eyes began tearing up. I looked outside and saw the rain had turned into a drizzle. "Max, get your backpack and a jacket. You're walking to school." This came out in my no nonsense police voice.

Tina looked at me, "But it's raining, I'll just drive him to school. It's almost a mile and I don't want him to get wet."

Maybe Max was related to the Wicked Witch of the West. His mother surely was. They might melt with a little water. "Well, you should have thought of that before you called the police. I walked ten miles to school, barefoot uphill, both ways, when I was his age. A mile won't kill him (thank you Mom for these pearls of wisdom you passed on to me). If Max doesn't walk, I'm writing you the citation. You have five seconds to decide. I'm too busy to stand here but I'll be following Max as he walks, so I can see he gets to school safely. If you call me back here again for a ridiculous reason, you will get a ticket. Is that understood?"

Max and I walked out the door and I followed, in my patrol car, as he walked to school. While my car crept along behind, I called dispatch.

A "10-16" denotes a crazy person. With all the calls I took that first year, few were actually crazy, but many complainants were, like this one, dumber than a box of rocks. I asked the dispatchers to make note of the new code on my special sheet. I called it an "11-16" -- code for a stupidity call.

Surprisingly enough, Tina never filed a complaint and no further incorrigible juvenile calls came from her house while I was on duty.

Chapter 21

Staying in decent physical shape was becoming my nemesis. Between the exhaustion of learning a new job, the changing work shifts, the eating on the fly, and the too many hours sitting at my desk or in my car, I had to make extra effort to find opportunities for even minimal exercise. I decided to walk through the park one day while on patrol. I had just been home for lunch and needed to walk off the left overs I had eaten.

A big kid ran up to me, apparently drawn by my uniform. "My name's Theo, I have a police record, and I've been to juvie twice."

"How old are you?"

"Ten and if you don't watch it, I'll kick your ass. I punched Officer Stephens in the face."

Now how could I not like this kid?

"Well, if you punch me in the face I'll probably cry, but then I'll take you to jail."

"Okay, I just wanted you to know." Theo ran away from our one-minute conversation.

He looked about fourteen years old with a stocky build and strange looking face. I would find out later, his face was a direct result of fetal alcohol syndrome, and kids born like Theo had similar physical characteristics.

I finished my walk at the park, went into the office, and decided to do a little checking on Theo. I pulled up reports that mentioned his name and began reading.

Theo's adoptive parents Claude and Marilee Bishop had two other children. It didn't say if they were adopted but it did say Theo punched Officer Stephens in the face.

I read the entire report and realized Theo was trouble and police were called to his home many times. All I could find were the two arrests, so I guessed he hadn't lied to me.

In one report, Officer Stephens pulled his Taser (after Theo punched him in the face) but had not deployed it. Theo must be having a good streak because I hadn't heard his name since starting at the department.

My luck held for another month.

During that month, I was finally issued my Taser. I took Taser training at the academy, but Sgt. Spears made all the officers go through his training too. The guys teased me and wanted to know if I was "taking the ride" as it was called. It wasn't required, but the last thing I would do was act like a baby in front of them. Sgt. Spears gave six hours of training before I was Tased. There were four of us taking the class, but I was the only Officer from Small Town.

Before the main event, the training room began filling with non-trainees to see the electrifying experience (this meant my guys wanted to gawk). When it was time, my hand went up first. I knew what was coming and I just wanted to get it over with. Alex and Spike volunteered to get on either side of me. Sgt. Spears asked if I was ready.

"Yes."

I didn't even get a chance to take a breath before the Taser was deployed. God it hurt. Five seconds may not seem like a long time, but when 50,000 volts are entering your body, it takes forever. I was laid down face first on the matt as the Taser continued to shock me.

When it finished the guys were laughing and Spike got the honor of pulling one of the probes out of my ass cheek, while Alex pulled the other out of my upper back. I didn't even feel the hooked probes as they came out. After telling me that I took it like a man, the guys wandered off. The show was over

Then I could talk, I explained, "That's because if I took it like a woman, it would have lasted twelve hours like child birth. You pansies!"

Everyone laughed and I officially received my Taser.

About a week later, I was sitting in the squad room and looking through police catalogs for another pair of handcuffs. My vest had slots to fit four pairs and I carried a pair on my duty belt. I already had a silver pair and a black pair. I saw pink ones in a catalog. They were slightly bigger than average cuffs and liking the way they looked, I ordered them. When they finally arrived I gave them the honor of residing in the front cuff case holder on my belt. I kept the silver and black in my vest.

It was a busy morning and I went from call to call. Nothing major, but it kept me hopping. A little before noon, a call came in that a juvenile was wrecking his home and an officer was needed immediately. Somehow I knew this was Theo.

I arrived at the address dispatch gave me, and could hear yelling and crying as I ran to the front door. The yelling was so loud I didn't try knocking, just opened the door. The room was in shambles and a small woman with short brown hair was crying. I could hear a crashing sound coming from the back of the house.

"Theo's brother and sister are locked in a bedroom so he can't hurt them. He got mad at me and I told the other two kids to carry out the safety plan." She was wringing her hands as she spoke.

I registered what she was saying, a safety plan for fear of a ten year old.

"Do you have any weapons in the house?"

"Not guns, but we have knives in the kitchen. I don't think he has a knife, but he broke a lamp and he's using it to smash up the house."

"I need you to stay here and not come up behind me. Can you do that?"

"Yes."

I radioed that I needed backup and then walked slowly to the back of the house. I could hear glass breaking. I pulled my Taser.

Theo was standing on a single bed and hitting the wooden lamp post into the window.

"Theo, it's me, Officer Ivy. We met at the park." Theo stopped long enough to look at me."

"What the hell are you going to do? If you come any closer, I'll kill you."

"I don't want to Tase you. I need you to put the lamp down."

"Are you going to make me?"

"If I have to."

"What are you going to do?"

"Tase you." I kept my voice calm and steady.

"I bet it doesn't hurt and you're too afraid to do it."

I turned my Taser on and squared the red laser light on his chest. "I'm not counting. I'm just going to fire. Put the lamp down!" My voice was soft and in my mind I had already made the decision to fire. My backup had not arrived and I didn't feel as if I had another alternative.

To my surprise, Theo threw the wooden club to the ground and then turned his body toward me while he remained standing on the bed.

"What are you going to do now?" He was breathing heavily and his face was scrunched up. Sweat saturated the front of his shirt.

I placed my Taser back in its holster, "I'm taking you to juvenile detention."

"How are you going to do that? I can kick your ass even without my bat."

"Well you can try, but then when we're done fighting, I will place you in my boring silver handcuffs. I have three different colors and if you behave, I'll let you pick the color."

"What colors do you have?"

It was that easy. I could see his body deflating, "Pink, black and silver. Get down here and I'll let you choose."

Theo got off the bed and I pulled out the pink cuffs. Before I got to the black ones, he said he wanted pink. Theo turned around and I placed the cuffs on him. My hands were shaking.

I walked Theo past his mother and told her I was placing him in my patrol car and needed her to check on the other children.

My backup arrived as soon as I shut the door on Theo. I asked the officer to watch him, while I went back inside and spoke to his mother, Marilee.

The other two children were fine and I could see by the looks on their faces that this was a common occurrence in their house.

Marilee was still crying, "I just don't know what to do with him. I can't give him up, but that's what my husband wants. We thought we could help a child by adopting, but it's just not working. I'm afraid of him."

I really didn't know what to say. I took down her personal information and then took pictures of the destruction and issued her a victim's rights form.

"Thank you for not hurting him."

"You're welcome." With lead shoes, I walked back to my patrol car.

I decided to drive Theo directly to juvenile detention so there was no risk of his becoming violent at the police department. I looked into my rearview mirror and a pair of brown eyes looked back at me with a single tear rolling down his cheek.

"Will you tell anyone if I cry in the back of your car?" It was said belligerently.

"No, but I've never arrested a ten year old, so will you tell anyone if I cry?" I answered using his same tone.

"No."

Not another word was spoken.

I walked Theo into juvenile detention. He knew the guard by name. I removed his handcuffs and he told the guard he picked the pink ones out himself. The guard raised his eyebrows at me, but didn't say a word.

Theo had to sit on a cement bench after emptying his pockets. I searched him before placing him in my car, but left him with two items, when I discovered they couldn't hurt me. The pack of gum and Hot Wheels car were taken out of his pockets.

I finished filling out the booking paperwork and then walked over to Theo and put my hand out. He put his hand out to shake mine and I couldn't help myself, I hugged him. Theo hugged me back and said he was sorry.

"It's okay. I'll see you at the park." I walked out.

I cried that night. I knew I couldn't help everyone, but how do you give up on a ten year old kid. I couldn't. I wasn't sure how I felt about Theo's parents giving him back to the state, but I hoped they didn't. I also knew I wouldn't blame them because they had two other children to protect.

That night, I called P-Rod, my academy bud, and cried as I told him Theo's story. The next morning, I called juvenile detention and asked about Theo. The guard said he was already on probation and was being kept in detention. In one way this was a relief. His Mom needed a break, but I still felt bad for Theo.

I knew this wouldn't be the last I saw of Theo and I knew he wouldn't be the only juvenile I would shed tears over, but he was my first. I've taken a lot of ribbing for my pink handcuffs, but for this alone they were worth it.

***

I had Superior court on Monday. Charles Fellows, the man that punched me during a domestic abuse call, took a plea bargain. He agreed to eighteen months in prison and three years of probation. It was depressing. Only eighteen months for beating your wife half to death and punching a cop. I learned before the sentencing hearing that Rachel, his wife, would be lucky if he served a year. Luck kind of sucked sometimes.

Rachel and I had spoken together several times since her release from the hospital. I wouldn't exactly say we were friends, but we enjoyed each other's company. I guess the fact that her husband punched both of us gave us something in common. I looked over at Rachel as Charles was led away. She mouthed, "Thank you." But even with her words, it was still hard to feel justice was served.

Chapter 22

Every community has eccentrics -- people who like to do things their own way. But some people just like to leave a trail of chaos and anger in their wake, whenever and where ever possible. For Small Town PD, Maxine Brown had become one of those people.

When I started working at the department, Maxine was staying with her sister in Phoenix for the winter. It was the longest time the PD had ever been without an emergency call from her.

Two days after her return, I was the lucky officer to take her complaint. My first mistake was answering the office phone while the secretaries were busy on other phone lines.

"Small Town Police Department, how may I help you?"

"This is Ms. Brown and I need an officer at my home immediately."

"This is Officer Ivy, what is your location?"

"I don't want to talk to you! I want a real officer."

I kept my voice pleasant, "I am a real officer and I can't help you if I don't know where you live."

"You're not a real officer; you're some ignorant bitch that doesn't know her way around town. Do you know who I am young lady?"

My voice tightened subtly as I answered, "I am an officer and if you will tell me where you live I can help you. I don't have a clue who you are, but if you persist in calling me names, I will hang up the phone."

"You're one of those colored people aren't you?"

Now, how was I supposed to answer that? I have blond hair, blue eyes and very light skin. I still felt I had color, it just didn't show after a long winter. I knew exactly what she was asking, and that pissed me off more than being called an ignorant bitch. "Yes, I'm a colored person."

"Then put me on the phone with someone that is smarter than you. It shouldn't be too hard."

I looked around and saw Sandy at her desk and she no longer had a phone to her ear. I placed Ms. Brown on hold.

"Who is Ms. Brown?" I asked.

The look on Sandy's face said everything. I figured I had just upset the mayor's wife or someone of equal importance.

"Is that who's on the phone? Who does she want to speak with?"

"She wants a white male officer at her house immediately, but wouldn't give me her address."

"Every person in town knows where she lives. We just avoid it like the plague."

"That good huh? Well what should I do?"

"I'll give you directions to her house. Tell her an officer will be there shortly."

"You don't want to talk to her?"

"God no! I'm afraid of her. She calls me a lazy cow and has made tons of complaints against me."

"Perfect, what's the address?" I did as Sandy directed and then gently placed the receiver back in its cradle.

Right before I left, Sandy said, "Whatever you do, don't go into her house."

I arrived on scene, called in my location and then walked up the path leading to the house.

The woman who opened the door, was about seventy years old, 5'4", a hundred and fifty pounds with enormous breasts put on display in a low cut top and an extra heavy-duty pushup bra. Did I mention she was seventy? On her forehead was a rhinestone encrusted sun visor to match her outfit. But most disturbing of all was the cosmetic facial surgery that left her with an ear-to-ear grin that was wide enough to rival the Joker in the Batman and Robin movie, without using makeup.

"Who the hell are you?" said "Joker" Brown, as she looked me up and down.

"I'm Officer Ivy. What seems to be the problem Ms. Brown?"

"Well, are you going to stand out there or come in?" She stood back and opened the door wide.

I hesitated a moment, remembering Sandy's warning, but entered anyway. The house was astounding. I had never seen so many figurines. Every possible surface was covered. There seemed to be a theme with each display, angels on one end table, dancing poodles on another.

"Don't touch anything." she warned, "I have no idea how clumsy you are and if you're as bad as Sandy Dunn, that cow, I won't invite you in again."

I was enraptured by the glass displays and didn't think to stick up for Sandy.

"Are you just going to stand there and gawk all day or are you going to do your job?"

I dutifully took out my notebook and pen. "What seems to be the problem?"

"Piss!"

"Uh, piss?"

"Yes, my neighbor's cat continues to piss on the hood of my car. The piss rolls down the windshield and I'm sick of cleaning it off. Has a cat ever pissed on your car?"

"No ma'am, where is your car?"

"It's in the garage."

"The cat gets into your garage?"

"They don't make cops very bright now-days do they?"

"Bright enough that we don't let cats piss on our cars." I just couldn't help myself.

"Oh, you think you're so smart in your blue uniform and shiny badge. I guess I'll need to tell you how to do your job. Now, take your fat ass and march it next door. I won't expect any speed because obviously that's beyond you, I won't expect brains either. Go tell my neighbor if their cat pisses on my car one more time, I'll hang it from a tree by its neck."

I stood there and gaped for a moment. Finally, I pulled myself together and replied, "I won't issue a threat for you, I have no proof that her cat peed on your car. If you want to show me the car, I can take pictures. Have you actually seen the cat on your vehicle?" I refused to give in to her biting remarks and lose my cool. But I worked to keep my tone level.

Ms. Brown walked over to her phone, watching me the entire time, picked up the receiver and dialed three numbers. Then spoke into the phone, "My emergency is that I have a dingbat in my house and I need another officer to remove her. Now!"

Ms. Brown had called 911 on me. I turned around, walked out the front door, and went to stand beside my car. I called dispatch on my radio and told them I was outside and to please send a supervisor to my location. I could hear laughing in the background.

Sgt. Spears arrived within ten minutes, but it seemed like an hour. Ms. Brown must have been peeking out her window because she was outside her door and in Sgt. Spears' face two seconds after he pulled up.

"I want that woman fired. I don't ever want her on my property again. Do you understand me? And if you don't fire her, I'll see that you're axed too."

"Now calm down Ms. Brown, what seems to be the problem."

She looked close to tears, but I wasn't fooled.

"Dora Longberger's cat uses my car for a litter box. The cat stands on top and relieves itself. The urine runs down the front window and I know it's going to ruin the paint. I've asked this woman," she pointed at me, "to speak with Dora, but all I got was rudeness along with a smart mouth. Is asking for help, to keep my car from being destroyed, too much to hope for around here? Aren't police here to protect and serve? I didn't think departments were allowed to hire fat people as officers. Boy the world has changed. Back in my day, if you had an emergency a police officer knew how to take care of business and protect you. All this woman could do, to stop a bad guy, is fall on him. I bet she's a lawsuit waiting to happen. Now stop standing there gawking. Do something!"

I couldn't help it. I was inching toward my car door trying to get away. With a gentle voice, Sgt. Spears began soothing the disgruntled bitc--ah woman, but it had little impact. I wasn't sure what to do. The police academy and field training neglected to teach me how to deal with the Joker.

Sgt. Spears finally looked at me and said to follow him. We went to Dora Longberger's house and knocked. She opened the door, carrying a baby on one hip, with another child holding her t-shirt and standing slightly behind her.

"May I help you?" She asked.

Sgt. Spears did the talking, "We've had a complaint from your neighbor, Ms. Brown. She told us your cat has been getting on her car and peeing on the window."

Dora rolled her eyes and sighed, "Hercules hates that woman. I think she puts poison out in the neighborhood because cats and dogs seem to die around here. My cat is old and smarter than average, but

I had no idea he could pee down a car window. I'm not sure what to do. I don't want her killing him. Is she sure Hercules is the culprit?"

"She says it's been happening for a while. Would it be possible to keep Hercules in for a while and let things calm down?"

"Yes, I'll talk to my husband and we'll try to keep the cat in."

"Thank you, we'll get out of your hair and let you get on with your day."

While this conversation was going on, the little boy was looking at me and gave a shy wave. I waved back and he buried his head in his mother' shirt.

We walked to the street and Sgt. Spears told me he was leaving and I needed to inform Ms. Brown of the conversation with her neighbor.

"You can't be serious, she called 911 on me."

"I'll meet you back at the PD and we'll discuss things, but yes, you need to go tell her we took care of her problem. Put emphasis on '*we*'."

With that, Sgt. Spears climbed in his vehicle and sped off. He didn't squeal his tires, but it was the fastest I had seen him drive. I walked up to the door, knocked and then stood and waited. Ms. Brown didn't answer. I rang the doorbell and waited some more. Still no answer. Maybe she fell and broke her neck. I knew I couldn't get that lucky. I knocked again and was startled when the door was suddenly thrown open.

"Get off my property or I'm calling the police!" I guess she meant her idea of the real police.

"The cat problem has been taken care of." I said it nicely then turned my back to Ms. Brown and walked away.

I was seething. I had never been a skinny person, but I was far from fat. Sandy wasn't fat either. She was beautiful. That old woman looked like a demon from hell.

I drove back to the department and went to Sgt. Spears' office. The door was open and he and the Chief were laughing. I stood still until they noticed me and then waited as they laughed harder.

Finally, Chief Varnett managed to get out, "This is the best news I've had in weeks. Where were you last year when we really needed you? Sgt. Spears will tell you about our solution to this problem because I've got a meeting in five minutes." He walked out of the room still chuckling.

Sgt. Spears was finally able to control himself but had to wipe his eyes before pointing to a chair. I got the message and sat.

"We've put up with that old biddy for years. The other officers do whatever she says and dread going near her. This is the first time an officer has been rude or fought back at her insults. Congratulations Ivy, you have now become Ms. Brown's personal officer. If you're on duty and she needs assistance, it's your call. Tell her there is no one else available. I'll handle things when she complains. Just do your job and take care of her problems if you can. Are we clear?" The gleam in his eyes was unmistakable.

What could I say? Chain of command and span of control had just been forced down my throat. What a day. It didn't take long for the guys to hear about the consequences of my run-in with Ms. Brown. Everyone thought it was hilarious.

The next day, I had thirty-two messages from Ms. Brown on my desk. They weren't real and it must have taken the night guys a while to write them all. The messages varied from, "I looked in the mirror and scared myself." to, "I need Officer Ivy to unclog my toilet; I think the neighbor's cat fell in."

Ha ha! They thought they were so funny. I gathered up the notes and placed them in a file in my drawer. I then went out to begin my patrol shift and prayed it would be a long time before Ms. Brown called again.

Chapter 23

During my first six-month on the street, Benito landed fifty pounds of marijuana in a simple "no turn signal" traffic stop. A large theft ring was operating in town and we used every officer on surveillance for over a month. I put my time in but was in Phoenix, visiting my daughters, when the bust finally went down. My fellow officers made me proud to be part of their team.

During that same time, I started to become more involved in sex crimes investigations. Much to the relief of my co-workers, who wanted nothing to do with child molesters. Spike and Alex were amazing at the interviews, but no one at Small Town PD "liked" dealing with sex crimes.

When my chance finally came to attend my first police training since graduating from the academy, I didn't voluntarily sign up. I was ordered to attend Basic Sex Crimes Investigations. Alex told me I would have a great time and meet others in the field of law enforcement, but I pictured my academy experience and was thoroughly terrified. I continued to stress over it as the class drew closer. The training information paperwork said I needed to wear business attire or my uniform. I decided to play it safe and go with the uniform.

The class was in Phoenix and the course would be Monday through Friday. I left home on Sunday afternoon and found the hotel without a problem. I saw other marked police cars in the parking lot but didn't see anyone that jumped out and shouted, "I'm a cop."

My paperwork said I would have a roommate but when I checked with the receptionist, she told me there was no one else assigned to my room. I woke up at 0500 and began getting ready. I had to be at the training facility at 0800 hours. I passed a Starbucks on my way to the hotel, the previous evening, so I made a stop before getting on the freeway and heading to class.

I arrived thirty minutes early and sat in my car enjoying my venti non-fat mocha with whip. There is no Starbucks in Small Town so this was a real treat. People started arriving and I realized none of them were in uniform. I saw everything from slacks to jeans. Not one other person dressed in their patrol attire. It was the opposite of having a dream where you're naked, but nearly as embarrassing.

I got out of my unit and went into class. Everyone was finding seats so I grabbed a chair close to the front. There was a large three inch binder for each student. I looked around, wondering if we needed to stand at attention when our instructor came in. I was having academy flashbacks and just wanted to be back on patrol.

The instructors finally entered. No one stopped talking. I wasn't sure what to do. The first trainer introduced himself and the room quieted. His name was Pete. He told us about his background as a sex crimes detective and told us, on the last two days of training, he would show us some actual case studies. The next instructor introduced himself; then asked us to stand one at a time, say where we were from, and how long we had been officers.

I was in the second row and when it was my turn, I stood up and gave the required information. Before the next person could introduce himself, Pete interjected, "It wasn't hard to figure out you were a rookie. Go out tonight and buy yourself human clothes if you didn't bring any. Be comfortable and enjoy yourself."

After that, I did relax. And I wore different clothes.

Certified officer trainings were very different from the academy. There was no homework for this class, though sometimes in more advanced training it is necessary. There was no test at the end. I learned so much without being yelled at or put under any other kind of stress.

The last two days were my favorites. True to his word, Pete showed videos of confessions by serial rapists. I was enthralled. Once these creeps started talking they didn't stop. They wanted to brag about their crimes. Their brains worked much like that of a serial killer. A few of the case studies had rapists that murdered their victims.

There were two comments I will never forget. One of the rapists was asked why he raped an eighty years old woman. He answered, "She had a hole." That was it. If we could have seen behind his eyes, the space for a soul would have been empty.

The other comment was the fact almost every rapist became a serial rapist or already is. This goes the same for child molesters. They don't stop until they are caught and put away. If they get out, they will do it again and again. It was scary and eye opening.

I tagged along with a few of my classroom tablemates for lunches. Two of the guys were also new officers. One told me he wore his uniform to his first training too. They invited me out to dinner on Thursday night. We went to a cowboy bar complete with an electronic bull. The guys were nuts and after beer started flowing they couldn't resist taking a turn. One after another the bull threw them off. They kept ribbing me to give it a try. They were out of their minds and I told them about my horse throwing me and my subsequent broken hip. No thank you. I didn't care if I looked like a tough cop or not, I passed on the bull.

I ended up being the one to drive us back to our hotel since I wasn't drinking. I walked into class the next morning with a smile on my face. The other guys walked in with a green tint to theirs. They were hurting. Friday, during police training, is hangover day. I haven't attended any class that hasn't followed this golden rule.

Class was released at 1400 hours, and I spent the night in Phoenix with my youngest daughter, Cassie. The next morning I got up and drove home.

***

I was far from being a sex crimes expert but the next child molestation case I responded to wound up being assigned to me. Alex and Spike were busy working a series of burglaries and Spike told me to call him if I had questions or needed help.

My victim was a thirteen year old girl. She told her mom that her step-father was giving her presents so he could touch her bottom. I had to drive mother and daughter to a professional forensic interviewer that was available an hour's drive from Small Town.

Neither the Mom nor child talked very much. I had strict instructions to not bring up the case in front of my victim.

I arrived at the Center and spoke to the specialist and a social worker first. I told them it was my first time at a forensic interview and they made me feel comfortable and walked me through their procedure.

I would sit in a small room with a two way mirror to observe the interview. I was to take notes and before the interview concluded, the interviewer would privately ask if I needed additional information from the child.

As good as my training was, it did not prepare me for what I heard when this child started talking about her life.

Her name was Julie and her tiny voice told the story of a monster living under the same roof as she, her mother, and her brother. The forensic interview process did not allow for Julie's Mom to sit in on the interview. I told her I would speak with her privately before we left. Her husband was at work and did not know what was happening.

Julie described how her step-father molested her. She painted a picture of text book "grooming." Child molesters seem to have built in knowledge to get them what they want. They start slowly and build up to their objective. In order to keep the child from telling anyone, they make them feel guilty and responsible for what's happening. These monsters hunt our children and they are masters at their craft.

After the interview, I sat down with Julie's Mom and told her the gist of the conversation. She cried and her hands shook as she told me how guilty she felt for bringing him into her children's lives. Her son was at his grandmother's house and she asked me to drop her and Julie off there. She wanted Ted Philips in jail as soon as we could get him.

I called Alex and explained what I had. He told me to get back to town and the three of us (he included Spike) would go pick up the "son of a bitch".

I dropped Julie and her Mom off and met up with Spike and Alex at the station. It was obvious Spike was in charge which didn't bother me at all. It was a relief.

Ted usually arrived home from work at 1730 hours. My job, while driving Alex's unmarked car, was to park on the road by Ted's place of employment and wait for his car. I would follow when he left, but stay back to avoid arousing suspicion. Alex and Spike would wait at the house. When Ted turned onto his home street, I was to drive past and go around the block. I would then enter the street from the other direction to cut Mr. Philips off if he decided to drive away when he saw the two cops waiting for him.

Julie's Mom had given me a description of Ted's truck and I spotted it when it pulled onto the main road. I followed two vehicles back. I called Alex on my cell and told him we were on our way.

Everything went like clockwork. It was frustrating to drive around the block and miss the fun. When I arrived, Ted was climbing into the back of Alex's unmarked car. Spike radioed dispatch and told them they had one male passenger, which pissed me off. My suspect was a passenger and not in custody. I remembered the earlier lessons taught by Spike but it was hard to remember the "why's" when I wanted this guy so badly.

I drove to the station and watched as Ted was placed in the interview room. Alex and I monitored the interview from his office. We sat and waited but I had no chance to ask Alex questions. He said to hold on and watch a pro at work.

First, Spike asked Ted if he wanted a soda. Ted said yes and Spike went and got one. I tapped my foot impatiently. Spike came back and handed Ted the soda.

"If you need to use the restroom just let me know. Soda goes right through me. This isn't like the movies where the cops are assholes. You just let me know if you need anything."

"Okay."

"So where do you work?" Spike already knew the answer.

"I work for Browning Construction."

"Well, do they at least pay you? They don't pay us shit here."

"Yeah, the pay's not bad."

"Do you work a four or five day workweek?"

"It depends on the job. They let us work four if we're not on deadline."

"So what do you do in your off time?"

"I don't know; this or that. I tinker on engines some."

"Hey, I have a 1975 Harley-Davidson Sportster. It's sweet and I tinker on that thing all the time. You ever work on a Harley?"

"Yeah, my brother has one. It's newer so he doesn't bring it by often, but I changed the oil a few months ago. I took it for a ride and that thing can move."

"I bet all the chicks were watching as you drove by?"

It was hard to tell through the computer screen, but I think Ted blushed. Spike gave him a pat on the back and told him he understood that old ladies cramp the style.

"So Ted, before I ask any questions, I like to read everybody their Miranda rights. People see it done on TV and they don't think anything is official unless I read their rights to them."

Spike began reading Miranda.

Ted said he understood his rights and Spike then went on and asked Ted about his brother's motorcycle. They continued to talk bikes for another fifteen minutes.

I was past impatient and began walking around the small office. Alex only smiled and told me this was the best thing I would ever learn.

Finally Spike asked, "So tell me about your family."

"My wife's name is Miranda. I have a son Conner and a daughter Julie."

"Are they your biological children?"

"Well no, but I'm the only dad they've ever known. Their real father is a SOB and they don't have any contact with him."

"So, do you get along with your wife?"

"Is that what this is about?"

"No, this is actually about your step-daughter Julie."

"What did she say?"

Alex whispered to me, "See how he doesn't ask if Julie's okay or been hurt. He just asks what she said."

Spike went on, "Well, she told Officer Ivy a few things and we're interested in hearing your side."

"What did she say?" Ted asked again, but he had a slightly wild-eyed look now and it was obvious he was getting nervous.

"She told Officer Ivy that you've been buying some things for her."

"I like buying her stuff. Can't a father buy something nice for his daughter? Is that against the law now?" His voice was becoming belligerent.

Again Alex whispered in my ear, "See how he attacks about buying things for his daughter. Spike has this guy."

"Hey, there's nothing wrong with buying pretties for your daughter. You and I both know that."

"I've never touched my daughter. I wouldn't do that. I'm not a sick bastard."

Alex whispered in my ear, "You're just a stupid one."

"So you never touched your step-daughter?"

"No, I told you I didn't."

"But I never asked if you did…" Spike let his words sink in before he continued, "Do you know why she would tell Officer Ivy about bad things?"

"She's just getting to that age. You know, bitchy. Wants my attention all the time and I'm a hard worker. I keep a roof over my family's heads and it takes long hours."

"I can understand that. I also know what thirteen year old girls are like. You know, just coming into their sexual maturity. I haven't met your daughter, but I know what they're like. Girls, now-days, develop breasts when they're ten. It's all those hormones in chicken and milk."

"Yeah, Julie drinks lots of milk and she really likes chicken. I didn't know that's what caused it."

"I think those hormones should be outlawed. They make our little girls become all sexual and everything. It's not right. I don't think you're a bad guy Ted and I just want to know your side of the story."

Ted thought for a moment, and then gave his first explanation, "Well, Julie was jumping on the bed a few weeks ago, and I told her to stop and get off. She asked me to come over to the bed. I sat down on the side and my hand was resting like this." Ted pulled his hand up from his side and had two of his fingers sticking up. "Julie jumped on my fingers. I didn't know she didn't have panties on, but she seemed to like it."

I couldn't help my reaction and feeling sick, I jumped out of my chair. Alex grabbed the sleeve of my uniform. "Keep watching, don't freak out Ivy. We have one felony count so far. Spike wants them all."

"Is that the only time you got a finger inside her?"

"No, she liked it. She was always asking me to touch her."

"How old do you think she was when it happened the first time?"

"I don't know maybe eight or nine."

"Did you just stick your finger in or did you start by doing other things?"

"Julie liked to get in bed with me. I would rub her back, but she was always rubbing her body against me. I couldn't help it. I would get hard. I told her not to do it, but she said she liked it. I didn't know how to make her stop."

"So, is this something she did all the time?"

"About once or twice a week. I tried to tell my wife, but she wouldn't listen."

Alex's whisper again, "See how first he blamed Julie and now he's blaming his wife?"

Spike continued, "So who do you think should be punished here?"

"I guess probably me. I'm the adult. I should have stopped Julie from behaving that way."

"So you understand I need to arrest you?"

"Yes, but can I call my wife and Julie to apologize?"

I couldn't believe I heard him right and shock was evident on my face.

"No, I don't think that would be a good idea right now. You need to talk to a lawyer and see what he thinks."

"Okay, do you know how long I'll be in? I have bills to pay and can't afford to miss work."

"Nope, it's not up to me. It's up to a judge. Hold on a minute and let me grab some paperwork."

Spike walked out of the interview room and closed the door behind him. He walked into the office and gave us each a high five, "That's the way it's done Ivy. If you want to catch the bastards you need to make them think you're as sick as they are. Now, you're going in there, handcuffing that bastard, and filling out the booking paperwork. I'm going home to sterilize myself in disinfectant. Then I'm going to drink myself silly. It's the only thing that works."

I felt my rage deflating. Spike was amazing. Ted would go away for a long time. I felt bad for Spike and I could see why he wanted to get drunk. It was hard to understand my own feelings. When I placed my pink handcuffs on Ted, I was angry but cuffing him gave me a sense of peace. I felt a sense of accomplishment when the jail door slammed behind him.

I was at every hearing until Ted finally took a twenty-five year plea. Julie's mother was at each hearing too. She came up and hugged me after they took Ted away for the last time. I admired Julie's mom for putting her child first.

Even sentenced to twenty-five years in prison Ted didn't get what he deserved. Maybe his prison mates would give it to him.

Chapter 24

Summers in Small Town are beautiful. People think of Arizona as one hundred and ten degrees Fahrenheit, plus. Small Town usually tops out in the low nineties at its hottest, but evenings go down into the fifties. There is little or no humidity. We live for summer.

In August, I celebrated eight months as an officer. One of our guys left for a job with a bigger agency in the city and we were sending a newbie to the academy. I hoped for a female, but none applied. When the new cadet graduated, I would be at my one-year mark as an officer and no longer the rookie. I couldn't wait.

The new guy, Joe Warling, was stuck with me for two days before he left to begin his journey at the academy. He accompanied me to my calls, frequently telling me how he always wanted to be an officer and couldn't wait to help people.

I remembered being that naïve. It wasn't even that long ago. I now knew I helped put bad guys in jail. A few people appreciated it, but most never even knew. I admit before I was an officer, I had no thought of crime in Small Town. I lived in la-la land like my neighbors. Joe went on and on about what kind of cop he would be. He told me he couldn't wait to kick some ass. I laughed and told him the academy would kick his ass first, and if he survived, he could come back and do lots of paperwork. It was obvious Joe didn't believe me.

I got a call from dispatch while Joe was telling me what a wonderful cop he would be. A woman reported a snake in her house.

I drove to the address and Joe followed me to the front door. A woman, close to my age, answered and told us her name was Cynthia. She invited us inside. Pointing to a couch, she explained that the snake slithered underneath. The house was dark, with a small amount of light coming in through the dirty living room window. The inside smelled musty and a little rank. I was looking around as I approached the couch. I like snakes, but I wanted to know where this one was, so it didn't surprise me. We didn't see too many rattlesnakes in our area, but better safe than sorry.

Next to the couch along the baseboard of the wall, I saw a thick black trail. I looked closer and saw mouse droppings everywhere.

"Do you have a problem with mice?" Duh!

"Yeah, I can't get rid of them. They're in the walls."

I told Joe to pick up the back of the couch to help me tip it forward. Joe didn't look happy but did as I asked. We brought the couch forward and sure enough there was a medium sized gopher snake underneath. It moved in Joe's direction and he screamed like crazy, let go of his side of the couch, and jumped back.

"It's a gopher snake Joe and perfectly harmless." I turned to Cynthia, "Are you afraid of snakes?"

"Not particularly, as long as they're not poisonous."

"Mice carry Hantavirus and it's more dangerous than anything you can catch from a non-poisonous snake. If I were you, I would call an exterminator, but if you're not going to do that then just leave the snake be. It won't hurt you and it will take care of some of your mice. I might add a cat or two to my family, the snake's not big enough to hurt them. If you decide to notify an exterminator, call me, and I'll come get your snake."

"I don't want it in bed with me or anything."

"It would only do that if it was cold and we have a few months of warm weather before you need to worry. I don't have a problem getting the snake now, but I'd be more worried about the mice."

We left the house, minus the snake, and Cynthia had a new pet.

Once we were back in my patrol car and clear of the house, Joe asked, "How do people live that way?"

I was learning a lot in this job. The way people lived had stopped surprising me. I saw garbage, knee-high, throughout homes. I couldn't believe the number of people I dealt with that didn't bathe regularly or brush their teeth (provided they had any). It was part of the job. I was getting used to seeing people at their worst. I tried to explain it to Joe, but he was still set on helping people and changing our town for the better. He thought he would ride in on his white horse and get rid of the drug dealers and child molesters. Didn't he know these elements of life regrettably provided job security for us cops? We would pound away and continue doing our jobs, but unfortunately we made only a small dent in crime.

I was becoming jaded.

A few days after he left for the academy, I went out to lunch with Spike and Alex. They made fun of Joe for being wet behind the ears.

"God, I was like that too." I said.

Spike looked at me, "You were never like that. Yes, you had a concept of what being a cop was but you learned, real quick, to throw that shit out the window. You had life experience, kids, been married and lived in the real world, not just the world controlled by mommy and daddy. I wish all the cops we hire could be like that. Joe will be a dick with a badge on the end. What's rule number five Ivy?"

I groaned, "Rule number five, two things will get you fired in this job; your dick and her pussy."

Spike slapped me on the back. He was proud. I was hoping no one else in the restaurant heard me.

***

I wish I could say that after eight months on the street, I stopped doing stupid rookie things. Just when I thought I was becoming a good cop, a bright light would flash in front of my eyes and I had to wake up from my fantasy.

In September, I went back on the night shift. I had been on days for the past three months. Nights have a different feel. Jared Stephens was on duty with me and I was less than thrilled. When I was out with the other officers we would sometimes ride together. Stephens and I never rode in the same vehicle.

I hadn't seen Alex in a while and he came in at the beginning of my shift. He told me he was working a big case. I got a call from dispatch and had to leave before I found out about the "big case" Alex had.

I went to my call and handled a minor theft. It was an ex-girlfriend squabble. I made a call to the ex and then did a civil standby while my victim retrieved his DVD's. We handle a lot of these type calls. It's part of the job.

I began patrolling town and getting into the feel of the dark streets. At around 2300 hours, I heard Alex on his radio, yelling for backup. I had no idea where to find him and was not aware he was still working. I asked dispatch to give me the address but they could only give me his vicinity. My heart was pumping as I sped his way. Stephens arrived two seconds behind me. We both had our guns out as we jumped from our vehicles. The night was quiet. Stephens took the lead and told me to go north and he would go south. We were in a neighborhood where the houses were closer together than most districts in Small Town. I walked to back fences and shined my flashlight over. I was scared to death for Alex. We had received no further communication from him.

About six houses down, I heard Alex yell, "Let me see your hands, let me see your hands!" I ran toward the sound of his voice and yelled into my lapel mike that Alex was north. I rounded the corner of the last house on the street and he was standing six feet away from a man curled up on the ground. I saw a large hunting knife by the man's knee. The knife was huge. The street light illuminated everything.

Alex was breathing hard. He again yelled, "Let me see your hands."

My eyes never left the knife.

It's hard to describe the feeling that comes over you when you know you might have to shoot your gun. It's like a final resignation that this is it. I had no doubt, if the man went for the knife, I would shoot him.

Alex put his gun back in his holster and drew his Taser. We knew, in a situation such as this, that it was better to have lethal and non-lethal force available. I was okay with Alex having the Taser; I wanted my gun in my hand.

Alex turned on the Taser and the laser light appeared on the man. He suddenly pushed himself backwards. My eyes continued to stay on the knife and I felt a moment of relief that he was further away from his weapon. It was just a moment because a short pop sounded and at the same time Alex fired his Taser. As the man screamed and rolled on the ground, I could clearly see a gun lying by his hands. He had fired the gun at Alex. I had tunnel vision on the knife and hadn't recognized the pop as a .22 caliber gunshot.

Alex was yelling, "Cover me, cover me," as he ran at the man, kicked the gun away, placed him on his stomach and put cuffs on his hands. Everything happened in less than five seconds.

I moved to the side so I had a clear shot. Stephens ran up on the scene and covered our suspect too. Alex told me to call Sgt. Spears and get him to our location. The man continued screaming. I was worried about Alex.

My training said, during incidents like this, some cops don't always know they've been shot because the adrenaline masks the pain.

"Are you all right?" I asked.

"Yeah, I felt the bullet go by my ear. You did good. Now holster your gun, everything is okay."

I holstered my gun. I didn't feel good. Alex could have been killed. I used my cell phone to call the sergeant.

We searched the man and left him on the ground, then collected the gun and knife. Sgt. Spears arrived and had the honor of removing the probes from the suspect that Alex identified as Frank Monty. The screaming got a little higher pitched when the last probe was removed. Talk about a sissy; willing to shoot someone but screams over Taser probes. He was lucky I didn't shoot him. He could easily have been beyond screaming.

I moved my squad car closer to the scene so we could use it for transport. I then helped load Frank into the back seat. Alex jumped in with me and we drove to the police department. Frank wanted his lawyer so there would be no interview. Alex told me to fill out the booking packet. What usually took twenty minutes was short and sweet because Frank wouldn't answer any booking questions. I wrote "refused" at the top of each page and then Alex and I took him to jail.

We dropped Frank off and drove away. Alex told me to drive to the park. My hands on the steering wheel were trembling. I did as directed. When I parked, I placed my hands over my face and began crying.

"What's wrong Suzie?" Alex never called me Suzie. I was Ivy.

I removed my hands but wouldn't look at him, "I never saw the gun. I only saw the knife. I should have shot him."

"Why do you say you should have shot him?"

"He shot at you, with a gun, and he could have killed you. I was your backup." My voice was angry.

"I didn't see the gun either or I never would have put my own gun away and pulled my Taser. You don't think I feel stupid right now? We could both be dead."

"I didn't fire after he shot at you. I barely even heard the pop and had no idea what it was."

"Then why should you have shot your gun? Do you know how much paperwork is involved when you shoot? It's bad enough when you use the Taser. The only difference is that you would have some time off with pay, so maybe you should have shot him." Alex was doing what Alex did best. He was putting things into perspective and also trying to lighten the mood. He went on, "I always thought you would cry if you did shoot someone and here you are crying because you didn't. You never cease to amaze me."

I couldn't help but give a short laugh. "I just can't believe all I could see was that knife."

"Well, it was a big-ass knife. I didn't want to get cut with it. Now stop your bawling and let's get some food before we begin the mountains of paperwork. I hate it when someone makes me Tase them."

Alex told me, while we ate dinner, about how he came to be on the corner holding Frank at gunpoint. Frank was the front guy for stolen property throughout the county. He had different people pawning and selling the hot merchandise. Alex arrived at the stash house and approached Frank. Frank ran. Alex said he called for backup as soon as Frank pulled up in front of the house, but then chased him on foot for about a mile.

When we finished eating, Alex had me drop him at his car and followed me back to the police department. He called and told Stephens to watch the house until we got a search warrant. I knew Stephens wouldn't be happy and that was the only thing that lightened my mood.

It was three hours before we had a signed warrant and were able to get inside the house. Again, Stephens did guard duty and I helped with the search. Several other officers were called in so things went fast. We recovered thousands of dollars' worth of stolen property. Alex was the cop of the year in my eyes.

I was exhausted when I arrived home, but couldn't fall asleep. I kept thinking about the gun and feeling stupid. What would I have done if Alex died? I knew I needed to learn from this experience. I felt like the rookie I was.

Chapter 25

Life as a cop never seemed boring to me. Days were turning into weeks and weeks into months. Before I knew it, I was celebrating my one year anniversary of graduating from the police academy. I think I was the only one who took notice since there was no mention of my one year performance review.

The day of my anniversary was cold like my first official day on the job. I was thinking about Mr. Piskett and his big-ass rock when a call came in from dispatch. The dispatcher said that a woman reported that her dog bit a male subject. I could hear the dispatchers laughing in the background.

The men and women in dispatch loved to gossip, and they always had the best information in town. I took donuts and coffee to them at least once a month and felt that might get me an explanation for their hilarity. When I cleared this call, I would drive by and find out why they were laughing.

I arrived at the scene, and walked up to a white, one story block house. It wasn't overly attractive, but wasn't a junk pile either. A woman, who appeared to be in her early thirties, came to the door. She didn't seem happy to see me. I introduced myself and she said her name was Kelly Gaylord.

"Look, my husband is an asshole and didn't want me to call the cops, but I want an official record of this. I don't want you touching my dog. She has all her shots and she's my protection. I'm glad you're female because my husband deserves this."

I was slightly confused, but if I learned anything this past year, it was to prioritize. "Does your husband need an ambulance?"

"Probably, but I wanted a police report first."

"Where is your husband?"

"In our bedroom, he has ice on the bite, but I don't think it's helping."

"I need to see him." Before I followed her, I asked, "Where's the dog?"

"I put Chewbacca in the back yard."

I followed Kelly to the back bedroom. Her husband was lying on his side, curled up tightly, with a towel over his midsection. From what I could see, he had nothing on but the towel. I noticed a pair of, what appeared to be boxer shorts, lying beside him. They were covered in blood. His eyes were barely open and it was obvious he was in pain.

"Hi Mr. Gaylord, I'm Officer Ivy. I need to talk to you and see if you need an ambulance."

Mr. Gaylord mumbled something, but I couldn't hear what it was. I stepped closer to the bed. "I'm sorry but I couldn't hear you."

Between clenched teeth I heard, "Her damn dog bit off my dick." Mr. Gaylord shoved the towel aside when he said this. The area in question was covered with an ice pack and blood was covering his midsection.

I don't think I've ever moved quite so fast. I jumped back at least four feet.

Okay, one year ago I started this job. I was told I would eventually be able to handle any call that came in, sort through the bullshit and make snap decisions. The bullshit in this case was a guy with his dick bit off and the snap decision was calling an ambulance. I also realized why dispatch had been laughing. I wasn't calling this over the radio so I took out my cell phone and did what any person faced with this situation would do.

I called 911.

"911 What is your emergency?"

"This is Officer Ivy; I need an ambulance at 2142 E. Butler Dr. I have a male approximately 30 years old. His penis was bitten off by a dog named Chewbacca. He is conscious and speaking to me."

"Please hold."

I hung up the phone. I could hear the "call out" for the ambulance on my radio. I asked Kelly to pack a bag for her husband, who was letting out loud moans from the bed. I pretty much ignored him. I had three children, was certified in first aid, but this one was beyond me. If he was making noise he was alive.

The ambulance arrived and I cleared out of their way. I had never been so relieved to see the emergency crew. They removed the ice. There was a lot of blood and I wasn't sure what I was actually looking at. It could have been a small penis or a large penis missing a big piece.

John Henly was on the crew and he was one of my favorite emergency medical techs. "Have you looked for the missing appendage?" He asked with a straight face.

Wow, I hadn't thought of that. I turned to Kelly, "Did Chewbacca eat it?"

"I don't know, I just pulled him off and Stan fell back on the bed. I cut his boxers off so I could see the damage." She had a smirk on her face.

Oh goody, I was going to go and search for a penis. I asked Kelly if there was some place she could put Chewbacca while I checked the back yard.

"The only person my dog doesn't like is him." Kelly said as she pointed to her husband, who just groaned some more.

I didn't argue. I love big dogs. If Chewbacca gave me any trouble, I could use my Taser.

I followed Kelly out the back door. Chewbacca came out of his dog house and ran to her. He was an eighty pound pit bull. He walked over to me and I let him sniff my legs, keeping my hands up. After a sniff or two I placed my hand down in front of him. Chewbacca rubbed his head under it and I gave him the desired pat. I had my flashlight in my other hand and I started shining it around the yard. We were standing under the porch light and I could see a few streaks of blood on Chewbacca's muzzle.

While I searched, I asked Kelly to tell me what happened.

"I got Chewbacca as a puppy. My husband abused him from the beginning. Chewbacca hates him, but he's always been afraid of him too. Tonight, Stan had a few beers and then wanted me to drive to the store and get more. I told him no and went back to the bedroom. Chewbacca was there with me. Stan came behind me and before I could close the door, he grabbed my arm and called me a bitch. Chewbacca growled and Stan kicked him. I told Stan not to kick my dog and he turned around and hit me. That's when Chewbacca attacked. I think he's just as fed up as I am. I had to pull him off. I've never seen Chewbacca act like that, but he was only protecting me. I've had it with Stan, and penis or no penis he's not coming home. I hope Chewbacca ate the damn thing."

I was kind of hoping the same thing. I mentally slapped myself. "Do you have any marks from Stan hitting and grabbing you?"

Kelly put her right arm out and I used my flashlight for illumination. I could see the perfect outline of a handprint on her upper arm. I turned her in the direction of the light, but I couldn't see anything else.

"I don't even know if Stan connected with the punch. Chewbacca attacked so fast it's hard to remember."

"I need to get pictures of your arm and I need to get a statement from Stan, but I will probably charge him with assault under the domestic violence statute. I would advise you to seek an order of protection from the court, especially if you're not allowing him back to the house. Now would you mind helping me look, I don't know what Stan's penis looks like." We both laughed, though it was shameful of me.

The ambulance loaded Stan and took him to the hospital. Fifteen minutes later, dispatch radioed to see if I was still on scene. I told them I was searching for a missing appendage. This got more muffled chuckles over the air and I knew I was in for a day of jokes from dispatch and the department.

I finally cleared the scene and called John Henly, telling him I needed to interview Stan. John told me Stan would not be up to it for some time. He laughed when he said "up to it" so yes, I got the pun.

I drove to dispatch and couldn't help laughing along with them. It was only the girls working tonight and the Lorena Bobbit jokes were flying.

"We can't believe you said the dog's name over the radio. Chewbacca, is that for real?"

"Yeah, and I couldn't find the appendage."

One of the dispatchers had gone to school with Stan. "He was a dick then, but he doesn't have one now," more laughter.

We added a last name to the dog. He became known as Chewbacca Bobbit. I know, for guys, this story is not so comical, but with all the domestic abuse I see on the streets, the women rarely leave their husbands or boyfriends. I would think of Chewbacca at every domestic call I took from here on out.

We talked and laughed for thirty minutes before I went back on patrol.

I took a neighbor harassment call and caught a couple of high school boys drag racing through the center of town. It's amazing how teenagers think they're invincible. They were both quite upset over getting a ticket and then having to call their parents. I told them they could go to jail for endangering the public. I could see by their facial expressions that my words were having little effect. I hoped the fine for the ticket and an increase in their insurance premiums would change their attitudes, but I'm sure, to them, I will always be the bitch cop that stopped their fun.

Their parents were grateful for the phone calls and ordered both boys to come home immediately. I decided to head back to the department and start writing reports. It always seemed like my shift was longer when I was the only person on duty. I picked up a burrito and diet Coke and ate them at my desk while typing.

What a year! I couldn't ask for a better place to work and a better job. Yes, the stress was high, but being an officer was everything I ever dreamed it would be. Our new guy would graduate from the academy in a few days and I would no longer be the rookie, at least not in name. I knew I still had a great deal to learn.

Like Mr. Piskett and my first call, I would never forget Mr. Gaylord and my one year anniversary at Small Town PD.

Chapter 26

Joe Warling made it through the academy. He was still pompous, but like the academy does to everyone, it changed him. It was nice to have a new rookie. I passed the title to him gladly. He also "passed" the rookie search warrant setup at the abandoned house, screaming the entire time he fired his gun. The guys teased him and I could tell it pissed him off.

A couple of weeks after my one year anniversary, I received my performance appraisal. It wasn't bad, but I was irritated because Sgt. Spears felt I needed to distance myself from my victims more. He used the words, "Too emotionally involved."

Like most of my fellow officers I felt the justice system helped the accused more than the victims. The accused definitely had more rights. I returned to the police department many times after court angry and upset. I was female. I wore my heart on my sleeve. I said as much to Sgt. Spears.

"Suzie, this appraisal reflects what I observed. Your psychological profile indicated that you are a caring person. According to research you and your "type" make up only six percent of law enforcement personnel. The reason for this is you take things too personally. It could be your undoing. I never let an officer read their psychological profile, but with you, I'll make an exception. Do you want to read it?"

This should probably have been an easy answer, but I wasn't sure I wanted to see what the psychologist thought of me. I remembered the feelings I had after taking the tests, they left me drained and confused. After several moments of reflection I answered, "Yes."

Sgt. Spears pulled a stack of white pages from my file. "I'll leave you alone while you read it. You can stay in my office. Please come and get me when you're finished. I'll be in the evidence room."

I looked at the front page after the door closed quietly behind Sgt. Spears. Stephen Crane, Ph.D. Licensed Psychologist, was at the top.

The psychological profile started with an assessment overview, saying it was used to determine my psychological fitness to function as a sworn officer. The words that jumped out at me were "keeping people in the community safe," this was my answer when asked what I felt the role of a police officer was.

Oh, to be that naïve again.

The reading got more interesting as the detailed report gave the analysis for "Intellectual Effectiveness."

"On the Wonderlic Personnel test, Ms. Ivy achieved an age adjusted score which yielded a 78th percentile ranking. Police officers average 21 (52 percentile) on this test. All percentile rankings referenced in this section are based on the general population working norms.

This candidate achieved at the 90th percentile in verbal comprehension, a measure of ability to employ words meaningfully in planning, thinking and communicating.

This applicant achieved at the 90th percentile in inductive reasoning, an index of an individual's ability to analyze generalizations, determine relationships, and to apply an overall rule or guideline to a sequential problem solving task.

This candidate received a 95th percentile in deductive reasoning, a measure of ability to organize information from a variety of sources and to make valid judgments.

Overall Ms. Ivy was functioning in the 'Well Above Average Range' of intellectual intelligence."

Wow, I remembered my feelings of inadequacy after finishing the tests. Who knew how smart these doctors really were? Next, the test gave opinions on my friendliness and approach to the tests themselves and my behavior with the Psychologist. The next part to get my attentions was the Law Enforcement Type Sorter.

"Ms. Ivy responded as an Intuitive/Feeling type. The Intuitive/Feeling type of officer comprises only 6 percent of law enforcement and up to 28 percent of the general population. They are somewhat uncommon in law enforcement. These officers tend to think globally in nature and may dislike routine and detail. They are responsive to people's needs, being concerned about what others think and want, and trying to handle things with due regard for people's feelings. Often these types of individuals drop out of law enforcement, feeling that the profession was not what they expected it to be. Peer officers may not see them as sufficiently 'tough minded.' In addition these individuals do well in behavioral sciences, art, music, religious service, psychology and teaching. Ms. Ivy views herself as morally and psychologically superior to most people.

My "wow," wasn't so strong this time. I kept reading. "Summary of Rating" was next.

"Overall Ms. Ivy received a given rating of "2" which placed this candidate in the 'Highly Recommended' category." Her areas of strength included a talent for leadership and being a good judge of what people think and feel. Her areas of concern show Ms. Ivy tends to tell others what she believes they want to hear. She is somewhat naïve and she may tend to withdraw after long periods of stress."

The evaluation was signed by the doctor.

I took a deep breath. I would need a while to sort out what I learned. I read an astrological chart for my birthdate one time. I am a Leo. In my opinion the chart was not very favorable for Leos. This profile was somewhat similar and then not so much. I was confused. I went to get Sgt. Spears.

He followed me back to his office. We both sat down and I handed him back my psychological profile.

He looked at me, "What did you think?"

"I'm not sure. You've seen more of these than I have so I was hoping you could tell me."

"Well, to begin with, we have never had anyone come close to the scores you received in Intellectual Intelligence. It was almost scary when we compared you to the other officers we have working in the department. For your Sorter Type, you also threw us for a loop. We had some long deep discussions about you as a candidate for the police academy."

"I guess I can see why." I really could. Police officers in general are not the Intuitive/Feeling types. They get the job done by using pure hard facts. I knew I was different. Alex was the only other officer whom I felt used his feelings to help on the job. I had never really thought about whether it was good or bad. I felt it took different types of people to make a well-rounded functional police department. I looked at Sgt. Spears. "What are your biggest concerns?"

"I…we, worry about the emotion you put into your work. It can be a great thing, but can just as easily be bad. I personally worry about your stress levels. One of the best things about you is the fact you truly feel for people, but this is a tough profession and sometimes there is no justice. Can you deal with that?"

I didn't answer his exact question, "But I do feel there is justice."

"I know and that more than anything is what worries me. What happens when you are faced with a situation, especially one involving a child, and justice does not prevail? I'm not asking you to give up being you. I just want you to try and step back and not take things so personally. You are probably the best woman we could have hired to show that female cops are needed in this profession. We got lucky the day you applied. We don't want to lose you. I don't know how else to explain what I'm saying, but it's meant to help and to keep you in law enforcement."

I took a moment to process what Sgt. Spears said. "Okay, I think I get it. I won't write a rebuttal to your review of my performance at this time." I smiled.

Sgt. Spears shook his head. "I always count on you to keep me in my place. I can easily say I would most likely have enjoyed the rebuttal."

We both laughed. I left the office. The bottom line was, regardless of the areas for improvement, I received a five percent raise. I was elated.

I left the office and hit the streets. Dispatch radioed me fifteen minutes later. I was needed at 175 W. Bass Street. I couldn't help the, "Oh shit," that came out of my mouth. Maxine Brown needed an officer at her house. How surprising. It had been two weeks since the last call. I knew everyone in town with a scanner was laughing.

I arrived and walked to the door. How could I possibly dread one old woman so much? Every time I dealt with her, I was determined to get the upper hand, but it never worked. I think I had finally reached the point where I was as terrified of her as the rest of the department. My knuckles connected with the door, three short knocks.

I had to step back when it was thrown open. Today's outfit was white with large red and blue rhinestones around the extremely low cut V-neck collar. Ms. Brown must be feeling patriotic. Her sun visor matched as always. Unfortunately, she was not happy to see me.

"I thought they fired you? I can't believe you haven't messed up enough to get your ass sitting in county lockup. They probably can't afford the amount of food it would take to keep you happy. You must be one of those depression eaters. What's wrong, not keeping your husband happy in bed? In my day woman knew how to keep their husbands from wandering. A good attentive wife and a nice pair of breasts kept a man from straying. They just don't make you girls the way they did in my day." She said this as she pushed her chest out.

I wanted to gag, "What seems to be the problem Ms. Brown? " I tried to say it in a friendly manner, I really did.

"You're standing at my door aren't you? That's a problem in my book. Come on in, but try to keep your butt cheeks from touching anything."

I wasn't going in. "Ms. Brown, if you have something to show me inside, I'll come in, but if not, I'm staying on the porch."

"Look here! You will be respectful in my home. I will not put up with your smart mouth." Her face was turning red.

"Ms. Brown, I'm worried I will knock something over. I'm doing you a favor. What can I help you with today?"

"I have fingerprints on my back window. They shouldn't be there and the only way for you to see them is to come through the house. I can't imagine you getting over my fence and if you did, it would probably break." She stepped away from the door and I had no option but to follow.

We walked through the figurine filled living room into the kitchen. This was the farthest I had been into the wicked witch's home. I looked for her broom. Off the kitchen there was a laundry room. I spotted the broom. The room had a door that led outside. There was a glass window built into the door and it appeared to slide up and down. Ms. Brown opened the door and told me to look on the outside of the glass and I would see the prints. I walked outside and sure enough I could see a bunch of fingerprints on the glass. There was also, what appeared to be a nose print, in the middle of two distinct handprints. What in the world? It looked like someone was peeking in Ms. Brown's laundry room window. As funny as this might be later, I was horrified. Who could possibly be that desperate?

"Well, do you see them, or are you blind? Do they train you women cops to do anything but paperwork? I think I need one of the real cops to come here. My life could be in danger. I could be sexually molested in my sleep. Someone was looking in my back door."

"I can see that, and I will get my fingerprint kit out of my car and lift the prints. I want to walk around the yard and see if there are any footprints. Have you had any workman here recently or even a meter reader?"

"My meter is outside the fence. There is no reason for anyone to come into my back yard."

"I'll check the rest of the windows too."

I got a "humph" for my trouble, but Ms. Brown stayed out of my way as I did my job. I discovered a shoe print and was able to take some good pictures. Unfortunately, our budget is low and we don't have casting material for footprints, but I put a ruler down and was able to get an approximate size. It was a big shoe and had to be well over a size ten. I wasn't able to locate fingerprints on any of the other windows. I walked back to my patrol car and got my printing kit. It wasn't the greatest, but would work fine on glass. Fingerprinting is a messy business. I worked like crazy to clean up the powder when I was finished. I told Ms. Brown I would let the other officers know and they could keep a closer eye around her neighborhood.

"It will be like living in a communist country. No privacy at all. What is this world coming to?"

"Well, I won't tell the guys to patrol more in this area if you don't want me to." This was a lie, but she was getting under my skin.

"What I want you to do is find this pervert and get him off the street. I suppose that's too much to ask. It would require you to do your job!"

"Yes, Ms. Brown, I'll try my best." I said as I walked away.

I drove around town for an hour and then went back to the department to write my incident report on the call to Ms. Brown's house. I was halfway through when Sgt. Spears walked over to my cubicle.

"Officer Ivy, we have a problem." His face looked stern.

"Yes sir, what's the problem?"

Sgt. Spears actually cringed a little. He hates when I call him sir at the department. I smiled.

"I have a complaint from Ms. Brown that you left black dust over everything you touched while at her house. She requested that you go clean it up properly."

"Yes sir!" I stood up and headed into our bathroom for cleaning supplies. We had one small bathroom in the back for all the officers. There was another one off the lobby for the general public. We all avoided it though I sometimes thought it might be cleaner than the one the guys used. I grabbed the cleaning supplies I would need and then marched by Sgt. Spears and headed out the door. He was a smart man and kept any snide comments to himself. It was evident I was one pissed off officer.

I drove to Ms. Brown's house. I knocked on the door when I got there. When she answered, I told her I was jumping the back fence and wouldn't come inside. I stomped over to the fence and threw the glass cleaner and roll of paper towels over first. I then took four steps back, and just like I was taught at the academy, I went over the wooden fence. I picked up my cleaning supplies and went to the back window. I washed the entire door and when I was done, washed it again. That door had never looked so good. I left the same way I came and went out to my car and drove away. I avoided peeling rubber but just barely. I had a splinter in my hand and a broken fingernail for my trouble. I truly hated that woman!

Chapter 27

I learned from Spike that Sgt. Spears was retiring by the end of the year and Alex, Detective Molinero, would be applying for the Sergeant position.

"Who will be the new detective?" I asked.

"Well," said Spike, "Alex and I have been talking and we don't think any of the guys want it, but we think with some extra training you might be ready."

I was stunned. I'd been assisting Spike and Alex on their cases more and more, but I had been a cop for only one year. "Does Sgt. Spears or the Chief know?"

"Nope and we're going to keep it that way. You might be ready, you might not, but Alex and I are going to try. What do you think?"

"I don't know if I can do the job. But I want it." I smiled.

"Okay. Alex and I are working a kiddy porn case. We need your help. What do you say?"

Of course, I said yes.

Spike gave me a rundown on what they had.

"Mrs. Jones works at The Dusty Shelf bookstore. She seems to be a nice lady, but we think her husband is downloading child porn. A man came to the department a few days ago and said he bought a computer from Mr. Jones last month. He was cleaning up the hard drive and some pretty bad pictures showed up. We now have the computer and we're sending it to the state lab. They said it will be at least eighteen months before the results are back. We also have not been able to do a criminal history on Mr. Jones. They don't own a vehicle. We haven't written him a ticket or warning. We're looking into the county's records for property ownership but Jones is such a common name it's slow going. We need a birthdate."

I was stuck on what Spike said before the birthdate comment.

"Eighteen months? As in a year and a half?"

"Yep, that's standard for the state lab. We need to see if you can make friends with Mrs. Jones and get a look inside the house or get that date of birth for us. We're not in a rush because of the lab, but it would be nice to know what computers are in the house and the layout if we do get enough for a search warrant. Do you know anything about books?"

Books aren't just my hobby they used to be my business. I owned a small bookstore in my twenties and early thirties. I love books. I've visited the Dusty Shelf a few times, but I'm a bookstore snob and didn't care for the shelves being just what they advertised, dusty. I explained to Spike about my book experience. He was thrilled, but I could tell the idea of sitting down and reading a book for pleasure was beyond him.

I had learned over the past year that Alex's words to me about Spike's intelligence were true. Spike had a gift for policing, but he didn't get his knowledge from books, he got it from the street.

Spike asked how much money I would need to purchase books and get a relationship started with Mrs. Jones. I told him twenty dollars would get me on the good side of her. I would be taking books in to trade, an important ingredient of a used book store, and Mrs. Jones and I spoke the same book lover's language.

Spike said he would get the money cleared with Sgt. Spears.

I drove home that night saying aloud the words, "Detective Ivy," over and over.

Spike rearranged the next afternoon's schedule enabling me to get off early from my shift, although technically, I was still working. I went home and took a quick shower and let my hair down. While in uniform, my hair was always up in a tight bun. Now, I wanted to appear less severe and not at all threatening. I drove to The Dusty Shelf, leaving a bag of used books in my car. I went in to see if Mrs. Jones was working. She was behind the counter waiting on another customer. I looked around until she was free.

I walked up, "Can you tell me how your trade system works? I've been in before, but I don't remember."

"Sure, we give you one-fourth book credit for each book you bring in, and you pay one-fourth in cash for each book you take out on a trade. Our books are priced at half price, if you just want to buy and not trade."

My own bookstore had been stocked with half used and half new books. The Dusty Shelf was entirely used books from what I could see.

Mrs. Jones went on and explained it a little more. I assured her I understood.

"Back in my younger years, I owned a bookstore. I don't think people understand what hard work it is." I told her.

"Aren't you the new female officer the police department hired?"

"Yes, but please don't tell anyone I'm a book nerd or the guys will never let me live it down."

"Oh I won't." she laughed "Where did you own your bookstore?"

"It was in Phoenix, a little smaller than this and not nearly as nice."

Lie, lie, lie. Have I mentioned cops can lie? I remember my polygraph test before I could enter the police academy and how afraid I was that I would be thought a liar. Now, the lies were rolling off my tongue. My bookstore had been twice this size and three times as nice. It also had a coffee bar and a children's play area. Now was not the time to give Mrs. Jones lessons on the book business.

"What made you decide to become a police officer?"

"Well, I wanted something more exciting in life. I sold my bookstore years ago and thought I could help people." Mostly true and all new cops think they can help people. What I learned in my first year was that most of the people I helped either got a fine or a jail sentence. They rarely appreciated police "help".

"What do you like to read?"

"I read everything, but I've always been a fan of mysteries. I have a first edition, signed copy of The Killing Floor by Lee Child, at home but I will never give it up."

"Did you meet him?"

"Yes, at a book signing. I've always been a fan." Another lie, He was signing books at my bookstore and I gave him a ride to Tucson from Phoenix when his flight was cancelled. He sent me the signed copy as a thank you gift.

"He's so good looking in his pictures, is he as gorgeous in real life?"

"Yes he is. Have you read his books?"

"Every one of them."

"Do you know of anyone that writes as good?" I asked, "I just don't have a lot of time to read anymore and I don't want to waste my money."

Beverly, which is what she told me to call her, showed me some other authors. I had read most of them and thought she had good taste in books. I hoped the "kiddy porn" didn't turn out to be her husband's. I liked her.

We talked for thirty minutes about the book business and books in general. I ended up buying two and decided to leave my books for trade until next time. It cost the department a little over five dollars and I told Beverly I would be back.

I left the store and then drove around to make sure no one was following me. Yes, it was unnecessary, but I was really getting into this detective thing and decided it wouldn't hurt to practice.

Alex and Spike were at the department when I arrived. I told them I would go back to the store in a few days. One of the books I purchased was something I had already read. I bought it on purpose so I could talk about it and go back to the store sooner. The other book was one I planned on reading. After all, I needed to be able to discuss it too. Boy, the perks of the job.

"I told her about a signed book I have and plan to talk about more of them on my next visit. I'll try to get her talking about her own collection and see if I show her mine, she'll show me hers."

"You don't want her at your house," this from Spike.

"Why not? Everyone in town knows where I live. If I can do it without taking her into my house I will, but it might be the easiest way. She will want me to see her collection of books too."

"You really have a lot of books at your house?" Spike said with a look of disbelief on his face.

"Yes, some of us actually get smarter by reading. I don't have the 'on the job training' you do. I need to read books."

"Books are for pussies."

"Is that rule number seven?"

"Yes, it can be rule number seven. Alex here only needed six rules, but I guess you'll need more."

"Smart ass," I said under my breath.

Alex and Spike both laughed. I joined in. I would add "Books are for pussies" to my list of Spike's rules of policing.

Alex looked at Spike and finally spoke up, "It could be worse. She could live to watch CSI."

We all hated CSI. It was a police joke. "How come none of their evidence has to wait eighteen months to come back from the lab?" I asked.

We talked shit about CSI for a while longer and then I went home.

Three days later, I went back to see Beverly at the bookstore. I took my copy of The Killing Floor for her to look at. The inscription read, "Suzie, Thanks for everything! Lee Child."

"What does 'thanks for everything' mean?"

I was ready for this question. "Oh, I held up the autograph line, telling Lee how I had read all his books, and I was a super fan. I think he wrote it to say thanks for buying all his books."

"Do you have anything else that's signed?"

"Yeah, I have a bunch. I was always going to book signings. How about you?"

"We don't get any big authors here in Small Town. Mostly just locals that think they can write. What other signed copies do you have?"

The conversation went on and I asked more and more about her books at home and what she collected. I knew from experience that most book people collected something. I also learned she managed the store for the owner who was an elderly woman in her eighties. Beverly told me she couldn't afford to buy the business or she would. She said her husband was a computer geek, but he was out of work and they lived off his unemployment check and her pay.

"Does your husband ever work in here?"

"No, he likes books, but the owner wouldn't want Barker working for her. This is more of a bookstore for women."

"Maybe we could go to a book signing sometime in the City. I still hear about some now and then and I'd be happy to drive."

"I don't know, it's hard for me to leave the store and Saturday is the busiest day. They probably don't have signings on Sundays."

We talked some more and I tried not to push my luck. "I think I'll find a book for my husband. His birthday is next week." Please God, let me remember all my lies.

Beverly took the bait. "My husband's birthday was two months ago. He wanted one of those Visa gift cards."

"My daughter's birthday is in November. When was Barker's?"

"It was November 11. When was your daughter's?"

"It was on the 20th right before Thanksgiving. How old is Barker?"

"He's fifty-five and I'm fifty-one. I always call him my old man."

We both laughed.

Right before I walked out with two more books in hand, I asked, "Where do you live. I'll make sure to do extra patrol in your neighborhood. There's got to be some benefit in having a police officer as a friend." I already knew the address, but I thought I would throw that last bit out. The sad part was, I really liked Beverly and I was starting to feel bad for investigating her husband with the possibility of putting him in prison.

I went back to the department. Alex was there, but Spike had already gone home. I told Alex I had the date of birth for Barker Jones. Alex told me he would run a criminal history and he wanted me to keep a log of all information I got. I was to write everything down.

"Not a problem but I feel guilty, I like her."

"I know Ivy. I've been there. What you're doing is not really detective work, its undercover work, though in this case, Mrs. Jones knows you're a cop. It takes a special officer to work undercover. I worked the drug task force for a few years and it wasn't my thing. I felt sorry for a lot of the people I dealt with, but I did my job and put the bad guys away. Can you do that?"

"I have no doubt I can do it, I just didn't think I would feel bad about it."

"Feelings are what separate detectives from street cops. It's not that street cops don't have feelings; it's that they think they're better than the bad guys and have no compassion for their circumstances. You do. I really think you will make a good detective. Enough of this talk. I have a small glass display case that needs fingerprinting. You want to give it a try?"

I tackled the display case and came up with some good latent prints. One print probably belonged to the bad guy and one to the owner who swore no one but he and the bad guy touched it. Again television CSI does police work no justice. It would be a month or two before we knew if the prints hit a match. I was learning Detective work took a long time.

Chapter 28

I was enjoying my change of pace, but I was still a patrol officer. I thought some of the guys resented the trust Spike and Alex had in me, and the extra time they spent on my training. I shared my concerns with Alex.

"I'm worried about the guys and all the time I spend with you and Spike."

"Every one of them is capable of becoming a detective. Being a good one is the hard part and they can't accept that today's suspect is tomorrow's victim. I get information because I treat everyone with respect. They talk to me. I don't pound them into the pavement over the little shit. The guys will get over it or they won't. It's not our problem."

He was right and all I could do was the job in the manner that worked best for me.

Officers Warling and Stephens were becoming good friends. I wasn't surprised. Joe had the same "I'm better than everyone else attitude" as Stephens. This attitude was becoming more and more apparent the longer Joe worked at the department. He was having trouble on field training and I heard that he would probably be on for much longer than it took me. It wasn't very nice of me to feel pleased but I did.

***

One day flowed into another, but the in-house training broke up the monotony. These were classes taught by officers who had been through General Instructor School and then trained in the advanced area they wanted to teach. You had to be an officer for two years before you qualified to apply for General Instructor certification.

To remain certified, all police officers are required to complete a certain amount of regular training hours and a certain amount of proficiency hours (advanced training) every year. Training never stops. We were also regularly required to qualify with our handguns, rifles and shotguns. I carried a shotgun, but had been unable to get into rifle training so could not carry one yet.

All the officers name their shotguns and rifles. But they didn't name their handguns. I started my own tradition with my handgun and named it Clint after Mr. Eastwood and Dirty Harry. My shotgun was named "The Rock" after Rock Hudson. Yes, he was a homosexual, but I was madly in love with him when I was younger. Most of the guys cringed when I explained Rock's name. It was kind of like carrying my pink handcuffs. I was not one of the guys; I was one of the officers and wanted to be sure they always knew I was female.

Mike and Benito taught high-risk stops for the department. I had attended the daytime class months ago, but we were also required to attend night training. I was currently on mid-shift working 1400 hours to midnight, Sunday through Wednesday. The night training would take place on Thursday at 1800 hours. It would be cold and on one of my days off. On average, I worked five hours of overtime each week. I was rarely on patrol Wednesday mornings, so I always worked overtime for court. It was normal to sleep for two hours on Wednesdays and then get up for two to three hours of court. It wasn't fun, but I grew accustomed.

My sleep was uninterrupted all day Thursday and I woke up ready to go. We use the airport for many of our tactical training classes. Few planes land in the afternoons and evenings, and we most often had the area to ourselves. Our location also helped keep the citizens in Small Town from observing our activities.

We stood on a line, had our guns checked and our slides taped open with orange tape. No loaded guns or weapons of any kind are permitted during tactical training. If you left the area, Chief Varnett was standing by to inspect your firearm before you could get back inside the secured area. Police take their safety very seriously. Our department did not have the funds to purchase blue guns, hard rubber facsimiles of duty weapons we used at the academy, so the orange tape was used.

There were three areas set up for scenarios. Each had an instructor. A few officers from a neighboring town were joining us to undergo training too. I was the first female cop in the area, so their guys didn't say too much to me. I was accustomed to it. I didn't get a lot of acknowledgment from the county deputies either. We were separated into three groups. As luck would have it, my group included Joe Warling, Jared Stephens and two officers from the neighboring town. Yes, that's me, Lucky Suzie!

We walked to our first scenario. The four men in our group talked among themselves. I listened to the instructions given by Benito and could hear the guys whispering behind me, obviously not paying attention. Benito told us to get into pairs. Of course, I had no one to pair with. Benito told the guys that one of them would need to team up with me when my turn came. Finally, they were silent.

It was like being in grade school and I was the least popular girl in school. It was good that I was older and could see the humor and the absurdity of the situation.

In the first scenario, we had to use two patrol vehicles to pull over the bad guy's vehicle. "The bad guys" were being played by the spouses and girlfriends of officers. Norman wanted no part of this which was too bad, because I think he would have had a great time. The two officers drove separate cars and then fanned out behind the suspect vehicle when it came to a stop. In this scenario, the license plate matched a bank robbery from an hour ago and the suspects were armed and dangerous. The first two trainees went and then the next two. I watched and it helped me remember my previous training. I saw what the guys were doing wrong, but knew I was sure to mess something up too. Tactical training was meant to teach us things we didn't know, remind us of what we did know, and it was almost a requirement that we never be perfect. At least if you weren't Officer Stephens.

Stephens made some big mistakes and was being an asshole when told what he did wrong. I wasn't aware there any problems between him and Benito until tonight, when it became obvious they didn't much care for each other. It made me like Benito even more.

My turn finally came and I did what I was taught, as best I could, and made sure to fix what I observed others doing wrong. I had the greater advantage in going last. One of the guys, from the neighboring department, partnered with me. He turned out to be pleasant to work with when he wasn't around his friends. Everything went smoothly. I was pleased with myself and when I finished.

Benito said, "Good job, Ivy," and turned away to go over a few things in general with everyone.

I couldn't believe when Stephens said, "What, not going to critique her performance like you did ours? She blowing you or something?"

Benito moved so fast I barely followed with my eyes. Stephens was picked up and thrown several feet through the air, landing on the tarmac.

"She's a better officer than you'll ever be, you son of a bitch. What the fuck is your problem? She didn't make any mistakes or I would have pointed them out. Unlike you, she follows directions and doesn't need to be a 'lone ranger' by doing it herself."

Everyone from the different groups came into our area to see what was going on. I was embarrassed and pissed off. Sgt. Spears tapped me on the shoulder and drew me away from the guys. I told him what Stephens said and Benito did. He immediately told me to go back to the office and make a written report. He sent Alex with me. As I walked away, each witness was being isolated. Alex told me they would be questioned one by one.

As usual, my tears kicked in but I was trying to hold them back. I wiped my eyes a few times and managed to make it to the department without breaking down. Alex asked me not to talk about what happened until I had everything on paper. After I was finished, he read what I wrote. I was expecting anything but the smile I received.

"You sure do get under his skin. No one here likes him except maybe Joe, but Joe's a rookie and still dumb. He doesn't count. The guys, including Joe, will back your story. They won't lose their jobs over Stephens. Benito will be in some trouble, but not as much as Stephens. This couldn't be better. He needs to go."

I felt better, but still worried about the fallout. This made our department look bad and I knew Chief Varnett would not be happy. I liked him, but he was very proud and wanted any dirty laundry at the department kept in the family. This would get out.

"Have there been any other problems with Stephens besides denying him a blowjob?" Alex asked.

"How did you know that? The only person I told was Sandy." Bing, the light went off.

"You never brought it up so we never brought it up. The guys respected you more for not tattling. I didn't agree, I think he should have been fired. Spike talked me out of saying anything. He told me it's hard enough to be a female cop. It's even harder if you get a male officer fired."

"Spike hates female cops."

"Yeah, he might, but he has a lot of respect for you. Just don't tell him I said so. Now come on and let's go finish training."

When we returned to the airport, Stephens was not there. He had been sent home. I was glad to see Benito was still instructing. I found my team. They all greeted me, even Joe. I finished the training saying very little to anyone. It was after ten when we were done and I went home.

Norman was still up and I told him what happened. He told me he always liked Benito. His dislike of Stephens matched mine, especially after I told him about what Stephens said to me during field training.

"Why didn't you tell me?"

"I was embarrassed and didn't want you being angry at one of the guys I worked with. I'm sorry. I should have said something. I stay away from Stephens whenever I can. He's a creep and makes my skin crawl."

I lay in bed with Norman for a while. He fell asleep but I couldn't get my brain to shut down. I finally got up and watched some late night television. I fell asleep at four in the morning. My phone rang at eight with instructions to come to the police department and speak with the chief.

It was a closed door meeting with Chief Varnett and Sgt. Spears. They had my written statement.

Sgt. Spears spoke first, "We have statements from all the officers in your area and also the spouses who witnessed the incident. The stories are the same. We would like your input on Stephens' punishment. How do you feel about what happened?"

I looked back and forth between the two of them. "I really don't want to have anything to do with Stephens' punishment. I just want to let it go."

This time Chief Varnett spoke, "It might seem easier to you, but Stephens could press charges against Benito and Benito could lose his certification. Stephens' father is on the town council and they will scrutinize everything we do. It helps that there were so many witnesses, but we still need to mind our P's and Q's."

I hadn't thought about the long term ramifications. "I would still rather have no input on what happens to Stephens. I feel bad for Benito, but he shouldn't have gone after Stephens. I can take care of myself."

"Okay, Stephens is suspended for one week without pay. In addition, he can't apply for a promotion for a year. This is standard department procedure after a heavy infraction. Benito gets the same punishment. I'm sorry this happened. We pride ourselves on behaving professionally which is what you have done. You are to let me know if Stephens so much as looks cross-eyed at you. When he returns, he won't work any shift you're on for at least six months." The Chief looked at me as he spoke and I could see compassion in his eyes.

I left the office as Benito was getting out of his car, arriving for his meeting. "I'm so sorry Ivy. I didn't think. I just reacted."

I hugged him, "I can take care of myself, but I feel the love, thanks."

Benito laughed and then walked into the department to face the music. As I drove away I saw Stephens pulling up. I refused to look the other way and we played the stare down game as I left. I can be childish too.

Chapter 29

Life went on and Stephens and Benito each survived his punishment. I heard rumors that Stephens was applying at other agencies. I crossed my fingers that someone was dumb enough to take him. Unfortunately, our county and surrounding agencies knew Stephens' problems and wanted nothing to do with him.

I had one full week where I received five calls from Maxine Brown. It was getting to the point where being armed in her vicinity was a catastrophe waiting to happen.

Along with my Maxine problems, there were a series of burglaries in town with similar MO's. Alex was getting called out approximately two mornings a week to investigate the scenes. I was still on mid shift and Alex would talk to me about the burglaries when I came in. It was driving him nuts. The crimes took place between four and five in the morning. After two a.m., we always reduced patrol to one officer and he never saw anyone on the streets.

The same shoeprint was found at all seven crime scenes. Alex felt that the small items stolen meant our suspect was hitting the businesses on foot. He was taking money and laptop computers, things that he could carry. The guy knew what he was doing and was staying well hidden while getting to and from his targets. The shoeprint was small for a man, a size eight, but Alex wore a size nine so thought nothing of it. I was not much help. I only gave Alex a sounding board for his frustrations.

Two weeks and three burglaries later, Alex was ready to explode. Chief Varnett wanted something done and the city council was on his back every day. Alex asked if I was willing to drive his unmarked car while he patrolled on his bicycle. Not his usual approach, but Alex felt he needed to be closer to the street. He asked for help from Spike but was flatly refused. If he wasn't working a shift, nothing got Spike out of bed that early.

Sgt. Spears gave permission for me to assist Alex and we met at the police department the next morning. I was in uniform and Alex was in jeans, a long-sleeved t-shirt and light jacket. It was freezing outside, but Alex said that bicycle riding would warm him up and he wanted to be able to toss the bike and give chase if needed.

We headed out at 0330 hours. Alex carried a radio, his duty weapon, and a pair of handcuffs as he rode through town. We decided to communicate using our cell phones and not the radios. Small Town residents owned too many scanners. We called dispatch and let them know what we were doing. Our first morning was a bust when we didn't come across a single person.

The second morning was much the same. It was too cold for the good or any citizens of Small Town to be out. The third morning was the charm.

I was tired and the past two mornings' patrol took place during my scheduled days off. I had to be back on shift at 1400 hours that afternoon. Alex stuck to his guns and said he would go out without me if I wouldn't help. He was determined to catch our guy or die trying.

We were both overly tired and forgot to notify dispatch that we were going out. Alex jumped on his bike and I took off in the opposite direction. About thirty minutes later, which put the time at 0400, I heard Alex shouting into his radio. He was out of breath and I had a feeling he was giving chase on foot. I immediately headed to the location he yelled over the radio.

From out of nowhere a person ran in front of my car and I slammed on my brakes.

The suspect was small and fast. Alex ran by next and was about thirty feet behind the suspect. I stayed in my car and decided to cut them off as they ran toward the elementary school.

Going through the streets took longer than I thought, and when I got to the school I couldn't locate Alex or our marathon runner. I got out of my car and heard yelling coming from the playground area. What surprised me was the feminine voice that was screaming over Alex's yelling.

I ran toward the voices and saw our suspect holding tightly to a tetherball poll, with Alex yelling for her to let go. Alex was trying to pry fingers off the pole, but was having little luck. The entire scene was hysterical but I tried to hold in my laughter. I took out my cuffs, walked up to the two of them and placed handcuffs on the suspect's wrists, securing them to the pole. Alex stood back.

For once, I felt I did something right the first time. It was a great feeling. Our suspect was crying and sat down on the ground hugging the pole. I recognized her. It was Becky from dispatch. Damn!

I retrieved my patrol car and drove it to the playground area. Alex was standing by his catch and still pulling air into his lungs. He'd run more than a mile. I walked up and said hello to the crying woman. She continued to sob. I told her I would let her stay attached to the pole as long as she needed, but Alex and I would wait in the car where it was warm. I turned and walked toward my car.

It's okay, I'll go with you." She said between sniffs.

I turned around and went back to the pole, un-cuffed one hand, kept it in a tight hold and brought it behind her back. Becky cooperated. We put her in the back of my patrol car and notified dispatch we had one in custody. They could figure out for themselves that we were on duty.

I drove Alex to where he dropped his bike and then followed slowly behind him as we went back to the office. Becky kept quiet except for the occasional sniffle and hiccup.

Alex read Miranda to her and we got the story. Becky was addicted to prescription drugs and needed money. Her work shift ended at 0400 and she lived five minutes from the dispatch center. She would drop her car at home and then hit the street, staying in the shadows. She carried a backpack for stolen items. She refused to give up the name of the person to whom she was selling the laptops.

We booked Becky into the county jail.

Afterward, Alex told me how he spotted her.

"I was riding my bike and saw a person walking. I rode up and said hello. I don't think Becky knew who I was, but I knew I had the burglar. I asked what was stuck to the bottom of her shoe. Becky looked down and lifted her foot. I think she realized, as soon as she looked, that she was caught and took off. I was still on my bike, so rode after her. I tried to call into my radio but hit something in the road. I went over the handle bars and rolled on the ground. I got up and started chasing her. That's when I was able to radio you."

Alex had the knee torn out of his jeans and I could see some small dark stains indicating blood. He had a minor case of road rash.

"Why were you trying to get her hands off the pole?" I asked.

"I don't know, I was pissed and my mind was just thinking about getting her hands behind her back. I felt pretty stupid when you cuffed her in place. Thanks a lot!"

I laughed and pantomimed the action to make it funnier. Alex laughed too.

The capture of our burglar caused some bad feelings between county staff and the police department. One of their own was a criminal. It didn't sit well with them. The chief was ecstatic that we took the city council off his back. To give credit where it was due, Alex solved the case. Alex was like a puppy with a chew toy and I was lucky to go along for the ride.

When I arrived at work at 1400, Alex had already told the guys the story of the pole. I guess he wanted to be the one to make fun of himself before I had the chance. I had fun embellishing the image of Alex and a stripper pole.

My first call of the day came in a little after 1500. It was Ms. Brown. "Shoot me now!"

Apparently a neighbor of hers was revving his car engine and disturbing Ms. Brown's peace. As always, she asked about her peeping Tom.

"Are you ever going to find that pervert? Is anyone in this town safe?"

"I look for a matching shoeprint everywhere I go. I have a picture on my cell phone to compare it with. I'm not sure when the fingerprints will be back from the lab."

"That's ridiculous! They probably have fat people working at that lab. Fat and lazy, that's what a lack of self-control gets you." She looked me up and down as she spoke.

I had determined that Ms. Brown was more prejudiced against "fat people" than "colored people" as she called them. She never made another "colored" comment in my hearing after I met her the first time. Alex told me she wasn't very fond of Hispanics either, but he agreed, anyone that was not skin and bones set her off the most.

I found the neighbor and spoke with him. He was repairing his car and said he would be done in an hour. I passed this information on to Ms. Brown and drove away. She wasn't happy.

An hour and five minutes later I received another call to her residence. I decided to break a rule and go to dinner instead. Over the next half-hour, Ms. Brown called dispatch four more times, then the calls stopped. I arrived at Ms. Brown's residence about fifteen minutes later.

The neighbor's garage door was closed and he was no longer working on his car. I walked up to Ms. Brown's door and knocked. It was opened for a split second and then slammed in my face. I cleared the scene and couldn't help my smile. For once, I thought I got the upper hand. I expected a complaint would come, just not in the form in which it arrived.

One week later, at the monthly city council meeting, Ms. Brown took her complaint to the board. City Councilman Stephens had a field day bad mouthing Chief Varnett and his inability to make his officers do their jobs.

Sgt. Spears called me on the phone and gave me a heads up. He was on vacation and not a happy person. I was hoping this was my lucky break from being the "go to" officer when it came to Ms. Brown. I didn't get my wish.

I was sitting in the chief's office the next morning.

Officer Ivy, from what I've heard, you have done very well in handling a big problem at the department. Ms. Brown has complained on you fewer times than any of the other police officers we have. I want to commend you for that. It would probably be better though if you make a more timely response from here on out. I don't like the city council messing in police business. Please don't give them the opportunity. Would you like to respond to my comments?"

What could I say? Ms. Brown won again.

I left the office thinking about my grandmother. When she was alive, during her later years, we took turns taking her to the grocery store. She enjoyed doing her own shopping but refused to wait in a line to check out. One of her "spells" would come on if there was more than one person in front of her. This got a chair and another cashier just for her. My brother commented, after his turn, saying the next time the clerk asked paper or plastic, he was choosing plastic and putting it over grandma's head. Though we loved grandma, it became our family joke. Ms. Brown was made for plastic.

Chapter 30

I continued to work on Beverly Jones at the Dusty Shelf bookstore. We were on great terms when it came to books and I enjoyed talking to her about authors. Alex had run a criminal history on Beverly's husband Barker, but he was clean. The biggest problem was Beverly's unwillingness to invite me to her home. I couldn't help my curiosity but was learning patience and knew eventually we would have the analysis back from the lab.

The more I got to know her, the more I was convinced that if her husband was downloading child porn, she was not aware of it.

The rumors of Sgt. Spears retiring finally came to fruition. He planned to leave in two months and we would miss him. Alex and Mike Compton were applying for the Sergeant's position. Mike was a nice guy, but no one really thought he had a chance. Alex was made to be sergeant. Benito and Stephens were out of the race completely due to their altercation. Spike did not apply.

No one mentioned anything about the next person to make detective. Again, Stephens and Benito were ineligible.

Alex was studying a sergeant's training manual he ordered online. He liked reviewing what he learned, out loud. I teased him for actually reading a book. He was nervous, though I didn't think he had anything to worry about.

I didn't know if I had what it took to be a detective and was worried when told by Spike that my name was on the short list. Alex and Spike had confidence in me, which helped relieve my anxiety.

One month before Sgt. Spears retired, Alex got the sergeant's position. He would spend the next weeks training with Sgt. Spears until his last official day.

Norman and I threw a going away celebration and promotion party at our house. Alex brought his new girlfriend. We were all in shock when Spike showed up with a lady. He wasn't married and had never mentioned Candice before. We were intrigued. Both the women were nice and we had a great time. Sgt. Spears was smiling but I could see he would miss us. He and his wife purchased a motorhome and had big plans. The department issued him a police badge that said, "Retired." It was shiny and new. We all pitched in and bought him his own Glock handgun. He would have to turn in his police issue weapon along with his other gear and we wanted him to have the same gun he used when working the streets.

***

Two days after Sgt. Spears retired, I was in my office typing a report when a 911 call came in from Ms. Brown. It was hard not to groan, again. I even hit my head against the steering wheel as I drove to her house. Would I ever be relieved from "Joker" duty?

I drove reluctantly to her home and knocked on the door. No one answered. I rang the doorbell and then knocked on the door again, but got the same result, nothing. I called dispatch and asked them to call Ms. Brown on the phone. They received no answer. They told me her voice was very faint when she called and she just asked for an officer.

I tried to look inside the front windows, but they were covered. I found this strange. Anytime I came to her house during the day, a gauzy inner cover showed with the dark drapes pulled back. I decided to jump my "fat ass" over Ms. Brown's fence. I would get some enjoyment by telling her I'd done so. I made a running leap at the fence and propelled my body over. I went to the back laundry room door and looked through the glass.

Part of the kitchen was showing and I could see two legs on the floor, though the rest of Ms. Brown's body was obscured. I tried the door. It was locked.

I called dispatch and told them to send an ambulance. I then took out my gun and used the butt to break the glass. The movies got something right for a change and it worked. As I worked to get my hand through the glass, I saw faint movement from Ms. Brown. The lock turned in my hand and I was inside.

Ms. Brown was barely conscious and I wasn't sure what was wrong. It was obvious her bowels had let go at some point and I didn't know how long she had been on the floor. There was no blood. I sat on my knees and began asking her questions. She opened her eyes and whispered her hip was broken.

I radioed the ambulance crew and gave them the update. I left her side long enough to unlock the front door and open it wide. When I went back to her side, I wasn't sure what to do so I went back to my knees and rested my hand on her shoulder. I continued talking and told her help was on the way.

The ambulance arrived, and I moved to the side. I broke my hip two years before and I can't begin to describe the pain. The paramedics placed Ms. Brown on a gurney and she made barely a sound. She was a strong old bat. I heard her throaty voice telling me to lock her front door as she was wheeled outside to the waiting ambulance.

Her stay in the hospital lasted three weeks. I later learned she had lain on the floor in the living room for two days. She managed to drag herself to the kitchen and the phone when she had no hope left. I felt awful for my bad thoughts when I first got the call. Just because I disliked her, didn't mean I wanted her to suffer.

   ***

Two weeks later, we had a department meeting. It was at two in the afternoon, the beginning of my shift. I hadn't slept well and hoped a good night's sleep was around the corner. It was the last day of my work-week and like the end of every week, I was ready for a break and grateful the meeting was not on my day off.

We sat down and Chief Varnett began with his list of complaints, mostly having to do with the condition of the squad room and bathroom. Every time he mentioned these problems, things would be clean for a week or two. They would then go back to messiness. Our new Sergeant was next to speak, and I was very proud of Alex as we listened to some changes he was implementing, which included vehicle inspections. The guys groaned but they were given fair warning. I missed Sgt. Spears, but Alex looked good sitting in his chair.

We next went around the room and shared cases, anyone we were looking for and problem traffic areas, etc. The mysterious fingerprints on Ms. Brown's window had finally come back from the lab, but there was no match. I let the guys know we still had a Peeping Tom on our hands.

Sandy was last to speak and she gave us a heads up on reports she needed immediately. We all began to stand when Chief Varnett told everyone to hold their horses and stay seated.

"There has been a lot of discussion about who will fill Sgt. Molinero's shoes as detective. Sgt. Spears, Sgt. Molinero and I have decided our next detective will be Officer Ivy.

I was shocked. Both Alex and Spike had grins on their faces and I was getting back slaps all around. I had been an officer for one year and eleven months. I had so much to learn and so much to prove. My new work schedule would be Monday through Fridays beginning the next week. No more uniform! I would be in plainclothes and Alex' unmarked vehicle was being cleaned out for me.

I followed Alex and the chief out of the room after everyone left. I turned over my officer chest badge and flat badge and received my detective badges. I pinned the new badge to my uniform and placed my new wallet in my back pocket.

Alex wanted me to come in the following day and begin moving into my new office. He told me we needed to sit down and go over a few of his open cases. I was no longer tired and didn't care that the following day was my weekend. I went home for dinner and gave Norman the news. He was pleased and relieved I wouldn't be on the street so much. I didn't burst his bubble by telling him how Alex continued to be in danger as a detective.

I went to sleep with the words Detective Ivy running through my head.

***

The next morning it was like my first day after graduating the academy, though I felt no anxiety only excitement. I walked into the office smiling ear to ear. It took a couple of hours to get my new digs in order. I now occupied a large office with a window. Alex and I went to a late lunch and then went back to the department to review his cases.

About an hour into our discussion, we overheard Benito being dispatched to a 911 call received from Rachel Fellows. I'd heard a few weeks before that Charles was out of prison and the two of them were back together. I couldn't help but feel bad for her even though it was her choice to go back to her abuser.

Dispatch informed Benito that Rachel was in her car and her husband was trying to kill her. Alex and I headed out and drove straight to the Fellows' residence. The car wasn't there, but Charles answered the door. I was relieved that Rachel apparently got away from him and hoped she wasn't beat up too badly. I could see Charles' right hand, which displayed bloody knuckles. "Where's Rachel?" Alex was doing the talking. I was paying close attention to Charles' demeanor.

"The bitch was on one, and went tearing out of here like a crazy person. I don't know where the fuck she went and I'm sick of her shit. She's drunk."

"If you hear from her, let us know. We'll be watching."

As we walked away, I called dispatch and asked exactly what Rachel said when she called 911.

"She said Charles was trying to kill her and she had to get away. She hung up after that."

"We know he beat her up and he needs to be arrested." I was desperate to put the son of a bitch behind bars until I was sure Rachel was safe.

"I'm sorry Ivy, but we don't have enough. We need to find her first."

I wasn't surprised, just pissed off because Alex was right. My biggest fear was that Rachel would come back home and Charles would finish what he started. We left and began our search.

After two hours, I called Norman and told him I didn't know when I would be home. It was now getting dark and we split up in different cars. Charles called dispatch several times. He was pissed that Rachel had not brought the car home. Rachel had no family or friends that we could find in Small Town. I was hoping that she had just started driving and wouldn't stop until she was out of Arizona.

Sometimes, even heartfelt wishes don't come true. At a little after nine, I was driving on a back road, and saw lights in the distance between two hills. As I got closer, I realized it was an upside down vehicle. I recognized the car. I shouted into my radio to send an ambulance and for all police units to respond. I ran up to the car shining my flashlight. Rachel's head was caught in the front window. I could see her blank eyes staring at nothing. She was covered in blood. Her face was unrecognizable.

I checked the pulse on her neck but felt nothing. I walked around to the passenger side of the car and managed to squeeze inside. I ignored the scrape of glass against my jeans and placed my fingers on her wrist, checking again for a pulse. I knew she was gone and there was nothing I could do. Sitting half inside the vehicle, I held her hand in mine and waited. I was too angry to cry. It wasn't Rachel's blood I wanted on my hands.

Alex was first to arrive but I could make out more lights heading up the road. Alex knew of my relationship with Rachel. He knew how upset I was when Charles got out of prison and Rachel went back to him. We all said he would kill her one day. We were right.

I let Alex have all my anger and frustration as soon as he was close enough to hear me. "He beat the shit out of her. Did you see his knuckles? That son of a bitch killed her."

"Are you okay Suzie? Can you handle this case? It's yours if you want it."

"Yes, I can handle it, that bastard is going away."

"You need to start processing the scene. I'll keep the ambulance back. I'll assist to make sure you're covered. Let's get started." Alex knew by bringing my police "thinking brain" into play, I would put everything else aside and do my job.

I refused to think of the person, hanging out of the window as Rachel. I took pictures of the scene and then drew in closer to get the body in death. Using Alex' evidence kit, I placed brown paper bags over her hands and secured them with rubber bands. Her body was growing colder as I worked. I wondered what time the accident happened and how long she was alive before death claimed her. Alex let me work alone unless I asked for his help.

When I finished, I had dispatch notify the mortuary. I helped get Rachel out of the car and into a large white zippered bag. I grabbed the straps and secured her waist and legs as the mortician gave me directions. Alex stood at my back and as the hearse drove away he placed his hand on my shoulder. His sympathy would only make me cry, and I had work to do. I walked away from the comfort he offered and waited as the car was towed from the scene.

The entire process took hours. We went back to the police department after midnight and I stood beside Alex as he woke up the county attorney's chief deputy and placed the call on speaker phone. I kept my feelings to myself as I listened to the difficulties this investigation posed. The attorney told Alex to put the case together. He informed the attorney that I was the lead investigator of record and now our new detective. I felt no elation with my promotion. Only one thing would make me happy at the moment. We went and picked up Charles.

Chapter 31

While riding in the car, Alex told me that Charles was coming with us one way or another and he had no problem placing him into temporary custody. We also decided not to tell him right away that Rachel was dead. Alex and I would interview Charles together.

We arrived at the house and Alex knocked on the door. "Hold your fucking horses, I'm coming." The door crashed open. "Did you find my car yet?"

His car, that's what he cared most about.

Alex spoke up, "We need to speak with you at the police department and you're coming with us."

"What's this all about? What's that fucking bitch saying this time? I didn't touch her. She's a lying bitch."

Alex grabbed Charles by the arm and I pulled my Taser. Drawing my gun would not be wise. I wanted to shoot Charles with something and high voltage was perfect.

Charles didn't resist after he saw the red laser light hit his chest. Alex wouldn't even let him get his shoes on. We escorted him to our car in his socks. It took five minutes to get him into our interview room.

Alex read Miranda, "You have the right to remain silent."

That was all I heard before Charles spit out, "I just want my fucking car. That bitch can leave me if she wants but I get the car."

"We don't want to talk about the car. We want to know about the cuts on your knuckles."

Charles looked down at his hands which were now free of blood. There were abrasions showing. I should have photographed them when we went to the house the first time.

"I was working on the car. I never touched her."

"Why did Rachel tell me you did?"

"She was drunk and had no business taking the car out. I hope you plan on charging her with drunk driving. It'll teach that bitch."

"How many times have you been arrested for domestic violence?"

"It doesn't matter, I'm taking my classes. I don't want to return to prison. That bitch begged me to come back."

I stood up and told Alex I was going to get a drink of water. If that wife beater called Rachel a bitch one more time, I wouldn't be able to control myself. I took several deep breaths and realized that Charles was winning. I was stronger than he but I was letting him get to me. Alex's voice sounded muffled from where I was standing. I took a last soothing breath and went back in.

Alex continued, "Tell me about your entire day starting when you woke up."

I listened to Charles drone on about his day. When he was finished I caught his blunder and so did Alex.

"You forgot to mention working on the car."

"Oh yeah, and I worked on my car."

We questioned him for more than an hour. I stayed in the room the entire time and kept my cool. Charles stuck to his story.

"So, am I getting my car back or what?"

"No, you're not getting your car back."

Charles got up from his chair but before he could blast Alex with more name calling, Alex spoke, "The car was totaled in an accident."

Charles sat down. "It's all I have, that bitch took all I have."

"Rachel was killed when the car rolled. You don't have her any longer either."

Charles sat in stunned silence for a few minutes. He looked at me with a sneer on his face. "You have nothing. I never touched her and she was drinking. I want my lawyer."

It took us an hour, but we obtained a physical characteristics warrant. It allowed me to take swabs of Charles' hands and pictures of his body. I had him take his shirt off. There was a scratch on his chest and I swabbed that too. Alex finally drove him home. I was not willing to watch him walk up to his front door knowing that Rachel would never again have the same opportunity.

I sat in my new office, cataloged the evidence and began downloading the pictures to my computer. I went through the photos of the scene, one by one. My heart broke for Rachel.

Alex came back to the station and walked into my office, "You know this will be a tough one. The chances of getting any kind of conviction are slim."

"I know, but I have to try. Somehow, that SOB needs to go away."

"The autopsy will take place sometime in the next few days. Are you up to going?"

Oh, the joys of detective work. I hadn't thought about an autopsy. Rachel would be my first. Of course I would be there.

Alex went home but I stayed and wrote the incident report. An hour later I pulled into my driveway. It was four in the morning. I was exhausted, but couldn't sleep. I was back at work the next morning at 0800 hours. I went to the county attorney's office and spoke with the chief deputy. Rachel's death would most likely be ruled an accident.

The autopsy was the next day. The medical examiner's office was a two hour drive from Small Town. I went by myself. Rachel's body was transported the previous day. I spoke to the doctor and told him Rachel's story. I was asked if I had my "T" test, but had no idea what it was and didn't want to appear as stupid as I felt. I told the Doctor no. I was in the room as they undressed Rachel and washed her body. I was able to take my own pictures. I hadn't thought to bring my camera into the building so I used my cell phone. Not a good idea, but I didn't care. I planned to download the pictures to my computer and erase them from my phone as soon as I returned to the police department.

Before the medical examiner began cutting, his assistant escorted me into a viewing room. I was able to watch through a window and on a television screen. As long as I distanced myself from thinking of Rachel, the autopsy was fascinating.

Her fingers made loud cracking noises as the medical examiner bent them repeatedly in order to get the rigor out so he could take fingerprints. He ex-rayed her body and before washing her face, he swabbed it in case her husband's or anyone else's blood was present. He finally used a sprayer to wash her face and hair. It was Rachel. She had never been strikingly beautiful but she had been pretty. The damage to her face hid any hint of beauty.

I watched everything they did to her body. The medical examiner stuck a large needle into her eyeballs to extract fluid. It was the only time I cringed. He cut her rib cage open with a saw and then used a different saw to cut open her skull and pull her scalp back.

Finishing up, he put her organs back into her chest cavity in no precise order. Pulling her facial skin back down, a semblance of a woman took shape. He then sewed the "Y" incision up, using a large needle threaded with yellow cord. The skin unevenly melded together. It barely resembled Rachel.

I left with a small bag containing her clothing, a gold wedding band and a ring from her pinky finger.

I went back to my department and wrote my first supplemental report to the case. Police reports from seven years back were included in the file, all the years Rachel suffered from Charles' abuse in Small Town. The medical examiner told me Rachel died from massive head trauma, likely caused from hitting the windshield.

Really, the only evidence I had were the small cuts on Charles' hand, the scratch on his chest, and Rachel's 911 call. The most I could probably hope for was him getting jailed for another aggravated assault. Even that was pushing it. My victim was dead with only her last phone call to tell her story. I had done all I could. The DNA analysis would take at least thirty days.

I drove home feeling the weight of the world on my shoulders. I heard dispatch send an officer to Ms. Brown's house. I guess she was back from the hospital. I was glad I wasn't taking the call and couldn't hold back my first smile in more than two days.

I was glum the entire weekend. Norman was leaving Monday and would be gone the entire week. I thought being a detective would be exciting. It was anything but. I spent hours reviewing Alex's cases. Tuesday the lab report from Rachel's blood came back. The medical examiner used a private lab and didn't need to wait on the State. Rachel's blood was over the legal alcohol limit for driving.

I took my case and lab report to the county attorney's office. I already knew the answer, but I had to give it one last try.

Unfortunately, Rachel would not even be a statistic for domestic violence. Her death was ruled an accident. Even if the DNA came back with Charles' blood mixed with Rachel's, he had not driven the vehicle and his actions were not the direct cause of her death, said the powers that be. I felt differently in my heart but logic told me they were right.

I managed to hold myself together until Thursday when Charles came to the department to pick up Rachel's personal items. I refused to hand them over and begged Sandy to do my dirty work. Everyone was walking softly around me and Sandy agreed. I went back to my office. More than anything I needed something to hit. The physical therapy gym was not available until after their normal business hours. I sat at my desk and hit my fisted hands against the top. I did it so hard it hurt, but that was the idea.

The first item I would buy with my extra detective pay would be a heavy bag. My desk and fists did not make a good combination. This was what Sgt. Spears was talking about when he worried about me and the first time justice failed. I could either move forward and do my job or give up. I wasn't a quitter. I worked hard for my promotion. I would learn from Rachel's death. I would be stronger and tougher. It was either that or find a new job.

I worked through the day and then went home to begin my weekend. I was mentally exhausted. I didn't expect Norman back home until late the next day. I looked around and realized that if I stayed home I would start to cry. If I started to cry, I wasn't sure if I could stop.

I changed into a pair of comfortable jeans, a t-shirt and winter jacket. I then went into the kitchen and grabbed a bottle of red zinfandel. The laundry room was my next stop where I found a canvas carrying bag. I didn't want anyone to see me walking the streets of Small Town with a bottle of wine in my hand. Thinking about it, I went back to the wine cupboard and took out another bottle. I then opened a drawer and extracted a deck of unopened playing cards and a corkscrew. On my way out the door, I added a bag of Hershey's Kisses. I took my house key off the hook and walked out the front door bypassing my car.

My destination was ten minutes away on foot. I didn't even try to talk myself out of going. I approached the house and walked up to the front door and knocked. I could hear the television.

"If you're not a salesman come in, if you are a salesman you better bring money because you're paying me for my time."

I walked in.

Ms. Brown was lying on the couch with her walker by her side. There was a glass of water and several pill bottles sitting on the coffee table. She didn't make any effort to sit up and I was glad. I knew how much a broken hip hurt.

"I brought wine for me. You can't have any because of your medication. I brought chocolate because I need it, but I'm willing to share. I brought playing cards in case you're in a bad mood and can't say anything nice. It's tempting, but I would rather not drink from the bottle. Where are your wineglasses?"

She didn't blink. "Cabinet next to the sink, on the right side, second shelf." She looked me up and down before I walked into her kitchen and got a wineglass.

I came back into the room, took the corkscrew out of my bag, and went to work on opening the bottle. I poured my first glass and gave a long sigh. "I've had a really shitty day and you were the only person that wouldn't give me pity and make me start crying. I plan on drinking at least one of these bottles. I just want to be able to walk home and not fall in a ditch somewhere. So what did you do in your younger years before you became the Wicked Bitch of the West?" I took my first long drink.

Ms. Brown smiled, "It's about time you grew a set of balls. If you can't have nice breasts like me, balls will do. I was a nurse in the Vietnam War. I saw a lot of things I wish I hadn't. I'm sure in your job you see them too."

Not what I expected, "Tell me about the war."

I managed to finish the first bottle and then half of the second. I did cry, but it felt good. Maxine understood. I stumbled home three hours later. That was the night I became friends with Ms. Brown. We're still friends, in spite of her bad moods, hatred of fat people and all her other prejudices. I don't take any of her shit and she doesn't take any of mine.

Life as an officer is never dull. I'm taking life as a detective one glorious day at a time, challenging the bad days and looking forward to the good...Sergeant Ivy, Lieutenant Ivy, Chief Ivy and President Ivy, a woman must have dreams.

Detective Ivy signing off

A note from Suzie,

Telling stories comes easy to me though writing them is more difficult. I write police reports and have a habit of continuing in the same vein when weaving my story.

Two people made this book possible, my mother who always gets first look and edits, and my friend, of more than thirty years, Linda Anselmi. They take my words and make me look good.

My husband understands my addiction to my laptop and forgives the time I spend writing, editing and cussing. He loves me or would never put up with the agonizing I do over each book. He pulls me away when I need rest and makes me play dominoes. He sometimes lets me win.

To all my Bad Luck Detective blog readers and the incredible women at BlogHer, thank you for your support, encouraging comments, tweets and emails. You are awesome!

All mistakes are my own.

Thank you for reading!

About the Author,

Suzie Ivy works as a police detective in a small Arizona town. She lives with her husband of thirty years, two dogs, horse and goldfish. When not at work or writing she loves to read, garden, and spend time with her grandchildren. She writes romance fiction (vampires & werewolves) under the name D'Elen McClain. When asked, "Why romance?" She replies, "Take me away from real life and give me a romantic fantasy any day." Suzie blogs about her police life at http://badluckdetective.com and her world of fangs at http://fangchronicles.wordpress.com. She loves to hear from readers at suzieivy@gmail.com

Book Group Questions:

What is your forgotten dream from when you were young?

Do you think you could go to the extent Suzie did and fulfill your dreams?

Did you know what the police academy entailed?

Would your family support you if you made the decision to do what Suzie did?

Are you Veronica or do you have a Veronica in your life?

Has your age ever stopped you from doing something?

Can you laugh at yourself?

Are you aware of the prevalence of domestic violence in your area?

Is there a safe house shelter in your town or section of the city?

Is there something your reading group could do to help out your local shelter? Items needed include diapers, blankets, bedding, toys, gas cards, food gift cards, clothing and money.

What was the saddest moment in the book?

What was the funniest moment in the book?

A preview of

Bad Luck in Small Town

By

Suzie Ivy

Due fall 2012 (eBook)

Summer 2013 (print edition)

Chapter 1
Death Before Sunrise

My cell phone rang at 0422 hours on Saturday morning. It's my sleep-in day so I'm extra groggy. A whispered, "Shit!" escapes me as my fumbling fingers find the answer button on my cell phone. I mutter an intelligent conversation starter with, "Yeah?"

My husband rolled over and seconded my intelligence with, "Grrrrrrr." We are quite attuned at 4 am.

A chipper dispatcher's voice began with, "Officer Garcia is requesting you at a death scene."

"Okay, who's dead?" My voice cracks slightly as my vocal cords wake up.

"We don't have the name on the victim yet, he's staying at the hotel."

"Okay, I'll be there in fifteen."

"What's up?" My husband's voice is a little more alert.

"It's a death at the hotel. I can't believe this." Without even realizing it, adrenaline is pumping into my body and reflects in my voice.

"You live for this crap. I'll see you next week or the week after." With that, he rolled over and went back to sleep.

If I truly had a homicide on my hands, we would be strangers in the night for a while. We've been through it before. I've been a detective for two years. In that time I've investigated and solved more homicides than Small Town has seen in the past twenty years. The nickname Bad Luck Detective is bandied by everyone at the department.

I grabbed my cold weather emergency bag which consists of everything I need to get ready in five minutes. My winter pack has underwear, sports bra, thermal underwear, comfortable jeans, blue long sleeved t-shirt with large yellow letters saying, "POLICE" on the front and back, socks and old comfortable tennis shoes that are accustomed to a little blood spatter. I also have a wide black belt for my jeans where I clip my badge and gun before I brush my teeth and throw my hair in a ponytail. My bag goes with me because it also contains essentials like an energy bar and two water bottles. At the bottom is an old bullet proof vest that can go over my t-shirt if needed. I've learned the hard way to be prepared.

I walk out my front door at the eight minute mark. It's cold but no snow fell overnight so I don't need to scrape down Esperanza's dark windows. She starts up immediately though she complains with a huff and puff from the cold as I pull her out of the driveway. She gets cranky when I don't have time to warm her up but she manages to sputter to the scene. I arrive twelve minutes after dispatch woke me up. I'm getting good at this.

Officer Benito Garcia is standing by his patrol car with his overhead red and blues flashing. He has one of our older vehicles that don't have new LED lights so they make a soft clicking noise as they turn. It's the only noise I hear when I exit Esperanza's still cold interior. He's one of my favorite officers and I'm glad he's the cop on duty. As I look around the parking lot, I glimpse the shadow of a head in the backseat of Benito's patrol unit. This does not look good and I realize that my husband will probably be cooking his own dinners for a while.

Chapter 2
Don't Mess With My Crime Scene

Benito walked over to me so we can speak away from his vehicle. "Whatcha got?" I asked.

"I was called at four. The spouse woke up and called 911 because her husband's body was cold. When I got here rigor was beginning to set in. A few things looked suspicious so I had dispatch call you. She said he was drinking last night and passed out on the floor. She thinks it was around midnight when she got up and helped him into bed."

"Okay, don't tell me what you think is suspicious. Did you mess up my crime scene?"

"I touched the body to check for a pulse. I had the wife step out of the room and stand at the door entryway so I could keep an eye on her and I walked through the room and quickly checked the bathroom. I didn't touch anything."

"You're going to be my second on this. Write your initial report and I'll take the rest. Call Denise out. I want her to sit with the wife at the station. We need the missus out of here. Did you call Alex?" (Alex Molinero is our sergeant).

"No, he's out of town and I figured you would want to call the chief yourself. I'll have dispatch get Denise over here. Do you want me to have anyone else called out?"

"Nope, not until I know what we're dealing with. I'm sick of stupid rumors leaking out of the department. I'm glad you're the one on duty."

Benito smiled and walked away a little to make his call to dispatch and I called the chief's phone and left a message. I knew he wouldn't answer but this way I adhered to policy, chain of command and all required procedure. I also call Sergeant Alex Molinero's cell. I hoped he would answer but it went straight to voicemail. I left a short message then walked to Esperanza's trunk and opened it to remove my large evidence bag. I placed it on my shoulder and grabbed the smaller one too. I walked them over near the door to the hotel room and laid them on the cement entry.

"Denise is on her way, what do you need me to do?" Benito said as he clicked off his phone.

"First, turn off your red and blues. It will cause less commotion in town and as soon as morning traffic picks up everyone will know something's up so let's keep it as low key as possible. I want the wife out of here before we start. I'll have a word with her before Denise arrives. Then when she's gone we'll run crime scene tape from pillar to pillar in front of the room to define our inner scene and then use our vehicles to run more tape about twenty-five feet out. No one gets past the outer tape without my say so. Got it?"

I flipped on the switch of my digital recorder and placed it in my left hand as Benito walked over and turned off his overhead lights. I asked Benito to unlock the backdoor so I can introduce myself to his passenger. She wasn't in handcuffs, which was good. She was crying but I know that doesn't prove innocence and a lack of tears do not prove guilt. I had no intention of questioning her fully until I could get her into our interview room.

I put out my right hand and introduced myself. "I'm Detective Suzie Ivy. I'm sorry we're meeting under these circumstances." She softly grasped my hand for a second and told me her name was Annette Lenman. Her hand was shaking. "What's your husband's name?" I asked.

"Gary, Gary Lenman."

"Okay, I'm going to be the investigator for the case and I will need to talk to you and get a full statement. I have another officer coming here to drive you to the police department. It's warm there and you will be more comfortable. We can provide food and coffee if you need it."

"I know this doesn't look good and we had a fight last night. I can't believe he's dead. I need to call my family. My cell phone is in the room and I don't know the phone numbers."

"I can't remove anything from the room yet but as soon as I can, I'll get your cell phone delivered to you." Out of the corner of my eye, I see another squad car pull up. "Officer Bullock just arrived and I need to speak with her then I'll bring her over and make introductions. She'll be able to help you with whatever you need."

I closed the car door and walked over to Denise. She was in full uniform and I realized I should have had her come out in civilian clothes. It's always the small details which hang you up and I didn't want Mrs. Lenman intimidated more than she already was. I was also glad I got her first statements on tape.

As I neared Denise I asked, "Are you ready for this?" She had been with us for a little over six months and this was her first death investigation. Sitting with the witness and or suspect is never fun because it can be hours before I'm available to begin the interview. Good rookies get this job.

"Whatever you need."

"You may not like me after this assignment but I need you to look after the spouse of our body. Take her to the police department and keep her comfortable and as calm as possible. If any of the other guys call, you know nothing. I don't want rumors leaking out." Handing over my recorder which is set on voice activation I explain, "Use this. Don't ask questions about her husband but if Ms. Lenman volunteers anything, I want it recorded."

"If anyone calls it'll be easy because I don't know anything."

Denise is going to be a great cop someday. Everyone wondered how I would feel working with another female. She's easy to like and Denise and I get along, there haven't been any cat fights. Some of the guys aren't happy about having another female in the department. Their testosterone-laden world is being encroached upon by estrogen.

I walked Denise over to the car for introductions and we then moved Ms. Lenman to Denise's car and asked her to get in the front passenger seat. I told Denise if she or Annette needed food to call Brett (our animal control officer) and ask him to pick something up. Brett works for us part time and prefers the company of animals. He doesn't talk much which is an excellent and desired quality in the midst of a death investigation. In a small department everyone is essential when we have a major case.

Made in the USA
Lexington, KY
16 May 2012